Private Members' Bills

The authors would like to thank the Nuffield Foundation for financial assistance towards the research on which this book is based.

Private Members' Bills

DAVID MARSH AND MELVYN READ

Department of Government, University of Essex

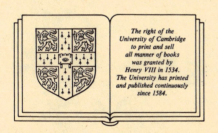

The right of the
University of Cambridge
to print and sell
all manner of books
was granted by
Henry VIII in 1534.
The University has printed
and published continuously
since 1584.

CAMBRIDGE UNIVERSITY PRESS

Cambridge
New York   New Rochelle
Melbourne   Sydney

Published by the Press Syndicate of the University of Cambridge
The Pitt Building, Trumpington Street, Cambridge CB2 1RP
32 East 57th Street, New York, NY 10022, USA
10 Stamford Road, Oakleigh, Melbourne 3166, Australia

Printed in Great Britain at the University Press, Cambridge

Britsh Library cataloguing in publication data
Marsh, David
Private members' bills.
1. Great Britain. Parliament –
Private bills
I. Title. II. Read, Melvyn
328.41'077   JN601

Library of Congress cataloguing in publication data
Marsh, David C. (David Charles)
Private members' bills.
Includes index.
1. Great Britain. Parliament –
Private bills – History.
I. Read, Melvyn. II. Title.
KD4242.M37 1987   328.41'077   87-15116
ISBN 0 521 33051 3

CE

6.5.88

Contents

Tables

Introduction

The last thorough study of private members' business was Peter Bromhead's *Private Members Bills* published in 1956.[1] Of course subsequently there have been various less detailed studies, but the aim of this book is to present the fullest study of the procedure since Bromhead's.

Many, if not most, studies of Parliament ignore, or at least give scant attention to, private members' bills.[2] Yet they do represent an important sub-category of legislation for a number of reasons. Firstly, more private members' bills are introduced into the House of Commons than Government bills, and while the majority of these are unsuccessful, a significant number do pass. So no understanding of Parliament could be complete without a study of these bills. Secondly, a certain amount of important legislation has originated from this procedure. Of course much of this legislation was passed in the period between 1965 and 1969 and dealt with social and moral issues.[3] However, such legislation has had a marked effect on many people's lives and even more recently a number of successful private members' bills have resulted in fairly major legislation – for example, the Chronically Sick and Disabled Persons Act (1970), the Rehabilitation of Offenders Act (1974), and the Housing (Homeless Persons) Act (1977).[4] What is more, while most successful legislation introduced by MPs is minor and uncontentious, it often affects quite sizeable elements of the population. Thirdly, even unsuccessful private members' bills often have a significance. They may draw attention to particular problems and concerns and perhaps encourage the Government to establish a Commission to investigate the area or even to legislate itself on the subject in a future session.

At the same time a study of private members' bills can also throw light upon broader questions concerning the nature of the relationship between the executive and the legislature. In British constitutional theory, the executive proposes and the legislature legitimates. There is little doubt that despite the reform of the select committee system in 1979 the legislature's scrutiny of the executive's administration is relatively ineffective.[5] At the same time, although there has been an increase in dissent in parliamentary voting,[6] on all except rare occasions the executive's proposals become law without significant amendment. Simply put, the executive dominates the legislature in the British system because of the existence of relatively strong party discipline. However, there is one category of legislation where the House of Commons both proposes and disposes: private members' bills. This is an area then which is supposedly the sole prerogative of the back-bench MP; the only area in which the ordinary private member plays a key role in legislation. As such it represents almost a base line against which to judge the influence of the individual MP in the British system. If, in this area, the Government still plays the key role, despite the constitutional position, then we have further important evidence of the limited nature of the legislature position. Very little would then be left to the ordinary MP.

One related facet of private members' bills also deserves attention. As we have emphasised in the past, on Government bills the vast majority of MPs in both the major parties vote in the way they are instructed by their party whips. In contrast votes on private members' bills are free votes – there is no party whip upon the vote so the MP is free to follow his/her inclinations. In such circumstances what factors affect an MP's voting? Is party still the key variable, which would suggest that it is not merely party discipline which keeps parties together but also a shared value system, or ideology, which in addition influences MPs' voting on private members' bills? If by contrast a study of these free votes indicates that factors other than party play a key role then, given the increase in dissent highlighted by Philip Norton, such factors may in the future have a growing influence on voting on Government bills.

We do have some good studies of aspects of the more recent period. Peter Richards's *Parliament and Conscience* and Bridget Pym's *Pressure Groups and the Permissive Society* deal with the series of social and moral bills passed under the private members' procedure during the life of the 1964–70 Labour Government. However, while these are solid books, they cover an atypical period in which a series of major private members' bills were given Government time. Without time they would have had no chance of success, as both Richards and Pym indicate.

Richards has also produced two very similar review articles on private members' business which deal with the period up to 1975,[7] but these articles are mainly concerned with three problems: whether bills passed; what type pass; and whether a bill received Government time. All these are important questions, but there are others of significance. In fact, we shall be dealing with a whole series of such questions in the body of the text, so one example of the advantages of a more detailed analysis than that employed by Richards should suffice. Richards presents no evidence about whether bills have votes yet the very existence of a vote on the Second Reading or Third Reading of a bill, that is on the bill's principles, indicates that there is opposition to it, and that the issue is, therefore, contentious. Our later analysis will show that such bills, even if opposed by only a handful of MPs, have virtually no chance of making progress.

Indeed, many important aspects of private members' bills are only revealed by a more detailed study of the sort offered here. For this reason, the main data in this book is derived from an analysis of all private members' bills introduced since the reintroduction of the procedure in 1948/9.[8] Each bill's progress through Parliament was traced using *Hansard*. This enabled us to determine amongst other things: whether the bill successfully passed or to which stage in the legislative procedure it progressed; the type of bill it was; the procedure under which the bill was introduced: that is Ballot, Standing Order 39, or the Ten-Minute-Rule procedures; who initiated them and the party to which that person belonged; whether the bill was voted upon at Second or Third Reading; and whether the bill received Government time.

This is not the only study which recognises the need for a more detailed analysis. Burton and Drewry are mainly concerned with Government bills but their analysis of the 1970–74 Government is very thorough and gives an excellent picture of the use of private members' bill procedure during that period.[9] Their material on the sessions since 1974, however, is much less thorough, dealing mainly with the success rate of bills, and giving brief details of the more interesting bills of this type which were introduced.[10] Our analysis is in one way less detailed than that Burton and Drewry provide for the 1970–74 Session in that we do not deal with private members' bills which originate in the Lords. However, our material has three major advantages. Firstly, as we deal with the entire post-war period we are in a better position to detect trends in the procedure than previous authors. Secondly, our aggregate material, especially upon balloted bills, is more thorough than even that provided by Burton and Drewry. In particular we have data upon the Government's role in relation to every balloted bill introduced since the Second World War which indicates just how crucial the Government's role is in relation to private members' bills. Thirdly, our study combines the fullest aggregate analysis available with case studies of four private members' issues: abortion, pornography, smoking and seat-belts. This is essential because aggregate studies such as that undertaken by Burton and Drewry tell us little about the politics of private members' business. There have been case studies of particular private members' issues or individual bills before[11] but no analysis which combines detailed aggregate material with extended case studies.

This book then is divided into two sections. The first section examines the aggregate pattern of private members' bills. Chapter 1 considers the three different procedures by which private members' bills can be introduced and establishes the extent to which these different procedures are used, and the strengths and weaknesses of each. Chapter 2 identifies the subject matter of private members' bills, the type of bill which is successful, and the way these patterns have changed over time. In Chapter 3 we consider the crucial role of the Government in relation to the procedure, while, by contrast, Chapter 4 looks at the role of interest groups and individual MPs. The second section of the book subsequently moves on to examine four of the more interesting and recurring private members' issues: abortion, pornography, smoking, and seat-belts. In the concluding chapter we shall then attempt both to summarise the main results of our study and to suggest how the private members' bill procedure might be reformed.

1   The aggregate patterns

1 Private members' bills: the procedure

The private members' bill procedure, like cricket, would baffle the intelligent alien. One MP summed up *one* aspect of the situation very well:

As a back-bench Member I am in somewhat of a difficulty when constituents ask why, after 30 years, I am for the first time introducing a private-member's bill on a Friday. It is difficult to explain to them that the privilege of standing here on a Friday is the result of getting fifth prize in a raffle.[1]

Clearly before we can assess the outcomes of the procedure it is essential to outline its complexities, for, as we shall see throughout this book, it is the procedure which ensures that so few controversial or contested bills succeed.

In fact there are three types of private members' bills: balloted bills, Standing Order Number 39 bills, and Ten-Minute-Rule bills. These types of bill differ only in relation to the procedure through which they are introduced. Once a bill has achieved a Second Reading it is subject to the same procedure, no matter what its type or origin. For this reason the first section of this chapter will look at the different procedures by which each of the three types of bill is introduced. The second section will then examine the procedure as it affects all private members' bills, no matter what type, once they have received a Second Reading. The final section will then quantify the number of bills introduced through each procedure and their success rates.

Introducing Bills

(a) Balloted bills

As pressure of work increased, the Government placed a premium on time and reduced the time available to private members. Standing Order Number 7 provides for ten Fridays each Session to be made available to individual Members who wish to introduce bills. However, each year a Sessional Order is passed replacing that part of the Standing Order 6 relating to private members' bills. It is thus possible that the amount of time available will vary year by year, but this is unusual. Extra time is usually only made available in an extended Session like 1979–80, when 14 days were set aside. Any back-bench member is entitled to put his name forward and a ballot decides who will introduce the bills. In most of the Sessions under discussion 20 MPs have introduced bills under Standing Order Number 7. Prior to the 1979–80 Session, private members' bills were discussed on specific Fridays between 11.00 a.m. and 4.00 p.m. So each day's debate lasts five hours at the maximum although it can be much shorter. Since 1979 a Friday sitting lasts for the same length of time, but from 9.30 a.m. to 2.30 p.m. Hence, only 60 hours are normally available to private members.

Standing Orders allow for a ballot to be held on the second Thursday of each Session, to decide which Members have first call on the limited time available. Any person who wishes may enter his/her name, by signing a book put in the 'No' Division Lobby in the two days before the draw is made. It is a convention that, while most back-benchers make use of this facility, Ministers and Opposition front-bench spokesmen do not. This means that in any Session between 400 and 450 MPs enter the ballot. It must be emphasised that at this stage the MP only enters his name into the ballot and need not have any specific bill in mind. Indeed, *most* MPs only seriously consider the matter *after* their name has been drawn. The Speaker is responsible for arranging the draw which takes place in a committee room. The number of names selected depends upon the amount of time allocated for the Session. Once an MP's name is drawn from the ballot, s/he has a month before the short title of the bill s/he intends to support is published. Obviously when an MP is successful in the ballot s/he will be inundated with suggestions for bills by other MPs and interest groups.

Since November 1971 the first ten MPs in the ballot have been entitled to £200 from public funds in order to cover some of the cost of drafting their bill. However, the amount has not increased since that time and hardly approaches the expense of drafting a complicated bill.[2] It is therefore surprising that relatively few MPs claim the allowance. Indeed Mr Biffen, Leader of the House, pointed out in reply to a written question, on 20 January 1986, that: 'During the last four sessions there have been five applications from Honourable Members for this form of assistance.'[3] Obviously some MPs receive help, financial or otherwise, from interest groups, or sympathetic lawyers, or, if theirs is a Government bill in all but name, from the Department, in drafting their bills. Others approach the Clerks of the House responsible for private members' bills who will help to get a bill into Parliamentary shape. In addition, once a bill receives a Second Reading, and appears to have a chance of success, the Department which will ultimately have responsibility for administering it if it becomes law will provide help with redrafting if the bill's sponsor asks.

Since 1970 Session orders in all except two Sessions have allocated 12 Fridays to private members' bills. The first six days are Second-Reading days, when the 'principle' of the bill is debated and one bill may well occupy a complete day. This means that only six balloted bills are guaranteed a Second-Reading vote. However, much depends on the nature of the bills under discussion on a given day. Often more than one will receive a Second Reading and go on to complete its passage, although some may be stopped at a later stage. Five of the other six days are used to provide time for the later stages of bills, that is Report stage and Third Reading, while the consideration of amendments suggested by the House of Lords usually occupies the final day available. These last six days are termed 'remaining-stages' days.

The first six MPs 'out of the hat' are thus certain of first place on the list on one of the six successive Fridays, since Members may select the day for a Second Reading of that bill according to their position in the ballot. When these six have made their selection, the remaining fourteen try to find the best day available, a task which becomes progressively more difficult. Given the limited time available, several bills will be down for a Second Reading on any day. If the debate on the first bill on the list fills the allotted time then all the other bills down for that day including non-balloted bills, are called over formally, but can make no progress if any member indicates opposition, normally by merely shouting: 'Object'. Sometimes an MP objects not because s/he opposes the bill but because if it progresses, less time will be available at Report Stage for some other bill s/he supports. In contrast a bill is given a Second Reading if it is called and no MP objects. In fact as private members' bills have become more limited, uncontentious and technical, a larger number of bills, including some non-balloted bills, achieve a Second Reading without debate. Some are nodded through at the end of a

Second-Reading day, others at the end of one of the 'remaining-stages' days. On occasion small bills are even nodded through at the end of the Fridays on which private members' motions have precedence over private members' bills. Bills which are objected to rather than being nodded through, or bills which are debated but talked out, can be put down again for a later Friday. However, deferment to a later date is almost inevitably fatal unless for some reason the objectors to the bill desist. This can happen as it did, for example, in the 1979/80 Session when William McKelvey's Married Women's Policies of Assurance (Scotland) (Amendment) Bill was objected to on five successive occasions by supporters of the Corrie Abortion Bill before it was allowed to pass unchallenged on the sixth occasion.

If on a given Friday there is time left after the discussion of the first piece of proposed legislation, then a second bill may be moved. The number dealt with will depend on the nature of the various bills. Thus any member who draws a place outside the first six has to make a shrewd choice involving an assessment of the time likely to be used up by the previous bill debated on a given day. Second position on a day on which an uncontentious, unopposed, bill is debated first might allow a bill to progress. This, together with the fact that some bills achieve a Second Reading 'on the nod', with no debate, means that a number of bills can receive a Second Reading on the same day. Indeed on 24 January 1975 five bills received a Second Reading.

Once a debate on a bill has commenced, the time it requires will depend very much on the nature, and the contentiousness, of the issue. If the debate is still in progress at 2.30 p.m. it is adjourned, and the bill is deferred to a future Friday. This procedure enables any opposition to talk out a measure. If this does happen, the Member sponsoring the bill can move a closure, by requesting that: 'the question be now put'. The Speaker will allow this only if he feels that there has been sufficient discussion of the principles of the bill. The motion normally will be accepted when there has been a full day's debate, but may be accepted with less debate. If such a closure vote is accepted there will be a division, which must be won by the sponsor with at least 100 Members voting in favour, otherwise the bill will fall. If the closure vote is successful, a second vote will take place to decide the fate of the Second Reading. Again, this must be won, although a simple majority is sufficient.

Table 1.6, which examines the use of private members' bill days in the 1979–80 Session, gives a good indication of the processes involved. In this extended session 14 days were allocated, seven for Second Reading debates and seven for the bills' remaining stages. On the third day, four bills progressed to Standing Committee, including one, the Licensed Premises (Exclusion of Certain Persons) Bill, whose sponsor had won seventeenth place in the ballot and which went through with no discussion. On the same day the Representation of the People Bill achieved an unopposed Second Reading, with 42 minutes' debate, and passed through Committee stage when it was approved, with no discussion, by the House acting as a Committee of the Whole House. This bill's Report and Third Reading stages were subsequently taken 'on the nod' on the fifth day. The last day on which Second Reading debate took precedence was the seventh day. Here two bills were debated, the second of which was adjourned after 49 minutes' debate and progressed no further. Subsequently six bills received Second Readings without debate, two of which were non-balloted bills. Of course bills can obtain a Second Reading on remaining stage days. Indeed, as Table 1.6 indicates, two bills, a Standing Order Number 39 (then 37) bill, the Import of Live Fish (England and Wales) Bill and the Married Policies of Assurance (Scotland) (Amendment) Bill obtained Second Readings on the ninth and eleventh days respectively. Both subsequently obtained the Royal Assent.

(b) Standing Order No. 39 Bills

After the 20 balloted bills have been presented on the fifth Wednesday of each Session, any Member can present a bill to the House, on any day on which there is a sitting. All that is required is at least one day's notice, and its presentation to the Clerk at the table at the correct time. Once presented, a Second Reading date is given, and the proposal is set down immediately below the other business for that day on the Order Paper. The major difference between the bills presented in this fashion and the ballot bills, is that the former have very little chance of any debate, since they follow the balloted bills, which have a prior claim on the limited time available, on the Order Paper.

Under Standing Order Number 39, any Member has a right to introduce a measure without the formality of a speech, or the need to obtain leave to have the bill read a first time. Any Member, who has previously indicated his/her wish to do so, is called by the

Speaker. The sponsor takes his/her 'dummy' bill to the Clerk of the House, who reads the short title. This action constitutes a First Reading. Once presented, the bill is then printed. However, this form of bill will make little or no progress without a good deal of luck. It can only make progress: if the bill is uncontroversial and unopposed, which is unlikely since, as we saw, a cry of 'Object' by any MP will block it; if there are few other private members' bills that day, which is unlikely as the backlog of deferred bills increases with each succeeding bills day; or if the Government makes time available, which might occur if Ministers are generally sympathetic, but is very rare as most Governments do not care to be officially involved.

(c) Ten-Minute-Rule bills

A third method of introducing legislation is by taking advantage of Standing Order Number 13, the Ten-Minute Rule. Each week, two Members are allowed to make a short speech, of not more than ten minutes' duration, in support of a motion calling for the introduction of a particular piece of legislation.[4] Reintroduced in November 1950, this procedure enables one bill to be raised, every Tuesday and Wednesday, at the end of Question Time by asking, 'that leave be given to bring in a bill'. A single speech, of a similar length, may be given in opposition to the motion. Where an opposing speech takes place, a division will decide if a First Reading is to be given, or not. If the motion is accepted, and the bill is read a first time, a date will be given for a Second Reading. Once again the bill follows any ballot bills on the Order Paper for that day. If the bill should prove to be particularly uncontroversial, it might achieve a Second Reading 'on the nod', without debate, and thus proceed to the Committee stage. If not, then failure is almost certain.

After Second Reading

If a bill is defeated at Second Reading, it cannot progress. However, if it receives a majority at Second Reading or is passed without a division, it then proceeds to its Committee stage. The successful bills proceed into Standing Committee in the order that they receive a Second Reading. At this stage it does not matter under which procedure they have been introduced, balloted bills enjoy no necessary precedence. However, any supporter of a balloted bill, which is not debated until one of the later Second Reading days, is unlikely to allow a non-balloted bill to progress 'on the nod' and thus delay the bill s/he supports getting into Committee. So normally the first balloted bills to receive a Second Reading are first into Committee.

At the Committee Stage the bill is considered clause by clause and amendments to its text can be introduced. In most cases this detailed examination is undertaken by a Standing Committee. Private members' bills have precedence over Government business in one Standing Committee, at present Standing Committee C. As we indicated, bills go into Committee in the order in which they receive a Second Reading. Only when the Committee has finished considering one bill does the next bill go into Committee, so there is a simple queuing system. In the other Committees, Government bills take precedence. However, if another Standing Committee is empty then an MP can ask for his/her bill to be referred there. The Speaker is responsible for the allocation of bills to Committees, but if the Government business managers object to the use of a Government committee for a private members' bill, or indicate that they will need the Committee soon, then the bill would have to take its position in the queue. The use of a Government Standing Committee is thus very rare. However, this was a tactic used by Enoch Powell in the 1984/5 Session. In this Session Standing Committee D had not been used by the Government so Powell asked for his Unborn Children (Protection) Bill to be taken in that Committee. The Speaker concurred when there was no objection from the Government's business managers. Powell, who was only fifth in the ballot, thus was able to bring his bill out of Committee more quickly.

An all-party Selection Committee chooses which 17 MPs sit on a given Standing Committee from a list of interested MPs drawn up by the Whips. If there is a vote at Second Reading then the composition of the Standing Committee roughly reflects the vote at Second Reading. So, for example, in the case of John Corrie's Abortion Bill in the 1979/80 Session, which was approved by 242 votes to 98 votes at Second Reading, ten members of the Standing Committee were supporters of the bill while five members were opponents. The other two members were an independent chairman appointed, as in the case with all bills, by the Speaker from a panel of senior back-benchers, and a Government Minister to safeguard departmental interests and provide the Committee with information. Given that Committee membership reflects any vote at Second Reading, opponents of a bill may deliberately not force a vote at Second Reading. In that case the Selection Committee chooses from among MPs who express an interest in the issue. So a group of MPs who oppose a bill can lobby the Selection Committee to become Standing Committee members and thus gain a larger representation than would have been the case if there had been a Second Reading vote. As we shall see later, this is what Peter Fry claimed happened in the case of his bill in the 1979/80 Session.[5]

Committees normally meet on Wednesdays between 10.30 a.m. and 1.00 p.m. However, any Committee is free to introduce a sittings' motion which can require it to meet more frequently. Indeed, the Standing Committee on the Corrie bill had 17 sittings lasting for a total of 43 hours. The Committee began by sitting for two-and-a-half hours every Wednesday morning. However, the vote on Clause 1 of the bill was only reached after six sittings and 15 hours of debate, and Corrie expressed concern that the bill would not be out of Committee in time for the first day set aside for the Report stage. He thus introduced a sittings' motion which was passed and required the Committee to sit on three mornings and three afternoons a week. What is more, if a Committee meets in the afternoon, no time limit is specified so the sitting can continue through the night. Of course, most Committee stages are much duller. Almost inevitably the bill's sponsor has a majority in Committee and most bills emerge relatively unamended for their Report stage, many with almost no debate.

There are two exceptions to this Standing Committee procedure. Firstly, any Member can move immediately after Second Reading that the Committee stage of the bill be taken on the floor of the House by a Committee of the Whole House (CWH). Although this tactic removes any delay caused by waiting for a Standing Committee, it is only of any real use for small, technical, non-controversial bills. This is because, unless the Committee stage can be completed by 2.30 p.m., any Member can object to any clauses, or move an opposed amendment, which will ensure that the Committee stage is deferred to a later day. Nevertheless, as Table 1.1 shows, somewhere around 20 per cent of the successful bills each Session have a CWH. Normally this means that the Committee stage is taken 'on the nod'. Secondly, any private members' bill which deals exclusively with Scotland (or much more rarely Wales or Northern Ireland) can be considered by a separate Standing Committee

Table 1.1 *Private members' bills and the use of a Committee of the Whole House (by decade)*

	Number of balloted bills considered by C.W.H.	Number of non-balloted bills considered by C.W.H.	Percentage of successful bills considered by C.W.H.
1950/1–1959/60	4	14	16%
1960/1–1969/70	5	20	17%
1970/1–1979/80	5	18	25%
1980/1–1984/5	7	6	21%

composed of 17 Scottish (Welsh or Northern Irish) members. In fact there are usually three or four Scottish bills each Session, and they often have the advantage of a faster path through Standing Committee.

The last six private-members'-bill Fridays are set aside for the 'remaining stages' of bills. The first of these days is normally six weeks after the last Second Reading day. On these 'remaining-stages' days bills are considered in an order governed by the progress they have previously made. So bills which have been reported back by a Standing Committee are considered before bills waiting for a Second Reading. It is at this stage that tactics become crucial and much manoeuvring occurs. Indeed, at Report stage a small number of determined and organised opponents can delay and thus defeat a bill. Of course, the Speaker is well aware of the variety of tactics available and is responsible for ordering the debate. He will normally not call any amendments which have been discussed and voted upon in Committee. At the same time, if there are a large number of amendments, the Speaker will often allow them to be considered in groups with each group being discussed for about two hours before the Speaker accepts a motion for closure. The Speaker, and indeed the Clerk of the House responsible for private members' bills, will receive representations from MPs on both sides concerning which amendments should be called. In most cases the Clerk will then prepare a draft list of amendments to be taken. However, this list will then be considered by the Speaker who makes the final choice.

All this means that the sponsors and opponents of a bill must be careful about the strategy they adopt at Report stage. Opponents of a bill must hold back amendments for Report stage; ensure that there are enough amendments to fill the time available; and ensure that there are enough opponents willing to speak to prevent any one speaker being accused of filibustering. If the debate upon a bill has not concluded during the five hours available for debate on any 'remaining-stages' day then the debate is adjourned. At this stage the promoter of the bill can ask for a closure motion. However, this is of no use if there are other amendments to be discussed, and anyway the request may not be accepted by the Speaker if he feels there has been insufficient debate.

Once a bill is adjourned at Report stage it is set down for consideration on a later 'remaining-stages' day. However, it has to take its place behind any bill waiting to begin its Report stage. In fact most bills only receive one day on Report and, while two days is not uncommon, it is very unusual for any bill to receive more time. At the same time the procedure is subject to a considerable amount of manipulation. So, for example, as we saw earlier when considering the McKelvey bill in the 1979–80 Session, supporters of a particular bill may 'Object' to a Second Reading for a minor technical bill in order to prevent that bill getting into Committee and taking time on Report which would otherwise be available for the bill they support. Similarly, supporters of a bill can attempt to delay a bill, in which they have no interest, in Committee, again in order to prevent it taking up time on Report. The main tactic available to opponents of a bill as we have already seen is the sophisticated filibuster.

Clearly then a bill's chances of success are partly determined by the number of amendments moved at Report stage, and the number of amendments is affected by three factors. These are, in descending order of importance: the strength and organisation of opposition; the size of the bill; and the skill with which it has been drafted. If a bill is uncontentious and not opposed then amendments, except for minor drafting amendments, are unlikely. This is particularly the case given that so many of the bills of this type are, as we shall see at length in Chapter 3, drafted within a Government Department. However, if a bill is contentious and opposed then it has little, if any, chance of success given the opportunities which exist for delay in the procedure. We shall deal with many of these points later, but there is one exception to this general rule. A small one-clause bill, even if it was contentious, might succeed despite sophisticated opposition. This is because only a limited number of amendments to a one-clause bill can be introduced and they might well be disposed of in one or two days' debate. There is little doubt, for example, that if John Corrie had introduced a short bill reducing the time limit up to which abortions could be performed then it would have passed despite the sophistication of the 'pro' abortion lobby. However, he introduced a large bill with four main clauses and this was talked out despite receiving an unprecedented four days' debate on Report stage.

The chances of a bill's successes are also affected by the existence of other bills due to be considered. We have already seen how this gives rise to manoeuvring. However, a brief consideration of the events in the 1979/80 Session give a good indication of the nature of the procedure. Table 1.6 provides a breakdown of the use of each of the private members' days in that Session, and indicates the fate of each of the bills introduced. Because the 1979 Election was in June, the 1979/80 Session lasted 15 months and the Sessional order specified seven 'remaining-stages' days. The Abortion (Amendment) bill was the first bill out of Committee. It was debated during the first two 'remaining-stages' days because the next bill, Neil Carmichael's Road Traffic Seat Belts Bill was filibustered in Standing Committee by its own opponents, notably Ivan Lawrence and Ronald Bell. The first eight hours of debate on the Abortion (Amendment) Bill was concerned with amendments to only one clause of the bill and no vote had been taken on any of the amendments to the second clause by the time the second day's debate was adjourned. On the third 'remaining-stages' day the Seat Belts Bill was considered but was filibustered by its opponents. Because John Corrie knew that he would have been behind the Seat Belts Bill on the third day, he had chosen the fourth day for his resumed Report stage. Once again progress was slow due to the large number of amendments and the sophisticated opposition and all but the last hour of the debate was concerned with clause two of the bill. The debate was adjourned with almost half of the bill still to be considered.

On the fifth day the Concessionary Travel for Handicapped Persons (Scotland) Bill had emerged from the Standing Committee which only considers Scottish bills. It was debated for 2 hours 39 minutes before obtaining a Third Reading without a vote. The Seat Belts bill was then considered for 1 hour 59 minutes. It was again filibustered and in effect fell when discussion was adjourned after a total debate of two hours 40 minutes on Second Reading and 6 hours 34 minutes on Report. By this time another balloted bill had come out of Committee, Robert Taylor's Child Maintenance Orders (Annual Up-Rating and Exemption) Bill (previously titled Affiliation Orders and Ailments Bill). However, as we shall see later, this bill was strongly opposed by the Government and after considerable pressure from them Taylor withdrew his bill. This meant that the sixth Report stage day was available for the Corrie bill. Again it was debated for five hours but adjourned with a large number of amendments not discussed.

This left one day available. The last 'remaining-stages' day in any Session takes place a month or more later (in 1979/80 almost four months). On this day Lords' amendments take precedence. One bill, the Licensing (Amendment) (Number 2) Bill, had been amended in the Lords and was considered first on the fourteenth day. Two other bills received some debate and three balloted bills passed through their remaining stages 'on the nod'. There was therefore no time available for the Corrie bill which thus fell after a total of 23 hours 58 minutes, or 40 per cent of time available for private members' bills in that Session. Clearly this Session was unusual in that it was dominated by one bill. However, during the Session six balloted bills did receive the Royal Assent although none of these received much debate: two of the bills were debated at Second Reading (one for 42 and one for 25 minutes); two were discussed on Report (one for 1 hour 41 minutes and one for 10 minutes); two were considered at Third Reading (for 58 and 51 minutes); and one had a debate on Lords' amendments (1 hour 38 minutes). Actually, as we shall see later, most bills which pass under the procedure are hardly debated at all. What is more, it is worth emphasising that the two bills which virtually monopolised the 'remaining-stages' days did not pass.

It is at Report stage that the fate of most contentious bills is decided. However, as we have indicated in passing, there are two further stages in the House of Commons before a bill receives the Royal Assent. As with Government bills, a private members' bill has to obtain a Third Reading, and in addition, if the bill is subsequently amended by the House of Lords, then these amendments have to be considered by the Commons. In most cases both stages are a formality if there is sufficient time available. If bills fail to receive the Royal Assent after passing their Report stage, it is almost inevitably because there is insufficient time for the matter to be considered by the House of Lords and reported back. Indeed, in any Session there are usually two or three bills which fail for this reason. In the House of Lords the bill must go through all its stages again. In theory the House of Lords could play a major role in relation to private members' bills, particularly in relation to contentious bills, because the House of Lords' procedure is such that it is much more difficult to restrict debate on bills than in the Commons. However, most contentious bills are defeated in the Commons and we have little indication of how the Lords might react, for example, to a bill to restrict the operation of the 1967 Abortion Act. In most cases the Lords are dealing with small technical bills passed by the Commons, thus their contribution is usually in terms of minor drafting amendments, if they make any change at all.

So far we have dealt with private members' ballot bills which progress in private members' time. However, there is no reason why such bills should not occupy Government time if the Government is willing, or Parliament's time if Parliament approves. The allocation of Government time is frequently discussed in relation to private members' bills; the allocation of Parliamentary time, to our knowledge, never arose as a question until the 1984/5 Session. As we shall see later, contentious legislation is very unlikely to pass using the procedure unless it is granted Government time. Two of the most celebrated post-war private members' bills, the Murder (Abolition of Death Penalty) Bill of 1965, and the Abortion Act of 1967, provide ample indication of this fact as neither could have been enacted within the time allotted to private members' bills. The Death Penalty Bill was actually a Standing Order Number 39 (then 37) bill. The House spent nine Wednesday mornings considering the bill in a Committee of the Whole House and an extra day was provided by the Government, from the time it controls but does not normally use, in order to allow the bill to complete its Report stage. The Abortion Bill required two all-night sittings to complete its Report stage, again in time which was provided by Government. As we shall see later, it is now much less common for Governments to give bills time than it was in the post-war period.

No book we have read, and no MP we spoke to prior to the 1984/5 Session, mentioned the other method by which the sponsors of a bill can hope to get extra time; that is by means of a Commons vote to suspend Standing Orders, utilising private members' motions' time. This omission is hardly surprising as in our detailed study we can discover only two instances in which this procedure was used. A motion to suspend Standing Orders cannot be introduced in the time provided for the consideration of private members' bills. However, it can be introduced as a private members' motion. In most Sessions twelve Fridays, alternating with the Fridays available for private members' bills, are reserved for motions introduced by private members. The time is allocated by ballots held periodically through the Session. On these Fridays the House of Commons usually acts like a debating society with the motions introduced most often calling upon the Government to take some action or another. However, in 1965 the procedure was used by a Conservative MP, Forbes Hendry, to suspend Standing Orders and recall consideration of the Committee stage of the Murder (Abolition of the Death Penalty) Bill from a Standing Committee C to the floor of the House. This particular tactic remained dormant until it was used, unsuccessfully, by supporters of Enoch Powell's Unborn Children (Protection) Bill, a bill which is discussed at length below, in 1984/5.

Money resolutions

Before we move on to discuss the use of the three procedures, it is important to deal with one other key feature of private members' bills. As Bromhead points out:

In 1706 it was resolved 'that this House will receive no Petitions for any sum of money, relating to public service, but what is recommended by the Crown.'[6]

The rule was made by Standing Order in 1713, and is now enshrined in Standing Order Numbers 109–12. This means that an MP cannot introduce a bill whose main object is a charge on the Exchequer. However, a private member may introduce a bill which incidentally involves the creation of a charge. In such instances the parts of the bill which involve such expenditure must be printed in italics and can only be dealt with if a Minister makes a resolution approving this while the Commons is functioning as a Committee of the Whole House. Put simply, the approval of the Government is a necessary precondition before any section of a private members' bill which creates new expenditure can be discussed.

As Table 1.2 indicates, money resolutions are not common. In the post-war period these have been an average of just over one per parliamentary Session. The figures also suggest that the numbers

Table 1.2 *Money resolutions 1951–1985*

Government	Number (No./session)	Percentage which are balloted bills	Percentage receiving Government time	Percentage receiving Royal Assent
CONSERVATIVE 1951–64	17 (1.3)	100	41	100
LABOUR 1964–70	18 (3)	72	39	78
CONSERVATIVE 1970–4	4 (1)	50	25	50
LABOUR 1974–9	5 (1)	100	20	67
CONSERVATIVE 1979–85	3 (<1)	67	–	67
TOTAL	45 (1.3)	89	38	87

are decreasing. Most of the bills which require and receive money resolutions are balloted bills, many need Government time and almost all pass.

The use of the three procedures

As Table 1.3 indicates, there has been a significant and continuing increase in the number of private members' bills in the post-war period. In the first ten Sessions under consideration, 1950/1 to 1959/60, an average of 32 bills were introduced per Session, whereas in the first five Sessions of the 1980s an average of 88 private members' bills were introduced. Perhaps more importantly, there has been a substantial growth in the number of Ten-Minute-Rule bills introduced. They represented only 27 per cent of the private members' bills between 1950–51 and 1959–60 but over 50 per cent of the bills in the last 15 Sessions under consideration. While the number of Standing Order Number 39 bills increased initially, it has remained constant representing around 20 per cent of the private members' bills introduced for the last 25 Sessions. In contrast the relative importance of the balloted procedure, if only in terms of the number of bills increased, has declined.

Table 1.3 *Types of bills introduced between Sessions 1950/1 and 1984/5*

SESSIONS	Ballot	Standing Order 39	Ten-Minute	Total
	Number (percentage of private members' bills introduced)	Number (percentage of private members' bills introduced)	Number (percentage of private members' bills introduced)	Number (average number per Session)
1950/1–1959/60	197 (62)	35 (11)	87 (27)	319 (32)
1960/1–1969/70	221 (33)	156 (23)	296 (43)	673 (67)
1970/1–1979/80	213 (27)	117 (23)	396 (50)	786 (78)
1980/1–1984/5	99 (23)	106 (24)	235 (53)	440 (88)
TOTAL	751 (39)	474 (21)	1014 (45)	2239 (64)

The main reason for these changes is clear. The number of balloted bills cannot increase given the nature of the procedure as enshrined in Standing Order Number 6. So if MPs want to air their legislative ideas, introduce a bill as the basis of a criticism of the Government, or attempt to gain publicity for a cause by introducing a bill, they have to use other procedures. The Ten-Minute-Rule procedure is preferred by MPs to the Standing Order Number 39 procedure for two reasons. Firstly, it involves less work as Ten-Minute-Rule bills do not need to be fully drafted, and are not printed until they are given a First Reading and thus formal approval by the House of Commons. Standing Order Number 39 bills by contrast have to be drafted and printed if they are to be debated. Secondly, while Standing Order Number 39 bills are rarely debated, Ten-Minute-Rule bills are by definition debated, if only briefly. Thus they have much more potential publicity value. The key point, however, is that the Ten-Minute procedure is rarely used with any hope of achieving legislative change. Rather such bills represent an attempt to gain publicity for an issue and test the feeling of the House upon the matter.

Table 1.4 *Success rate of bills introduced under the three procedures*
(Decades – Sessions 1950/1 to 1984/5)

Decade	Ballot	Standing Order 39	Ten-Minute-Rule	Total
	Number of bills Percentage of balloted bills successful (Number of bills successful expressed as percentage of total number of bills successful)	Number of bills Percentage of S.O. 39 bills successful (Number of bills successful expressed as percentage of total number of bills successful)	Number of bills Percentage of Ten Min. bills successful (Number of bills successful expressed as percentage of total number of bills successful)	Number of successful bills (Number of bills successful expressed as percentage of number of bills introduced)
1950/1–1959/60	n= 73	n=13	n=26	n=112
	37	37	30	(35)
	(65)	(12)	(23)	
1960/1–1969/70	n= 78	n=44	n=22	n=144
	35	28	7	(21)
	(54)	(26)	(4)	
1970/1–1979/80	n= 65	n=24	n= 4	n=93
	31	14	1	(12)
	(70)	(26)	(4)	
1980/1–1984/5	n= 42	n=11	n= 4	n= 57
	42	10	2	(13)
	(74)	(19)	(7)	
Total	n=258	n=92	n=56	n=406
	34	19	6	(18)
	(64)	(23)	(14)	

As Table 1.4 indicates, balloted bills have a much higher success rate than bills introduced under the other two procedures, and while the success rate of balloted bills has remained high, that of bills introduced under the other two procedures has fallen. More specifically, the success rate of Ten-Minute-Rule bills has declined dramatically. In the first decade under consideration, 30 per cent of the Ten-Minute-Rule bills introduced (26 out of 87) passed, and, indeed, 23 per cent of the private members' bills passed during that period were introduced under the Ten-Minute-Rule procedure (26

Table 1.5 *The politicisation of the Ten-Minute-Rule procedure 1975–6 to 1984/5*

SESSION	Number of Ten-Minute-Rule bills with votes	Percentage of Ten-Minute-Rule bills with votes	Percentage of these bills which deal with overtly political subjects
1975/6	26	60.5	27
1976/7	11	28	18
1977/8	24	63	17
1978/9	11	58	36
1979/80	21	36	10
1980/1	19	59	16
1981/2	8	31	13
1982/3	5	28	20
1983/4	6	11	33
1984/5	2	2	100

of 112). By the 1970s while 396 Ten-Minute-Rule bills were introduced, only 4 (1 per cent) were successful, and such bills represented only 4 per cent of the total number of private members' bills
passed (4 of 87). The figures for the 1980s are similar. Once again the
reason for this pattern is evident. While more Ten-Minute-Rule bills
are introduced, they have become more party political and contentious. They are introduced to promote debate and publicity with no
thought of success. This is clear from Table 1.5. A limited, but
significant, number of Ten-Minute-Rule bills are politically contentious enough to have votes and some of these are party political in
subject matters. However, while such bills represent an important
sub-category of Ten-Minute-Rule bills, they appear to be very much
in a minority and despite what Burton and Drewry say, that
number does not appear to be growing.[7] Of course, any conclusions
must be circumspect because it may be that many Ten-Minute-Rule
bills which are introduced are contentious but are not opposed as
the bills' opponents know that such bills have little chance of
progressing and that any vote would increase the publicity given to
the bill.

Table 1.6 *Bills making progress 1979–1980*

		Section A: Second Reading days		
Day and date	Time during which bill discussed	Bill	Position in ballot	Stage and vote
(1) 13 July	11.34– 4.00	Abortion (Amendment)	(1)	2R to Com.; V: 242–98
(2) 20 July	11.50– 2.30	Road Traffic (Seat Belts)	(2)	Closure 139–48; 2R V: 139–59
(3) 9 Nov.	11.05–12.07	Child Maintenance Orders	(3)	2R to Com.;
	12.07– 3.18	Youth and Community	(8)	2R to Com.;
	3.18– 4.00	Representation of the People	(11)	2R to C.W.H.;
		Licensed Premises (Exclusion of Certain Persons)	(17)	2R to Com.
(4) 16 Nov.	11.47– 3.42	Protection of Animals (Scientific Purposes)	(4)	2R to Com.
	3.42– 3.59	Deer	(10)	2R to Com.
(5) 23 Nov.	11.10– 4.00	Social Security (Maternity Grant) (Amendment)	(5)	2R Adj. Closure 95–0
		Representation of the People	(11)	Report and Third Reading
(6) 30 Nov.	11.15– 4.00	Licensing Etc. (Amendment)	(6)	2R Adj. Closure 68–13
(7) 7 Dec.	11.18– 3.11	Indecent Display (Control)	(7)	2R to Com.
	3.11– 4.00	Representation of the People (Amendment)	(20)	2R Adj.
		Coroners	(12)	2R to Com.
		Concessionary Travel for Handicapped Persons (Scot.)	(16)	2R to Com.
		Highways (Road Humps)	(18)	2R to Com.
		Ground Game	(19)	2R to Com.
		Gaming (Amendment)	H. of L. Bill	2R to Com.
		Licensing (Amendment) No. 2	S.O. 37	2R to Com.

Table 1.6 (*cont*)

	Section B: Remaining stage days			
Day and date	Time during which bill discussed	Bill	Position in ballot	Stage and Vote
(8) 8 Feb.	9.45 – 2.30	Abortion (Amendment)	(1)	Report: vote on new clause negatived 256–159
(9) 15 Feb.	9.45 – 2.30	Abortion (Amendment)	(1)	Report Adj 3 votes
		Import of Live Fish (England and Wales)	S.O. 37	2R to Com.
(10) 22 Feb.	9.35 – 2.30	Road Traffic (Seat Belts)	(2)	Report Adj
		Import of Live Fish (England and Wales)	S.O. 37	Report: Third Reading
(11) 29 Feb.	9.35 – 2.30	Abortion (Amendment)	(1)	Report Adj 3 votes
		Married Women's Policies of Assurance (Scotland) (Amendment)	(24)	2R to Com.
		Gaming (Amendment)	H. of L.	Report: Third Reading
(12) 7 Mar.	9.53 – 12.32	Concessionary Travel for Handicapped Persons (Scotland)	(16)	Report: Third Reading
	12.32 – 2.30	Road Traffic (Seat Belts)	(2)	Report Adj
(13) 14 Mar.	9.30 – 2.30	Abortion (Amendment)	(1)	Report Adj 6 votes
(14) 4 July	9.30 – 11.13	Licensing (Amendment) (No. 2)	S.O. 37	L/A
	11.13 – 12.04	Married Women's Policies of Assurance (Scotland) (Amendment)	(24)	Report (no debate)
	12.04 – 2.30	Youth and Community	(8)	Report Adj
		Deer	(10)	Report: Third Reading
		Highways (Road Humps)	(18)	Report: Third Reading
		Ground Game	(19)	Report: Third Reading

2 The introduction and fate of private members' bills

In this chapter we shall begin by identifying the changes in the type of private members' bills which have been introduced, and in who introduces them, in the post-war period. Although a large number of bills are introduced, a much smaller proportion are passed, so the second section of the chapter will highlight those changes which have occurred in the type of bills which are successful. The third and longest section will then examine the factors which affect the likelihood of a bill receiving the Royal Assent. In this chapter we are almost exclusively concerned with balloted bills.

What type of bills are introduced

Before examining the post-war period in some detail, it is worth saying something about the type of bills which were introduced earlier in the century. The main change is a very important one. From the 1930s there was a marked decline in the introduction of party political bills using the private members' procedure. Before the First World War bills upon Home Rule or Land Reform were commonly introduced by Irish MPs. Similarly, in the 1920s and indeed into the 1930s, Labour MPs brought in a series of overtly party political bills. So a Prevention of Unemployment Bill was introduced in 1919, 1922, 1923, 1925, 1926 and 1927 while a bill to nationalise the coal mines was put down in 1924, 1925, 1936 and 1938. Indeed, as Bromhead emphasises:

During the 1920s and 1930s it was the rule rather than the exception for the Labour Members who had obtained the highest places in the ballot to introduce bills which represented fundamental Labour Party policy.[1]

This use of the ballot procedure was not restricted to Labour and Irish MPs. During the 1920s Conservative MPs introduced a series of bills aimed at restricting the operation of trade unions in one way or another. However, Bromhead indicates that private members' procedure became depoliticised in the 1930s; the bills introduced subsequently were more often technical, non-partisan and uncontentious. He argues:

The evidence for this is to be found not only from a study of the trend in the matter of the type of bills introduced, but also in other ways. We see the tendency for the number of Members voting to decline, for Ministers and Opposition leaders to take less and less part in divisions, and for the whole atmosphere of the debates to become less and less controversial.[2]

The reasons for this change are clearly complex. As far as the Labour Party was concerned, the split in their ranks caused by Ramsey McDonald's defection to lead the National Government probably meant that the remaining Labour MPs were more concerned with Party unity inside and outside Parliament than with proselytising Party policy through private members' procedure. At the same time, once the Labour Party became a party of Government then, periodically at least, they had the chance to legislate. In the case of the Conservatives, they had always been less disposed to use ballot places to forward party policy, partly because their party had usually been in Government. At the same time, Bromhead suggests that Conservatives were strongly influenced by Baldwin's speech on the Trade Union Bill of 1925. The bill aimed to regulate trade unions, in particular by abolishing 'contracting out'. It was strongly supported by most Conservative back-benchers. However, after the opening speeches of the Second Reading debate, Baldwin moved an amendment arguing that big and controversial measures should not be introduced as private members' bills. Bromhead suggests that this strong assertion of the primacy of Government, while it merely confirmed existing trends, did mark a turning point in the attitudes of Conservative back-benchers.[3]

Bromhead also points to the influence of the report of the Select Committee on Procedure (unofficial Members' Business) in 1927. This report, which resulted in a revision of the Standing Orders, recommended the allocation of specific time for the consideration of the later stages of private members' bills. This reform offered more chance of success for bills but only if those bills were relatively uncontentious and therefore unlikely to be filibustered. So the change encouraged MPs to introduce limited 'constructive' bills which now had a real hope of success.

Despite all this the main reason for the depoliticisation of private members' business surely lies in the changing nature of relations between the executive and the legislature. As the executive came increasingly to dominate the House of Commons so it reduced the time and discretion available to private members. This argument is well summarised by Bromhead:

The fundamental argument is related to the modern conception of governmental responsibility. We have moved so far, in Britain at any rate, from the principle of the separation of the legislative and executive powers, that there is a widely held supposition – not, perhaps, explicitly stated, but clearly recognizable – that the Government of the day, because it will be responsible for administering any new Act of Parliament, ought not to be expected to have to take responsibility for administering any new Act that it had not itself decided to introduce. The obverse side of this argument is that it is wrong for individual Members of Parliament, as individuals, to introduce measures for the administration of which they will themselves have no responsibility. It may be suggested that the legislative work of Parliament in any one session should be regarded as a single whole, and that the allocation of priorities among different proposals ought to be decided entirely by the Government, whose responsibility for the whole of the legislative programme should be undivided.[4]

Bromhead treats this argument as a question. On this basis he asks: Does private members' procedure serve a useful purpose? This book is also concerned to address that question. However, our point here is that a variant upon the argument Bromhead cites has come to dominate both the executive's and the legislature's view of the ballot procedure. The procedure should be used to deal with non-partisan issues, either moral issues (broadly defined) which are political but cut across the party divide, or technical issues which are in most senses non-political. As most MPs came to accept this convention then the procedure inevitably became depoliticised.

So far we have paid little attention to the type of bills which are introduced. The first point to confirm is that in the post-war period party political ballot bills have been unusual. There have been some. Bromhead himself indicates that a number of Labour members introduced bills on party matters in 1954–5 in the run up to the 1955 general election. In the later period partisan balloted bills have been rare. However, in contrast, as we suggested in the last chapter, there has been a clear trend for Ten-Minute-Rule bills to become more partisan. So Burton and Drewry report after their review of the 1977/8 and 1978/9 Sessions:

The increased number of Ten Minute Rule motions taken to a division continued. More and more these divisions take place over bills whose titles deliberately flaunt partisan attitudes to contemporary political issues and which are in no sense serious legislative endeavours.[5]

Bromhead in examining the post-war period identifies four types of private members' bills, those concerned with: constitutional reform; moral and social betterment; legal reforms; and the regulation of professions.[6] Richards extends the list by introducing a category for bills concerned with local authorities.[7] However, even these five categories no longer seem adequate and retaining them would mean that a large number of bills were left in a miscellaneous category or were assigned to a category into which they do not happily fit. In fact it is clear that the type of bills introduced have changed, if only slightly, and the number of subjects involved have increased in the post-war period. This is one reason why we have used the ten-category classification developed by Burton and Drewry.[8] However, this classification has another advantage. It was produced mainly as a basis for categorising Government bills. Thus it is relatively easy to see both which type of subject is rarely dealt with through the ballot procedure and also which topics are more frequently the subject of private members' than of Government bills.

It is clear from Table 2.1 that most balloted bills fall into four categories. Three types of bill, those dealing with the administration of the welfare services, relations between individuals and the state, and relations between individuals and groups, have fairly consistently made up 20 per cent each of the balloted bills introduced. Bills dealing with constitutional and administrative law have also been common, although, as we shall see later, the number of such bills has been decreasing over the period studied. There have been very few bills indeed dealing with the regulation of the economy, foreign affairs, or relations between foreigners and the state. Private members thus have concentrated upon the broad area of the relationship between the citizen and the state, the bureaucracy, or his/her employer/trade union. In comparison Government bills deal much more frequently with economic policy and foreign affairs and much less frequently with welfare services and with relations between individuals and groups, or individuals and the state.

There have been fewer changes in the type of bills introduced than we would have expected, given the changes in society and social attitudes, and the massive increase in legislation, which has occurred in the post-war period. One change has involved a reduction in the number of bills dealing with constitutional and administrative law. These made up almost 20 per cent of the bills

Table 2.1 Types of bill introduced under the ballot procedure in the post-war period

(Figures are number of bills in category expressed as a percentage of total number of balloted bills introduced in given period – raw numbers in brackets)

Period of Government	Constitutional and administrative law	Public finance and the regulation of the economy	Administration of welfare services	Administration of non-welfare services	Land use environmental control and transport	Relations between individuals and the state	Relations between individuals and groups	Relations between foreigners and the state	External relations	Animals	Total
Conservative 1951–64	20 (54)	3 (8)	13 (36)	2 (6)	10 (28)	21 (58)	24 (66)	0 (1)	0 (1)	6 (16)	100% (274)
Labour 1964–70	19 (28)	1 (2)	20 (29)	3 (4)	6 (9)	26 (37)	17 (24)	0	2 (3)	6 (8)	100% (144)
Conservative 1970–4	10 (8)	3 (2)	20 (16)	6 (5)	5 (4)	19 (15)	31 (25)	1 (1)	0	5 (4)	100% (80)
Labour 1974–9	14 (15)	6 (7)	23 (25)	6 (7)	6 (6)	21 (23)	20 (22)	3 (3)	0	1 (1)	100% (109)
Conservative 1979–84	13 (16)	5 (6)	12 (15)	11 (14)	12 (15)	12 (15)	26 (32)	2 (2)	0	4 (5)	100% (122)

introduced between 1950 and 1970, but up to 10 per cent less of the bills in the subsequent period. This reduction is probably related to the increase in Government involvement in this field. The 1960s and 1970s after all saw Government attempts, some of them successful, to restructure Government departments, reorganise local authorities, reform the House of Lords, enter the European Community, and establish devolved government. As private members, as we have seen, tend to legislate in fields avoided by Government, the increased Government activity in this reduced the need for, and the appropriateness of, private members' legislation.

Most of the changes have been small and transient with MPs apparently responding to a mixture of their perception of the need for legislation, interest group activity, ideological changes and the increased role played by Government in the procedure. So, for example, while in the 1964–70 Parliaments 26 per cent of the balloted bills introduced dealt with the relationship between the individual and the state, the subsequent period between 1970–4 witnessed a 7 per cent decline in this figure. This decline appears to have resulted from the fact that the 1964–70 period witnessed a considerable amount of liberalising legislation in this field. Thus the impetus towards, and the perceived need for, liberal reform in this area was less in the subsequent period. In contrast the number of bills dealing with the protection of the individual against various groups increased from 17 per cent in 1964–70 to 31 per cent in 1970–4 before getting down to a level nearer 20 per cent. In particular during this later period there was a spate of landlord and tenant and consumer-protection bills. This growth probably owed a great deal to the increased activity of interest groups, particularly those concerned with the rights of the consumer, in the late 1960s and the early 1970s.

More recently the number of balloted bills dealing with the administration of welfare services and relations between the individual and the state have declined since 1979. A number of related reasons for this can be suggested. The Conservative Government elected in 1979 has an ideological commitment to the reduction of the 'Nanny' state. This rhetoric may well have had an effect on the thinking of MPs when it comes to the introduction of balloted bills, particularly given that the number of Conservative MPs has increased and the number of Liberal opposition MPs has decreased, especially since the 1983 election. At the same time, as we shall see later, after 1979, and particularly since 1981, the Government has

Table 2.2 *Party affiliation of MPs introducing private members' bills under the three procedures – 1951/2 to 1984/5*

(broken down by Governments)

Period of Government	Ballot (number and percentage)			Standing Order 39			Ten-Minute-Rule			Total
	Con.	Lab.	Other	Con.	Lab.	Other	Con.	Lab.	Other	
Conservative 1951/2–1963/4	153 (60)	92 (36)	10 (4)	51 (67)	21 (28)	4 (5)	61 (33)	117 (64)	7 (4)	516
Labour 1964/5–1969/70	84 (58)	53 (37)	7 (5)	48 (44)	45 (42)	15 (14)	63 (33)	113 (59)	17 (8)	445
Conservative 1970/1–1973/4	38 (47)	40 (50)	2 (3)	25 (45)	30 (54)	1 (1)	28 (22)	98 (76)	2 (2)	264
Labour 1974–1978/9	61 (56)	42 (39)	6 (5)	57 (62)	31 (30)	4 (8)	101 (45)	103 (46)	18 (8)	423
Conservative 1979/80–1984/5	83 (62)	42 (32)	8 (6)	60 (49)	56 (42)	12 (9)	98 (34)	153 (54)	33 (12)	545
Total	419 (58)	269 (38)	33 (4)	241 (53)	183 (39)	36 (8)	351 (35)	584 (57)	77 (8)	2193

played a larger role in the origins of balloted bills. The combined effect of the increased Government role and its rhetoric may explain the decline in bills designed to increase welfare position or require a greater Government involvement in relation to the individual.

Which MPs introduce bills?

Are MPs of one party more likely to use the procedure? Table 2.2 indicated some clear and interesting patterns. Conservative MPs have made considerably more use of the ballot procedure than Labour MPs. Of course, given the great element of chance in the ballot, no MP can ensure s/he will be able to introduce a bill. However, only in one period of Government – the 1970–4 Conservative Government – did Labour MPs introduce as many bills as Conservative MPs. In 1974–9, for example, despite the fact the Labour Party was clearly the largest party, 56 per cent of balloted bills were introduced by Conservative MPs and only 39 per cent by Labour MPs. This is because a lower proportion of Labour back-benchers enter the ballot than Conservative back-benchers. The pattern is similar though much less definite if we consider Standing Order Number 39 bills. Indeed in the case of such bills there is a tendency for Opposition MPs to be more likely to introduce bills regardless of which party is in power. So Conservative MPs introduced more Standing Order Number 39 bills in the two periods of Labour Government 1964–70 and 1974–9 while Labour MPs introduced more such bills during the 1970–4 Conservative Government.

Despite this, perhaps the most interesting pattern of all in Table 2.2 concerns the much greater use of the Ten-Minute-Rule-bill procedure by Labour MPs. During the life of every Government since the war, Labour MPs have been more likely, and in most cases *much* more likely, to use this procedure than Conservative MPs. We had expected that because this procedure is used to provoke political debate then, as is to some extent the case with Standing Order Number 39 bills, it might be more used by Opposition MPs regardless of the party in Government. However, it is clearly a procedure which has a great deal of appeal to Labour MPs. Certainly Labour MPs tend to be more likely to dissent generally and perhaps are less respectful of the traditions of Parliament than Conservative MPs. It may be, therefore, that while Conservative MPs are more concerned to use the procedure, less frequently, to promote 'causes', Labour MPs see the procedure as a means by which either to criticise the Government of whatever party or promote party policy. As Bromhead indicated, there is certainly a tradition throughout the century of Labour MPs specifically using private members' bills to promote party policy and bills. Perhaps what has happened since Bromhead's time is that Labour MPs have realised that the ballot procedure is, more or less, reserved for uncontentious bills and have shifted their focus to the use of the Ten-Minute-Rule procedure in pursuit of combative and publicised debate.

What types of bills are successful?

Of course, while it is interesting to discover the type of bill introduced and which MPs introduce them, most private members' bills never reach the statute book. So we also need to know which types of bill are successful. In fact, the data reveals only one major pattern (Table 2.3). There has been a decline in the success rate of

Table 2.3 Success rate of bills introduced under the ballot procedure in the post-war period

Figures are number of bills receiving Royal Assent in category expressed as total number of bills introduced in that category

Period of Government	Constitutional and administrative law	Public finance and the regulation of the economy	Administration of welfare services	Administration of non-welfare services	Land use environmental control and transport	Category of bill — Relations between individuals and the state	Relations between individuals and groups	Relations between foreigners and the state	External relations	Animals	Total
Conservative 1951–64	57%	38%	25%	67%	39%	45%	50%	0%	100%	50%	46%
Labour 1964–70	25%	0%	14%	75%	34%	16%	25%	n/a	67%	13%	22%
Conservative 1970–4	38%	50%	19%	20%	25%	27%	36%	0%	n/a	0%	28%
Labour 1974–9	27%	14%	33%	0%	50%	39%	50%	33%	n/a	0%	34%
Conservative 1979–84	43%	17%	27%	36%	60%	41%	34%	0%	n/a	60%	30%

private members' balloted bills generally. In the 1951–64 period 46 per cent of the bills introduced received the Royal Assent. Subsequently the success rate has dropped below 30 per cent. Interestingly enough the rate reached its lowest level, 22 per cent, during the 1964–70 period of Labour Government which tends to be viewed as the 'golden age' of private members' bills. The success rate has improved since to around the 30 per cent level. Why have these changes occurred?

The period of Conservative Government between 1951 and 1964 and the subsequent period of Labour Government 1964–70 were both atypical, although in different ways. It is often suggested that the Conservatives ran out of ideas or policies in their third term so that private members' bills in some senses expanded into the vacuum. Certainly it is clear as we shall see below that this Conservative Government was much more willing to grant Government time to balloted bills than any later Conservative Government has been. Both these factors, although especially the latter, probably helped increase the success rate of bills. The Labour Government between 1964 and 1970 was also willing to grant Government time for the consideration of private members' bills. However, there were two short Parliamentary Sessions, in 1966 and 1970, during this period which prevented the passage of bills.

The declining success rate in the post-war period is mainly a consequence of the increased reluctance of Governments of both parties to grant time, a feature we will return to at length later. This reluctance ensures that at present there is little chance of any major contentious legislation reaching the statute book as a private members' bill. Given this change, the success rate has only remained at somewhere near the 30 per cent level because the types of bills which are being introduced under the procedure have become much less ambitious, less contentious and more technical.

However, the declining success rate also owes something to an increase in the knowledge of procedure among back-bench MPs. One point which emerged consistently from our interviews was that a large number of MPs were aware that it was relatively easy to obstruct a private members' bill by putting down a large number of amendments at Report stage, and by sophisticated filibustering. There is no doubt that the best example of the use of this strategy concerned the 1979 Abortion (Amendment) Bill. Here opponents of the bill had clearly learnt lessons on the use of procedure from previous experience, particularly, although not exclusively, in dealing with prior abortion bills. At the same time the scale and the success of the efforts of the opponents of the Corrie bills made other MPs not interested directly in abortion, aware of the limitations of private-members'-bill procedure. Now many MPs, even if they do not have our figures at their disposal, know that almost any opposition can defeat a private members' bill.

Two other minor patterns emerge from Table 2.3 which are worthy of brief comment. Both constitutional and administrative law bills and bills concerned with relations between individuals and groups have a noticeably higher success rate than the average. Many of the first type of bill are based upon reports by the Law Commission and have active Government involvement or support. They are often technical and uncontentious. All these factors help ensure success. In the case of bills concerned with relations between individuals and groups once again most are uncontentious, often concerned with updating previous legislation or improving the position of the consumer or the handicapped. In most cases the commercial or professional interests whose affairs are being regulated have been consulted and often Government has been actively involved in the drafting of the bill.

Why do bills succeed or fail?

There is an adequate one-word answer to this question. Private members' bills fail if they are opposed in Parliament, if they are any way contentious. In fact almost any degree of opposition will prevent a bill becoming law. So any balloted bill which has no time for debate at the Second Reading stage, and any non-balloted bill, can be prevented from having a Second Reading if one member shouts 'Object' at the relevant time. What is more, the MP who thus opposes the bill may, in fact, have no interest in it, but merely be opposing it to prevent it progressing, and thus taking up time which the MP hopes will be spent on a bill in which he is interested. In this way in the 1979/80 Session the progress of a number of bills of MPs with lower positions in the ballot was affected by the objections of supporters of the Corrie Abortion (Amendment) Bill who were attempting to ensure that their bill had the maximum amount of time possible at Report stage. It is not only bills with lower positions on the ballot, however, which can be defeated by minimal opposition. In the period since the Second World War only 10 bills which have had votes on Second or Third Reading, that is, bills whose principles have been clearly contentious, became law. Of these, only three did not receive Government time, and the last of these three bills was successful in the 1958/9 Session. As a rule of thumb, therefore, we can say that bills which are opposed, that is, which are contentious, have little chance of passage without the aid of the Government. A brief look at the history of the abortion issue, which we shall consider at length later, amply confirms this point.

The abortion issue is an unusually contentious and recurring one. The original Abortion Act was passed in 1967 only because David Steel's private members' bill, which was opposed throughout its passage by a growing number of MPs, received significant and consistent support from the Labour Government. Since that time three major balloted bills have been introduced to amend it, and each has been unusual in the amount of interest it has generated, with on each occasion over 300 MPs voting on the Second Reading. What is more, each of these bills has received a comfortable majority, in the case of the Corrie Bill a majority of 144, at Second Reading. Yet none of these bills has become law, although the Corrie Bill had an unprecedented four days of debate at Report stage. The main reason is a simple one. Private members' procedure is such that a small number of well-organised MPs can block any private members' bill, even one with overwhelming support. There are no guillotines on debate and the Speaker will allow a certain amount of debate on all amendments before he will accept a closure motion. Thus the opponents of a bill merely need to put down a significant number of amendments and speak at length without too much repetition to ensure that any bill is effectively filibustered.

This happened in the case of the Corrie Bill, as Marsh and Chambers show, but it also happened to Neil Carmichael's Seat-Belts Bill in the same Session. The bill received strong support at Second Reading and had one-and-a-half days' debate on Report stage, but was, in effect, filibustered by two MPs, Sir Ronald Bell and Ivan Lawrence.

Abortion bills and seat-belts bills are unusual in that they provoke enough interest to ensure that a large number of MPs stay at Westminster on a given Friday. However, most private members' bills are not of this sort, and on most Fridays more MPs are in their constituencies, or elsewhere, than are in Westminster. This presents another problem for opposed bills as an MP needs to muster 100 MPs to support it if a closure vote is called either at the end of the Second Reading debate, or at the end of debate on an

Table 2.4 *Position in ballot–success rate (decades)*

	1948–60		1960–70		1970–80		1980–5	
	N	percentage	N	percentage	N	percentage	N	percentage
1–6	36	54.5	21	35.0	23	34.8	15	50.0
	(66)		(60)		(66)		(30)	
7–12	17	25.7	26	43.3	21	32.8	9	30.0
	(66)		(60)		(64)		(30)	
13–20	30	35.3	27	35.3	20	25.3	14	40.0
	(85)		(76)		(79)		(35)	
20+	1	100.0	4	16.0	1	25.0	n/a	
	(1)		(25)		(4)			

amendment at Report stage. In fact, many bills fail to achieve a Second Reading not because they are defeated on a vote but because their supporters cannot persuade 100 MPs to support a closure. As an example, Kevin McNamara's Social Security (Maternity Grants) (Amendment) Bill failed to get a Second Reading in the 1979/80 Session because he could not win a closure vote. In fact 95 people voted for the closure with no one against but there were not the requisite 100 voting. The Speaker refused to allow a Second Reading vote so the bill in effect fell. This is just one of many examples. Once again it can hardly be emphasised enough that the whole procedure is such as to prevent non-technical and/or contentious bills progressing without Government support and as we have already indicated, Government time is largely a thing of the past.

The ballot position

Some observers perpetuate the idea that as far as balloted bills are concerned the position in the ballot is the crucial determinant of the success or failure of a bill.[9] This view is based upon the fact that only bills in the first six places in the ballot are guaranteed a full debate, and thus almost guaranteed a vote on Second Reading. The data presented in Table 2.4 do not confirm this position.

In the initial post-war period bills drawn in the first six were almost twice as likely to pass as other bills. Subsequently, however, the position a bill drew in the ballot had virtually no influence upon its passage. The reason for this follows naturally from our previous discussion. Individual MPs drawing high places in the ballot became increasingly likely to take up a controversial bill because, with such a position, they were virtually guaranteed a Second Reading vote. At the same time, such bills were less likely to be given Government time in the later period, and these controversial opposed bills were almost certain to be defeated. MPs with lower positions in the ballot are usually less ambitious: they often take bills which are Government bills in all but name, and, as such, have a fair chance of success.

3 The Government and private members' bills

In many ways the term 'private members' bill' is a misnomer. Many of the bills, and increasingly more of the bills, which are introduced and passed are, in all but name, Government bills. In addition the Government's attitude to those bills which they do not introduce, while it does not completely determine their fate, is crucial. In this chapter we shall examine the type and extent of the Government's involvement with bills. The first section will attempt to establish how many private members' bills originate in Government departments. The second section will then look at how the attitude of Government can affect those private members' bills which don't originate in a department. The final section will then examine the question of Government time in order to show how the amount of time given by Governments for the consideration of private members' bills has significantly decreased.

The origins of private members' bills

We have identified four major sources of private members' bills – Law Commissions, Committee reports, the Government and interest groups. However, before we discuss the methods used and report our results, it must be emphasised that the type of bills from the various sources is significantly different. Bills which originate from one of the first three sources share crucial features – they are generally non-partisan, minor, technical and uncontentious. In contrast bills which are sponsored by interest groups are much more likely to be broad, contentious and sometimes even partisan. Some empirical confirmation of this general point can be found in Table 3.1. As we have said before, there are relatively few votes on private members' bills on the floor of the House. In Table 3.1 we examine those bills upon which there were votes in the post-war period. It is clear that most of the votes, and increasingly more of the votes, occur on those bills which are sponsored by

Table 3.1 *The origins of balloted bills upon which there were votes*

(Expressed as a pecentage of the total number of bills on which there were votes – raw numbers in brackets)

Period	Government	Official report/ Law Commission	Interest Group	
1948/9–1950/1	n/a	29	29	
		(2)	(2)	(7)
1950/1–1963/4	8	15	3	
	(1)	(2)	(3)	(13)
1964/5–1969/70	n/a	n/a	38	
			(10)	(26)
1970/1–1973/4	n/a	n/a	100	
			(2)	(2)
1974–1978/9			58	
			(7)	(12)
1979/80–1985/6	7	n/a	64	
	(1)		(9)	(14)

interest groups. In contrast, few of the bills, and since 1964 almost none of the bills, on which there are votes are bills which derive from the Government directly, or from Government reports or the Law Commission.

What leads an MP to sponsor a bill from a particular source? MPs choose a departmental bill for a number of related reasons. In fact almost inevitably such bills are chosen by MPs who draw a position outside the first six in the ballot and are thus not guaranteed a debate and vote on Second Reading.[1] This means that the only realistic chance of getting their name on the Statute Book is by taking a small non-contentious bill with Government support. In such circumstances an MP will often approach the Whips who have a list of small bills. These are bills which departments are anxious to see passed, but which are generally regarded as of too little importance to merit inclusion in the Government legislative programme. The MP can consult this list and choose a bill, probably one which affects an area of the country, or a sphere of policy, with which he is concerned.

William McKelvey's Married Women's Policy of Assurance (Scotland) Bill provides a revealing, if slightly unusual, example of this process. As we have already said, the 1979/80 Session was a long one and the names of 24 MPs (instead of the more usual 20) were drawn from the private members' ballot. William McKelvey, the new Labour MP for Kilmarnock, drew 24th place. As a new boy he had little idea of the procedure, but at least knew that his chances of success were limited. For this reason, after consultation with more experienced colleagues, and despite the fact that he was an Opposition MP, he approached Nicholas Fairbairn, Solicitor General for Scotland, and asked if they had any non-partisan, humane bills which he might promote. After a day or two Fairbairn came back with a number of suggestions from which McKelvey chose his bill, which, for the first time, allowed Scottish women to take out an insurance policy on their husband's life with a Scottish firm. The Scottish Office drafted the bill and their civil servants and lawyers briefed McKelvey throughout its passage. After being initially delayed by supporters of the Corrie bill, McKelvey's bill received an unopposed Second Reading, was discussed for only 51 minutes at Third Reading, and received the Royal Assent.[2] Such bills, being uncontentious and enjoying Government support in drafting, almost inevitably succeed. This case was slightly unusual only because an Opposition MP was involved.

On rarer occasions a Whip, or a Minister, may approach an MP with a place in the ballot and ask him to introduce a Government bill. In the 1980/1 Session Robert Banks, Conservative MP for Harrogate, won 14th place in the ballot. He knew he had no chance of success with a controversial bill so he initially approached the whips who gave him a list of 15 or 20 bills that the Government would like introduced. He was considering the list when William Whitelaw, then Home Secretary, approached him in the House of Commons Smoking Room. Whitelaw suggested that he might sponsor a licensing bill which the Home Office wanted introduced. Banks talked to the Home Office and to various brewing interests. The Licensing (Alcohol Education and Research) Bill was drafted by the Home Office, although Banks was consulted. Throughout the passage of the bill two or three fairly senior civil servants provided Banks with briefs on any amendments which were introduced to the bill, and indeed serviced him in the same way they would a Minister piloting through a Government bill.[3] The bill was minor and uncontentious. It passed Second Reading with no vote after a one-and-a-half-hour debate. Its Committee stage was taken in a Committee of the Whole House which lasted 45 minutes. The Third

Reading followed immediately and took 25 minutes. In fact this represents a classic example of the type of private members' bill which is successful currently.

The Law Commissions Act 1965 established the statutory duties of the Law Commissioners. They were required to eliminate anomalies, repeal obsolete bills and generally simplify and modify the law. The investigations which followed took some time so the major flow of bills which resulted from the Law Commissions' Reports occurred in the 1970–4 Parliament. The bills which originate with the Law Commission, or even in Government committees, are without exception minor and technical. The bills drafted by a Law Commission are concerned with statute law revision and almost inevitably pass with little discussion, unless their progress is delayed for tactical reasons by supporters of other bills. The Law Reform (Miscellaneous Provisions) Bill in the 1970/1 Session presents a typical example of the type of bill involved.[4] It was introduced by A. Probert, Labour MP for Aberdare, and was based in part upon a Law Commission Report on the Limitations Act (1963). It extended from one to three years the time limit for claiming damages for personal injury or death and established that the fact or prospect of remarriage should be discounted when widow's damages were assessed under the Fatal Accidents Acts.

We shall deal with the role of interest groups in the ballot procedure at length in the next chapter. However, it is clear both that they play an important role and that the bills which are sponsored by interest groups tend to be more substantial and contentious than those which have other sources. In fact, any MP who wins a prominent place in the ballot is inundated with mail and approaches from interest groups anxious to promote legislative change. This process is very graphically portrayed in Austin Mitchell's account of the fate of his House Buyers Bill introduced in the 1983/4 Session:

nearly all backbenchers enter the annual ballot for Private Members' bills. Many are pushed into it by the Whips, a few have a cause to push, most enter because this event, symbolically a lottery, is one of the few prospects of achievement, a rare escape from that impotent futility which is the backbencher's life. Like most MPs, when I entered the first ballot of the new Parliament in June 1983, I hadn't a legislative idea in my head. Until lunch time on 30th June, when Mary Whitehouse grabbed me as I emerged from the gents toilet in the Commons' basement, saying 'I want you', I had even forgotten I'd entered. Suddenly I was courted, I had won sixth place.[5]

Table 3.2 *Origins of balloted bills (by parties of Government)*

Government(s) in power	Law Commission	Reports rec.	Interest groups	Government	Misc.	None
Labour 1948/9–1950/1	–	1 (4%)	10 (40%)	1 (4%)	4 (16%)	9 (36%)
Conservative 1951/2–1963/4	–	15 (9%)	50 (20%)	12 (7%)	9 (5%)	88 (60%)
Labour 1964/5–1969/70	–	1 (1%)	33 (34%)	6 (6%)	6 (6%)	71 (68%)
Conservative 1970/1–1973/4	8 (13%)	11 (29%)	17 (27%)	6 (10%)	2 (3%)	19 (30%)
Labour 1974/5–1978/9	–	22 (27%)	24 (29%)	10 (12%)	–	31 (38%)
Conservative 1979/85–1985/6	3 (3%)	25 (23%)	25 (23%)	19 (18%)	8 (7%)	28 (26%)

Few people appear to recognise the scale of the Government's involvement in the process. Bromhead devoted a chapter to 'The Government and Private Members' Bills'.[6] However, he was most concerned to quantify the involvement of Ministers in the debates and divisions upon a bill. Bromhead did discuss the weapons available to Government for use against bills they oppose, but he said little about the use of the procedure by Governments to get through minor pieces of their own legislation.[7] In contrast, almost all recent observers mention the Government as a source of private members' bills but none give an accurate indication of the scale of the Government involvement. In fact, Burton and Drewry, whose work is the most thorough, acknowledge the limitations of their data when they claim: 'It is common knowledge that some bills (*we have no evidence of how many*) are officially drafted.'[8]

In contrast, Table 3.2 is based upon an examination of the origins of all those balloted bills introduced between the 1948/9 and 1985/6 Sessions which made any progress. This material is derived from a reading of the *Hansard* reports of the debates upon each bill. In these debates either the bill's sponsor, or the Minister who speaks in the debate, usually indicates the origins of the bill and the Government's attitude towards it. Of course, such data has its

limitations because sometimes a bill is not debated or the origin of
the bill is not discussed. However, it was impractical to interview all
those MPs who introduced bills in this period so our data is the best
practically available. Nevertheless we did interview, or correspond
with, all MPs who introduced bills in the 1979/80 and 1980/1
Sessions and this enabled us to test the reliability of the results of
our primary method and to provide more detailed information
about those two Sessions which are used for the case studies in this
book.

As we have already said, there are four major sources of private
members' bills – Law Commissions, Committee reports, the
Government and interest groups. However, Table 3.2 also includes
both a miscellaneous category and a category for those bills whose
origins could not be identified by the method used. The latter
category is particularly large in the earlier period when sponsors
tended to be less forthcoming in their speeches as to the origins of
their bills. There is no indication, however, that these sponsors
were particularly reluctant to admit Government assistance and
anyway as we also monitored the speeches of the responsible
Government Minister in each debate this served as a check upon the
Government's role. As such it is unlikely that our results are unduly
affected by our failure to specify the sources of so many of the
earlier bills. Nevertheless our data is limited. Despite this Table 3.2
reveals interesting patterns. Interest groups have declined in
importance as a source of bills while reports, mostly Government
inquiries, have increased in importance. The role of the Law
Commissions was only really significant in the 1970–74 Parliament,
a fact which probably caused Burton and Drewry, whose book dealt
with this period only, to over emphasise them as a source of private
members' bills.[9] Nevertheless the most interesting pattern to
emerge concerns the growth of bills which originate directly in
Government departments. Indeed 18 per cent of the bills introduced in the lifetime of the Thatcher Government to the end of the
1985/6 Session had their origins in a department. What is more, that
figure certainly vastly under emphasises the role of the Government in the drafting of bills. Many bills, while based on the reports
of Committees appointed by Government, are in fact prepared by
Government draftsmen. Some idea of the truth of this assertion can
be gleaned from Table 3.3 which indicates that the vast majority of
bills whose origin we have categorised as Reports or the Law
Commission, are supported by Government. In contrast, many

Table 3.3 *Government attitude to all private members' bills originated by pressure groups or in Law Commision or Committee Reports (by party in power)*

Party in Power	Percentage of bills originating with pressure groups which Government supported	Percentage of bills originating in Law Commission or Committee Report which Government supported
Labour 1948/9–1950/1	20	0
Conservative 1951/2–1963/4	32	57
Labour 1964/5–1969/70	14	0
Conservative 1970/1–1973/4	33	80
Labour 1974–1978/9	33	73
Conservative 1979/80–1985/6	24	86

fewer bills sponsored by interest groups receive the Government 'seal of approval'. If our interpretation is correct, and there seems little doubt that it is, this means that it is conceivable that by the 1980s almost 40 per cent of private members' bills have important origins in a department.

The pattern is even clearer in Table 3.4 which deals exclusively with successful bills. During the Thatcher Governments a third of the successful bills emanated directly from Government Departments while a further 31 per cent had their origins in Reports, most often Government Reports. Once again the role of interest groups has declined significantly in the post-war period while that of Government and Reports has substantially increased. The reasons for these changes are clear. If an MP introduces a bill because of personal interest, or after an approach from an interest group, it is, as we have indicated, often broad, non-technical and contentious. Thus it has little chance of succeeding without Government time. As we shall see later Governments are now much less willing to grant time than in the past so the chances of such bills succeeding

Table 3.4 *Origins of successful balloted bills (by parties of Government)*

				Origins			
Government(s)	Law Commis- sion	Reports etc.	Interest groups	Government	Previous bills	Misc.	None
Labour 1948/9	0	1 (10%)	3 (30%)	1 (10%)	0	2 (20%)	3 (30%)
Conservative 1951/2–1963/4	0	10 (10%)	31 (31%)	5 (5%)	0	2 (2%)	53 (53%)
Labour 1964/5–1969/70	0	1 (2%)	15 (29%)	3 (6%)	0	1 (2%)	31 (60%)
Conservative 1970/1–1973/4	8 (23%)	7 (20%)	6 (17%)	5 (14%)	0	0	9 (26%)
Labour 1974/5–1978/9	3 (7%)	14 (32%)	4 (9%)	10 (23%)	0	0	13 (30%)
Conservative 1979/80–1985/6	1 (2%)	19 (31%)	5 (8%)	20 (33%)	0	5 (8%)	11 (18%)

are slim. In contrast, bills from a Government department or based upon a Government or Law Commission Report are narrow, technical and non-contentious. They have, therefore, much more chance of passing and MPs, increasingly aware of the limitations of the procedure, have become more willing to introduce such bills.

The Government's attitude to bills

Burton and Drewry argued that:

A major determinant of the success or otherwise of any backbench bill is the Government's attitude towards it.[10]

Our figures confirm this assessment. As we have already seen, many bills are drafted in the Department. However, Tables 3.5 and 3.6 indicate that even in the case of those bills which Governments do not draft their attitude is important. The Government attitude to balloted bills has fluctuated considerably over the period but since the election of the Conservative Government in 1979 63 per cent of the bills introduced received support from the Government. This is more than ever before and indeed this level was only approached in

Table 3.5 *Government attitude to balloted bills (by parties of Government)*

Government(s)	Government attitude					
	strong support	support	ambivalent	neutral	opposed	none
Labour 1948/9–1950/1	–	10 (40%)	–	4 (16%)	11 (44%)	–
Conservative 1951/2–1963/4	37 (18%)	87 (43%)	11 (5%)	19 (9%)	47 (23%)	–
Labour 1964/5–1969/70	20 (19%)	26 (25%)	6 (6%)	15 (14%)	38 (36%)	–
Conservative 1970/1–1973/4	2 (3%)	32 (52%)	8 (13%)	2 (3%)	17 (27%)	1 (2%)
Labour 1974–1978/9	7 (12%)	11 (19%)	3 (5%)	4 (7%)	27 (46%)	7 (12%)
Conservative 1979/80–1985/6	18 (17%)	49 (46%)	5 (5%)	10 (9%)	18 (17%)	6 (6%)

the 1951–64 period of Conservative Government. Again this would suggest that MPs are now more willing to introduce technical non-contentious bills which the Government can support. The pattern is even clearer in Table 3.5 which concentrates upon successful bills. If a bill is opposed by Government it has very little chance of success.[11] In the entire post-war period only seven bills to which the Government expressed any opposition passed, and the last of these was the Mental Health (Amendment) Act in the 1974/5 Session. Indeed, even if a Government is ambivalent or neutral, few bills succeed. So in all the periods of Government over 70 per cent of the bills passed had Government support or strong support. Again Table 3.6 also confirms the impression of other tables that the importance of Government has increased in the recent period, with 90 per cent of the successful bills since the 1979 election having Government support. There is little doubt over all then that the Thatcher Conservative Governments, despite being reluctant to give Government time as we shall see later, have played a more active role in relation to private members' bills than any previous Government.

Our tables have shown that even if bills don't originate in a Government department, the Government's attitude to them is

Table 3.6 *Government attitude to successful balloted bills (by parties of Government)*

	Government attitude					
Government(s)	strong support	support	ambivalent	neutral	opposed	none
Labour 1948/9–1950/1						
Conservative 1951/2–1963/4						
Labour 1964/5–1969/70	11 (22%)	26 (51%)	4 (8%)	8 (16%)	2 (4%)	–
		78%				
Conservative 1970/1–1973/4	3 (9%)	25 (74%)	6 (18%)	–	–	–
		82%				
Labour 1974/5–1978/9	7 (17%?)	26 (62%)	7 (17%)	–	2 (5%)	–
		89%				
Conservative 1979/80–1985/6	14 (24%)	38 (66%)	3 (5%)	3 (5%)	– (5%)	–
		90%				

crucial. However, once again the aggregate pattern gives little idea of the detail of Government involvement. In almost all cases the department which the bill will affect gets involved in improving the drafting of the bill while it is in Committee or between Committee and Report. In some cases, although these are much rarer, it will play a much more active role. Probably the best example of this in the entire post-war period is the Rehabilitation of Offenders Bill passed in the truncated 1974 Parliamentary Session.

As Burton and Drewry emphasise:

The Rehabilitation of Offenders Bill was an extraordinary measure: a controversial Private Members' Bill presented in the truncated session of a minority Parliament and soon shown to have substantial drafting faults, would not normally be thought likely to succeed.[12]

The bill's object was to help rehabilitate convicted criminals by preventing the disclosure of a spent conviction. It had its origin in the 1970 report of a committee established by the Howard League, *Justice* and NACRO which had been the subject of both a private peers' bill and a ballot bill in previous Sessions. The bill was sponsored by Piers Dixon, Conservative MP for Truro, who obtained fifth place in the ballot. This did not ensure a Second Reading in this truncated Session when only five days were allocated for private members' bills. Nevertheless the bill got an unopposed Second Reading with Government support for its principles. So far little about the bill was unusual.

However, in Committee the bill was heavily criticised by two powerful interests: the Guild of British Newspaper Editors, who were concerned about the possibility of libel actions against newspapers, and a significant group of lawyers, who were afraid the bill would encourage lying in court. As a result of these and other criticisms the bill was largely rewritten by the Government draftsmen between Second Reading and Committee and between Committee and Report. The bill which emerged at Report stage bore little resemblance to the original bill. All seven clauses of the bill approved at Second Reading were negatived in Committee and they were replaced by eight new clauses. All the new clauses were put down in the name of the Minister concerned, Alexander Lyon, Minister of State in the Home Office. Lyon formally introduced most of these clauses and talked for 77 minutes (over 25 per cent of the time spent in Committee). Many of the amendments put down by the Minister were drafting amendments. However, the bill was also changed in more substantial ways. At Committee stage the Government introduced an amendment which excluded crown courts and above from the provisions of the bill. At Report stage this exclusion was extended to the magistrates' courts. In addition, the Government introduced an amendment to allow a public interest defence in relation to any civil action for defamation over a spent conviction. The bill was thus radically changed after Second Reading and indeed it was subsequently significantly amended in the Lords. When it returned to the Commons the Government provided time, in all half an hour, for the consideration of the Lords' amendments. This was the only bill given time in this Session. Overall the key point is that while it did not have its origins in the Home Office, it quickly became a Home Office bill. The Government's actions were not Machiavellian. Rather they supported the cause, responded to criticisms of the bill by amending it, and then found themselves committed to a bill which few, if any, wanted. They carried it through rather than lose face but the case illustrates both that a government often interferes with private members' bills, although this is an extreme case, and that it doesn't always know what it is doing.

In contrast the case of Nigel Spearing's bill, the Industrial Diseases (Notification) Bill introduced in the 1980/1 Session, indicates both that Government's attentions are not always well received by a bill's sponsor and that they can be repulsed. Nigel Spearing introduced his Industrial Diseases (Notification) Bill in the 1980/1 Session.[13] It is one of the few bills which we can classify as originating almost exclusively from the member's personal interests, as the main impetus for the bill was provided by a case which involved one of Mr Spearing's constituents. Spearing was well aware of the limitations of the procedure so he chose to introduce a one-clause bill which tightened the regulations for the certification/notification of industrial diseases. The bill was narrow and non-contentious and passed unopposed after a short debate. However, between Second Reading and Committee stage he was approached by the Minister and some of his senior officials who asked him to extend the scope of his bill and include a number of the recommendations of a Royal Commission which had reported on the area in 1972. Spearing refused, largely because he was afraid a larger bill might be delayed and thus defeated. However, in Committee the Minister pushed for an extension of the bill and had considerable support. In response Spearing used a novel procedural tactic. He moved the adjournment of the consideration of his bill by Standing Committee C until after it had considered the next bill in order. This motion was approved. He then wrote to the Secretary of State pointing out that he refused to widen the bill and that problems had arisen in Committee. He was assured that the matter would be sorted out. In the end the Minister on the Committee was changed, the bill was processed and passed on the nod through Report and Third Reading.

Of course, Table 3.5 only deals with those bills which were successful. However, the Government can play a major role in preventing the passage of a bill it opposes. Bromhead deals with this issue at length.[14] However, he is mainly concerned to emphasise that the Government can defeat a bill on a vote by informally mobilising its supporters, whipping the vote, or bringing out the 'payrole vote', that is ensuring that Ministers vote against the bill. This emphasis sounds the wrong note at least as far as the post-war period is concerned. At present votes on private members' bills are unusual so each of these tactics is of limited utility. In fact, if the Government wishes to defeat a bill it uses more covert tactics. The type of strategies the Government can adopt are amply illustrated by a consideration of two bills in the 1979/80 Session.

We have already come across Robert Taylor's Affiliation Orders and Ailments Bill. His bill was not welcomed by the Government but was passed unopposed on Second Reading. The Government then introduced a series of amendments to the bill in Standing Committee. However, Taylor succeeded in winning six votes in Committee against Government advice. The Government was not impressed. Indeed, when the bill came out of Committee he was approached by the Lord Chancellor, Lord Hailsham, who told him that unless he withdrew the bill the Government would ensure its defeat in the House of Lords, either through filibustering it or by whipping Government supporters to vote against it.[15] At the same time, while facing the stick, Taylor was offered an illusory carrot. Lord Hailsham promised that the whole matter would be referred to the Law Commission. Taylor was well aware that there was no chance of anything coming from such a referral but saw little point in persevering towards a certain defeat. The bill was thus withdrawn before its Report stage.

The fate of Trevor Skeet's Youth and Community Bill in the same Session shows the Government playing a much more overtly obstructive role in Committee and on Report. Skeet's bill would have required local authorities to make more provision for young people who had left school. In Committee the Government sought to delete all its major clauses, but were defeated on a number of occasions because the bill was supported by the Conservative back-benchers on the Committee. In response the Government tabled 77 amendments at Report stage and the bill was talked out.[16]

All this means that any MP introducing a bill is very concerned to persuade the Government to take a favourable, or at worst neutral, attitude to his/her bill. Any consideration of the Corrie Abortion Bill from the 1979/80 Session clearly demonstrates this point. In this case both John Corrie and one of his chief supporters, William Benyon, went to considerable efforts to try to win the support of Dr Gerald Vaughan, the Minister of Health, in the Standing Committee. Such a strategy, which ultimately failed, affected the unity of

pporters of the bill on Committee and did something to
its passage.[17]

1984/5 Session the history of Enoch Powell's Unborn
(Protection) Bill which is considered at more length below,
indicates how Governments can indirectly have great influence
on the fate of a private members' bill, and, perhaps more importantly, reveals much about the executives' attitude to such bills.[18] At
Second Reading and in Committee the Government did not support
the bill, not because they opposed its principle but because they
intended to legislate with a broader bill in a later Session. The bill
seemed to have been effectively killed by a filibuster when its
Report stage was talked out. However, as we saw earlier, at this
point the bill's supporters pulled the proverbial rabbit from the hat.
Andrew Bowden, Conservative MP for Brighton, Kemptown, introduced a private members' motion to suspend Standing Orders and
require Parliament to sit if necessary over a weekend in order to
complete the Report stage and Third Reading of the bill.

The Powell supporters' belief was that given the overwhelming
vote for the bill at Second Reading such a move would succeed.
Unfortunately for them they reckoned without the tactical sophistication of the opposition or the antipathy of the Government to such
a move. The Government, which, as we have indicated, was not
happy with the bill, was even more concerned about the likely
future consequences for Parliamentary procedure if the Bowden/
Powell tactic succeeded. After all, in theory at least, it could have
meant a major extension of private members' time and altered the
balance between the executive and the legislature. In the end the
Government turned a blind eye when Dennis Skinner, Labour MP
for Bolsover, used another procedural device to restrict discussion
and prevent a vote on the Bowden motion. This bill is discussed at
more length below; however, the whole affair indicates both how
difficult it is for private members to succeed, even with procedural
innovations, given the present parliamentary procedure and also
the opposition of the executive to increased power for the legislature.

Government time

Until this point we have been mainly dealing with bills which are
non-contentious. For a large, non-technical, contentious bill to get
through it needs Government time. All the classic private members'

legislation of the 1960s obtained Government time, and none of the bills involved would have received the Royal Assent without the additional time.[19] It is worth considering two of these bills – those which abolished the death penalty and legalised homosexuality – briefly. The Abortion Act of 1967 is examined at some length later.

The Murder (Abolition of the Death Penalty) Bill was introduced by Sydney Silverman as a Standing Order Number 39 (then Number 37) bill.[20] The Labour Government had indicated its support for such a bill in the Queen's Speech in 1964 by saying: 'Facilities will be provided for a free decision by Parliament on the issue of capital punishment.' Such a guarantee of time for a private members' bill was unprecedented, at least in the post-war period. The bill received its Second Reading on 21 December 1964, by 355 votes to 170. A subsequent resolution that the bill be considered by a Committee of the Whole House was defeated by 247 votes to 229. If this move had been successful it would have effectively delayed the bill unless the Government had granted its own time for the consideration of the Committee stage. The Labour Government supported the bill and would have felt obliged to grant time but it saved face by informally whipping its MPs to oppose the move. The bill was considered for five meetings in Standing Committee and while discussion was heated, all amendments to the bill were defeated by sizeable majorities. Of course, this was hardly surprising given the Second Reading vote which meant that there were twice as many supporters of the bill as opponents on the Committee.

The next move was a surprise. On 5 March 1965, an opponent of the bill, Forbes Hendry, Conservative MP for Aberdeenshire, West, who had been successful in the ballot to move a private members' motion, used this opportunity to propose that Standing Orders be suspended and the bill recalled from Standing Committee to the floor of the House. The motion took the bill's supporters by surprise and too few were present for the vote. Hendry's motion was thus passed by 128 votes to 120. The Government's reaction to this procedural device was immediate: it introduced one of its own. The Government proposed an amendment to Standing Orders so that the House would sit on Wednesday mornings to consider the bill. What is more, the Government whipped the division which was carried by 299 votes to 229. In fact, the House met on nine Wednesday mornings and all the amendments to the bill were substantially defeated. The only defeat suffered by the bill's sponsors was on an amendment which established that the bill would remain in force for only five years, subsequently it would need an affirmative resolution in both Houses to ensure its continuation. It is for this reason, of course, that the death penalty is a recurring topic of debate and voting in the House of Commons every five years. The Report stage lasted two days, one of which was provided from Government time, and the Third Reading was agreed on 14 July 1965, by 200 votes to 98. Throughout the passage of this bill then the Government's involvement, and particularly its decision to provide time, and whip its supporters to support the provision of that time, was crucial.

Leo Abse's Sexual Offences Bill was first introduced as a Ten-Minute-Rule bill in the 1966/7 Session.[21] It received a First Reading by 244 votes to 100 but did not subsequently progress. However Abse, heartened by that success and by the success of a similar bill introduced into the House of Lords by the Earl of Arran, approached the Government asking it to provide time. The Government was sympathetic and, as the draw for balloted bills for that Session had already taken place, it agreed to find time for a debate on the bill if it was reintroduced under the Ten-Minute-Rule procedure. Using this opportunity Abse reintroduced the bill. The Government then introduced a procedural motion to extend debate beyond 10.00 p.m. which was easily carried. The bill was debated and given an unopposed Second Reading. Abse subsequently persuaded the Government to allow the bill to be considered in one of the Standing Committees in which Government bills take precedence. This ensured that the bill reached Report stage much quicker than it would otherwise have done.

A number of Conservative MPs tabled amendments and new clauses at Report so it appeared that, given the shortage of time, the bill would fall. Once again the Cabinet agreed to the provision of an extra Friday but the Report stage remained incomplete due to a filibuster by the bill's opponents. Further time was necessary and strong pressure was placed upon Richard Crossman, the Leader of the House, to provide it. In the event, probably because Roy Jenkins, the Home Secretary, was a strong supporter of the bill, and Crossman was a sympathiser, the Government agreed and the debate was resumed at 10.00 p.m. on Monday 3 July. The House sat until 5.50 a.m. the next morning before the bill was finally passed. As in the case of the Death Penalty Bill, this bill could not have passed without substantial help from Government.

Table 3.7 *Government time for private members' bills*

(Divided by party in office)

Period	Type of Bill			Why time given			Number of bills failing despite being given Govt. time
	Balloted	Standing Order No. 37	Ten-Minute-Rule	Percentage of *Balloted* bills given time	To discuss Lords' amendments	Other reasons	
Conservative 1951–64	35*	5†	4	12.8	37	6	2
Labour 1964–70	17*	3*	8	11.8	20	7	1
Conservative 1970–4	2*	n/a	n/a	2.5	1	n/a	1
Labour 1974–9	6	n/a	n/a	5.5	6	n/a	n/a
Conservative 1979–85	4	n/a	1	1.6	n/a	5	n/a
Total:	64	8	13		64	18	4

*Includes 1 balloted bill which did not pass
†1 S.O. 37 bill which failed.

Table 3.8 *Extra time granted by Government for balloted bills*

Government in Office	Number of bills receiving time	Number of Sessions	Index (average per Session)
Labour 1948/9–1950/1	4	2	2
Conservative 1951/2–1954/5	7*	4	1.75
Conservative 1955/6–1958/9	8	4	2
Conservative 1959/60–1963/4	20	5	4
Labour 1964–1965/6	1*	2	0.5
Labour 1966/7–1969/70	16	4	4
Conservative 1970/1–1973/4	2*	4	0.5
Labour 1974	1	1	1
Labour 1974/5–1978/9	5	5	1
Conservative 1979/80–1985/6	4	7	0.4
Total	68	38	16.75

*Includes 1 bill which failed

We have examined two of the cases where the provision of Government time was crucial for the passage of private members' bills. However, the provision of such time is not common and indeed is becoming rare, as Tables 3.7 and 3.8 indicate.

The Government controls the allocation of most parliamentary time. It can provide extra time for further discussion of a private members' bill by allowing the bill to be considered in the time which is at its disposal, but which would not otherwise have been used.[22] Governments are reluctant to grant such time, but as Table 3.7 indicates, in the earlier period under consideration as many as 12.8 per cent of the bills in a given Session received Government time. In most cases the time provided is limited and most often, as Table 3.7 shows, it is used merely so that the Commons can consider the Lords' amendments to the bill. In the more recent period, however, the provision of Government time has become much less frequent, particularly, although not exclusively, when the Conservative Party are in power.

In fact, although most observers have regarded the Labour Governments between 1964 and 1970 as unusual in their willingness to grant time, the 1951/64 Conservative Governments were more generous to MPs. As Table 3.8 indicates, in the 1959/64 Parliament the Conservatives allowed 20 bills extra time in the five Sessions (an average of four per Session) while in the two Parliaments between 1964 and 70 the Labour Government only allowed 17 bills time in six sessions (an average of less than three per Session). In fact, as Table 3.7 indicates, 48 (12.8 per cent) of balloted bills introduced between 1951 and 1964 received Government time while only 11.8 per cent of the bills received time in the 1964/70 period. These figures, however, are a little misleading. The 1965/6 Session was very truncated because of the 1966 general election, so no bills progressed far. In addition, although slightly fewer bills were granted time, they were allowed *more* time. So in the period 1951–64 in 87 per cent of the cases where the Government gave time it was given solely in order that the Lords' amendments to a bill could be considered. In contrast, between 1964 and 1970 in 26 per cent, as distinct from 13 per cent in the earlier period, of the cases where time was allowed it was given for a longer consideration of the bill at the Second Reading, Committee or Report stages. Perhaps more importantly, as we have already seen, the time granted in this later period was often for the consideration of important social legislation. What is more, the 1964–70 Labour Governments, unlike their predecessors or successors, made it clear that they were willing to grant time for bills of which they approved. Indeed, Richard Crossman, then Leader of the House, explained how the 1964–70 Labour Government decided whether to grant time:

The considerations include the state of the Government's own programme; the prospect of the Bill in private members' own time and the effect on other private-members' legislation; the amount of interest in and support for the measure and possibly the progress the Bill has made. The Government's attitude to the Bill is also relevant.[23]

Nevertheless the most striking fact to emerge from Tables 3.7 and 3.8 is the extent to which the provision of Government time has decreased. In particular the Heath and Thatcher Conservative Governments proved very reluctant to allow time. In fact, on 18 February 1971, Mr Whitelaw, the Home Secretary, told the House of Commons, 'I wish to stick to the principle that the Government do not wish to give time to private members' bills.'[24] Between 1970 and 1974 the Conservative Government's resolution remained firm. So, for example, the Government allowed the Divorce (Scotland) Bill to be lost, despite the fact that it supported it and there was a large majority for it at Second Reading. In Burton and Drewry's view this allowed the 'continuance of inconvenient and indefensible anomalies between divorce laws of England and Scotland'.[25]

The attitude of the Thatcher Government was similar. On only four occasions up to the end of the 1984/5 Session was extra time found. In all cases this was for what are best described as 'technical' reasons. So, for example, the National Health Services (Family Planning) Bill was given time as a result of a technical fault during the Lords' amendments. After two days of pressure, with points of order being put to the Speaker, sufficient time was given to allow a division to take place, and the bill was completed.[26]

It appears then that Governments are becoming increasingly reluctant to give time, but when they do give time which type of bills benefit? With relatively few exceptions time is granted to balloted bills rather than Standing Order Number 39 or Ten-Minute-Rule bills. Indeed, during the post-war period, Government time was granted to only two Standing Order Number 39 bills (one being the Death Penalty Bill) and eight Ten-Minute-Rule bills (one being the bill to legalise homosexuality). As far as the subject matter of the bills allowed time is concerned, the picture is a little surprising. In the 1950s the bills given time were drawn from a wide spectrum of categories. However, in the next two decades most Government time has been granted to bills concerning moral issues, and this despite the fact that it has often been remarked that Governments avoid such contentious issues as they are inevitably vote losers. In the 1960s, 23 per cent of the bills granted Government time were of this sort, while in the 1970s the proportion increased to 33 per cent. Yet in these two periods only between 7 per cent and 8 per cent of all private members' bills were of this type. Obviously Governments are under a great deal more pressure to grant time from interest groups on these issues. In addition, given everything we have seen about the procedure it is this type of bill which is more contentious and as such needs time. At the same time since the 1960s most of the moral bills which have been granted time have been relatively minor bills and only one has been contentious enough to generate a vote on their principle.

In conclusion

The pattern which emerges is clear. The Government is crucially involved in the private members' bills legislative process. In fact, it is the key actor. Most importantly, it is evident that most successful back-bench bills are now Government bills in all but name. None of this means that the Government is totally omnipotent. As we shall see later, the MPs and interest groups involved with promoting private members' business have some ways of fighting back – but they are very limited.

4 Interest groups, individual MPs and private members' bills

We saw earlier that, while the departments, Government Reports and the Law Commissions are the most important sources of private members' bills, interest groups and individual MPs also play a key role. However, while interest groups are an important source of bills, the success rate of such bills is considerably less than that of bills which originate from the other two sources. This is clearly because bills which are promoted by interest groups are likely to be larger and more contentious than bills which emanate from Government departments or the Law Commissions. With such contentious bills there are almost inevitably interest groups, and strongly committed MPs, on both sides. Given the procedure, and without Government time, this invariably means that such bills are defeated. Perhaps not surprisingly, the difficulty of achieving success through the private members' bill procedure has consequently led interest groups, and the MPs who sponsor these bills, to explore other methods of achieving their aims. This chapter is thus divided into two sections. The first section examines the role of interest groups and individual MPs in promoting and obstructing private members' bills. The second section then looks at the strategies and tactics which interest groups, and interested MPs, can, and do, adopt when faced with the frustration of procedure.

Interest groups, individual MPs, and the private members' bills procedure

The best analysis of the role of interest groups in relation to private members' bills is to be found in Bridget Pym's book, *Pressure Groups and the Permissive Society*.[1] However, the picture Pym gives is restricted partly by the fact she deals only with bills focusing upon moral issues, but mainly because she concentrates on the atypical 1964–70 period. Nevertheless, her chief conclusion carries considerable conviction:

The weight of evidence is that government and Parliament exercise a decisive control over the business of law making and that the role of pressure groups is at best indirect, at worst negligible.[2]

This conclusion is flawed in two main ways. Firstly, it probably overestimates the influence of Parliament and underestimates the role of Government. This point merely reiterates the theme of the last chapter. Secondly, the conclusion misconceives the role of interest groups in relation to private members' bills. Governments rarely defeat bills, or cause bills to be defeated. The chief Government sanction is to withhold time and obviously that is a crucial sanction. However, as we saw earlier no private members' bill which has been opposed in principle, that is which has been voted upon at Second or Third Reading, has passed, without the provision of Government time, since 1959. So opposition defeats a bill. Sometimes such opposition stems from the personal conviction of individual MPs, as was the case with the objections by Ivan Lawrence and Ronald Bell to the Seat-Belts Bill. Often, however, the opposition is inspired or coordinated by an interest group outside Parliament, as has occurred on the abortion issue. Pym's emphasis is a direct result of her concentration upon the 1964–70 Labour Government. When Governments grant time, interest groups, and indeed individual MPs, can initiate, and hope to get enacted, controversial legislation. If a Government won't create time then an interest group, or an individual MP, can only successfully promote legislation, which doesn't originate in a Government department or a Law Commission, if that legislation is not opposed. In contrast interest groups can fairly easily use the procedure to prevent private members' legislation being enacted. In this section we shall look first at the positive influence of interest groups in effecting private members' bills, and subsequently at their attempts to defeat bills using the procedure.

Interest groups achieve success

Although many private members' bills in which interest groups play a key role are sizeable and controversial, most of those which are successful are minor and technical. The Insurance Brokers (Registration) Bill introduced into the 1976/7 session by John Page, Conservative MP for Harrow West, is a fairly typical example of this process.[3] When Page won a place in the ballot he was approached by a wide variety of interest groups. He told them all: 'No animals, no sex'. However, he was very impressed by representations from the British Insurance Brokers Association (BIBA). When he approached them, their Chairman sent a car around immediately and explained to Mr Page what bill they had in mind. Page had some prior interest in the subject because he had had three cases of constituents who had been defrauded by 'cowboy' insurance companies. The BIBA, like most professional organisations, favoured self-regulation. They wanted a bill which would allow them to establish a register of legitimate insurance brokers which they could police. BIBA and Page had discussions with the Insurance Division of the Department of Trade and Industry who approved the principle of the bill. The interest group paid for the drafting, in this case the parliamentary draftsman charged £5,000 because it was a long bill. In addition they provided a certain amount of secretarial and research help to Page. The bill was passed without a vote although there was considerable debate and the Government granted time for the consideration of Lords' amendments.

In contrast, only between 1964 and 1970 was major legislative change achieved through the private members' bill procedure. Such change occurred in large part because the Labour Government granted time to the various bills. Nevertheless interest groups and individual MPs did play key roles in the passage of these liberal reforms. The clearest example of interest group influence came then, as it has since, on the abortion issue. Indeed after his analysis of all the conscience issues dealt with by Parliament in this period, Richards claims: 'Of all the pressure groups noticed in this study, ALRA (The Abortion Law Reform Association) has been the most influential'.[4]

ALRA was founded in 1936 and its history until 1967 is well documented by Simms and Hindell.[5] It has never been a large organisation – even during the passage of the Steel bill ALRA had only around 1,000 members – but it had a small number of well-informed, well-connected, activists. ALRA thus had excellent contacts within Parliament, where its main efforts were focused, and a solid knowledge of the procedure. However, it might be argued its greatest success was in getting the issue of abortion reform onto the political agenda. As Pym argues:

... the business of making laws is not exclusively confined to the passage of a Bill. There must first be a demand for a Bill, the forming of a suitable climate of opinion. It is here, arguably, that groups make their major contribution. Campaigns like that mounted by the Homosexual Law Reform Society between 1958 and 1965 or that of ALRA from 1963 onwards made people rethink their attitudes towards homosexuality and abortion. These groups' activities stimulated wider and more liberal coverage of the issues in the mass media, and though it would be a mistake to imagine that every working man in Wolverhampton became a champion of, or even interested in, abortion law reform, these vigorous campaigners cultivated a public climate in which reform was possible. Their pamphlets also reached MPs, and if the ground was already receptive these pamphlets must have had some confirmatory influence. The final decisions and wordings lie with the parliamentarians, but on the whole there is a feeling that parliamentary Acts should embody public opinion.[6]

When David Steel won third place in the 1966/7 private members' bills he was not at first sure what type of bill he would sponsor. Not surprisingly, he was approached by a number of interest groups, among them ALRA. ALRA impressed Steel, and they provided him with a draft of the Medical Termination of Pregnancy Bill,[7] which he introduced. This meant that ALRA established the agenda around which other groups had to argue. So, despite the fact that some amendments were made to it, the bill incorporated a major part of ALRA's programme.

ALRA also played a key role during the passage of the bill. As Pym says:

Groups may besiege a citadel, but its walls can only be stormed within Parliament and by parliamentarians. As legislation gets under way, groups tend to become mere spectators unable to control the process of drafting, debating and voting. They may, though, and frequently do, make an effective contribution to the administrative side of getting a Bill through by providing secretarial facilities for the sponsor, lobbying MPs and by supplying any necessary statistics. ALRA and the National Campaign for the Abolition of Capital Punishment were particularly strong in these services.[8]

ALRA thus provided information and expertise to be used by the bill's sponsors. In addition they organised a write-in campaign to MPs from their constituents, and provided pro-reform material to the press throughout the campaign.

Nevertheless ALRA's success also owed something to the absence of an effective opposition lobby. The first of the two main anti-abortion interest groups, the Society for the Protection of the Unborn Child (SPUC), was not formed until 11 January 1967, after the Second Reading of the Steel bill. It was initially poorly organised and had little effect on the passage of the Abortion Act. Indeed, Richards argues: 'Compared with ALRA, SPUC was very unsuccessful'.[9] Perhaps more surprisingly, the Roman Catholic Church played a minor role in relation to the Steel bill. This allowed Barker and Rush, who were undertaking a survey of Parliament Members' sources of information at the time of the Steel bill's Committee stage, to conclude:

On the basis of our limited information from the 1966–7 Session we would speculate that the Roman Catholics were on this issue at least, less monolythic in their reaction (than might be expected) and that local priests are moving towards Anglican priests in their individual freedom either to preach and organise against legislation which official Catholic teaching opposes, or to keep quiet.[10]

Such a conclusion, as we shall see, would be difficult to substantiate for the later period when Parliament was considering private members' bills to reform the 1967 Abortion Act.

At this stage the most effective opposition came from the medical profession. Both the British Medical Association (BMA) and the Royal College of Obstetricians and Gynaecologists (RCOG) were opposed to abortion being performed on social grounds, and in general wanted the grounds on which it was legal to perform abortion to be restricted. David Steel had several meetings with representatives of the BMA and the RCOG. Subsequently he himself introduced an amendment, and withdrew two clauses. This appeared significantly to restrict abortion on social grounds. These concessions were opposed by leading reformers; however they revealed both the influence of the medical profession, and the political astuteness of Steel. Indeed, even Simms and Hindell, who were advocates of a more liberal reform than that enacted, admitted, when referring to Steel's concessions to the BMA and the RCOG: 'In view of the tremendous effort which was later needed to get even the amended and watered-down version through Parliament it is very difficult to fault Steel's political judgement.'[11]

The successful passage of the 1967 Abortion Act is seen by Richards as a classic case of interest group influence on private members' procedure. Yet even here, as we have seen, ALRA was not omnipotent. The medical lobby was very important, the opposition was surprisingly weak, and the role of David Steel, and his supporters among MPs, was substantial. What is more, we must emphasise again that the bill's failure would have been inevitable if the Government had not provided 25 hours of Government time.

If we look at the other successful liberal reforms during this period, the role of interest groups was significant but less so than in the case of abortion. As Pym argues:

... groups do play a role. They give evidence to committees, they stimulate public opinion, and they educate by campaigns while Bills are in the offing and more generally over a period of years; yet when all is said and done their contributions tend to be confined to the periphery – to the supportive campaign, negotiations over details, the watching brief of ineffective huffing and puffing. It cannot be said that every reform Bill receives effective contributions from even two or three groups. The Abortion Bill was an exception. The Divorce Act found the Church of England fairly directly involved, but the interventions of other groups were largely monitory, or weak and ineffective. In the Sexual Offences and Murder Bills the most important group contributions were indirect – the opposition of the police over the years, the sterling work of the National Council in converting left-wing opinion in the 1920s, and the efforts of the Homosexual Law Reform Society to create a climate favourable to change. When it came to the Bills themselves, neither of these groups nor any others were able to do anything effective, despite their willingness to help.[12]

With these other bills even more than with the Steel bill the role of individual MPs was of paramount importance once the bills had been assured of sufficient time. In fact one MP, Leo Abse, Labour member for Pontypool, was a dominant force in ensuring the passage of both the Sexual Offences Bill and the Divorce Bill.[13] The Divorce Bill was formally introduced by Alec Jones, Labour MP for Rhondda, West. He obtained ninth place in the ballot in the 1968/9 Session and was persuaded by Abse to introduce a bill to reform divorce law.[14] As Richards says:

Leo Abse was the dominant figure. His colourful personality, his boundless energy, his contacts with the press and his close acquaintance with some Ministers were all of greatest importance.[15]

The MPs closely involved with bills often have links with interest groups. However, as Pym says:

The extra-Parliamentary group is entirely dependent on MPs and peers for its success but the reverse is not true.[16]

MPs are jealous of their status and independence. At the same time they are often wary of being too identified with a group which may be pushing for a more radical reform than Parliament is likely to accept. So in the case of the Sexual Offences Bill, while Abse was glad of the support he received from the Homosexual Law Reform Society, he was also anxious to preserve his independence from them. Indeed as Pym indicates:

... the Homosexual Law Reform Society would have wished him to employ a looser definition of 'in private' and also to have lowered the age of adulthood from 21 to 18. Abse refused to yield on either count, however, partly because he was convinced that a more liberal Bill would not get through the House, and also because of his own belief that sexual orientations are not fixed at 18 and that the law should 'encourage' a youth to turn in heterosexual rather than homosexual directions.[17]

In the later period there is only one area in which legislation has been supported by an interest group and passed despite being potentially contentious – that is in the field of pornography broadly defined. We shall deal with this area at length later. Here it is important to emphasise that neither the 1978 Child Protection Act nor the 1984 Video Recordings Act was a narrow, technical, non-contentious piece of legislation. They did not originate in a Government department, they involved the restriction, many of course would argue a quite justifiable restriction, of individual freedom, and the need for legislation was hardly clearly estab-lished. However, both bills were passed with no vote and with little opposition. In fact in both cases the main reason for the bills' passage was the generation in the media of a 'moral panic' which was in large part orchestrated by Mrs Mary Whitehouse and the National Viewers and Listeners Association. As our case study below indicates, such an atmosphere was created that it was impossible for individual MPs, and even in the case of the Child Protection Bill, the Government, to object. So the *Guardian* summed up the atmosphere well when it argued in relation to the Video Recordings Bill that:

Anyone getting in the way too quickly risks being lumped together with the child-molesters and sadists.[18]

Such 'moral panic' can only be manipulated in the absence of a coherent opposition. Given such opposition as we have seen repeatedly, it is easy to use the procedure to block bills. The anti-pornography lobby itself found to its cost the truth of this when Winston Churchill introduced a much broader obscenity bill, in the 1985–6 Session. The bill involved restrictions on artistic freedom which affected television and the theatre. In this field powerful and organised interests were involved, and, as we shall see later, they successfully orchestrated a filibuster of the Churchill bill. In other areas, such as abortion, where interest groups attempt to amend liberal legislation partly by creating a 'moral panic', they are also faced by well-organised opposition groups which are skilled in the use of parliamentary procedure. Here we are back to one of the main themes of this chapter. It is opposition which defeats private members' bills and much of that opposition is itself organised or informed by interest groups.

On defeating a bill

Of course, given the procedure, one MP can defeat any balloted bills with a low position in the ballot, and any Ten-Minute-Rule bill or Standing Order Number 39 bill, merely by shouting 'Object' when they are called after previous balloted bills have been debated on a Friday. However, the more newsworthy opposition to bills is usually broader and better organised. Once again it is the abortion issue which offers the most direct example of how an interest group can play a major role, using the procedure to defeat a bill.

After the success of David Steel's bill, the anti-abortion lobby became much better organised. The second of the two major anti-abortion interest groups, LIFE, was formed in 1970. SPUC and LIFE became very active in the constituencies and have organised write-in campaigns, petitions and demonstrations whenever a bill attempting to restrict abortion was being considered by Parliament. In fact there have been nine attempts to use private-members'-bill procedure to amend the 1967 Abortion Act, making it more restrictive. None has succeeded. The failure of such attempts doesn't result from the inadequacies of the anti-abortion lobby or those MPs who support it. Rather it is almost impossible to achieve success using this procedure without Government support in the face of well-organised opposition. At present the pro-abortion lobby is probably the best organised parliamentary lobby partly because, given the large number of attempts to reform the Steel bill, it has had plenty of practice and has learnt its lessons well.

Before we consider the organisation of the pro-abortion lobby it is worth saying a little more about the weaknesses of the anti-abortion side. Its main problem is that while it is well organised in the constituencies, it is less well organised in Parliament, while the coordination between the parliamentary and extra-parliamentary arms is limited, although improving.[19] What is more, its ability to 'deliver' a large number of supporters who will write to MPs or attend lobbies or demonstrations is of limited utility, and becomes of decreasing importance with repetition.

One of Richards's conclusions is particularly interesting here. He argues:

One firm generalization about the influence of pressure-groups emerges from the six case-studies: the greater the public interest in an issue, the more numerous the organizations concerned with it, the less significant will be any campaign designed to affect the form of legislation. The weapons available to a group seeking reform are information and argument. Where mass interest is aroused the group will have inadequate resources to influence the flood of opinion – and perhaps of emotion. Further, the more widespread a discussion the more varied the levels at which it will be conducted and the information which a campaign group can supply tends to be less heeded. In these circumstances a campaign makes less impact on the public; the impact on Westminster is also lower since parliamentarians are subjected to a wider array of competing pressures. Capital punishment stimulated such public interest that no *ad hoc* campaign could have more than a limited effect on either public opinion or the legislature. Discussion on divorce was quieter: the issues were more complex; nevertheless, they were debated by a wide range of organizations. The Divorce Law Reform Union played some part in these discussions, but it was insufficiently strong to have a major effect. As one moves towards the topics with a lower coefficient of public involvement, the campaign-groups became more significant. The Lord's Day Observance Society had some impact on events through the activity it helped to generate at constituency level. The Abortion Law Reform Association and the Homosexual Law Reform Society worked quietly and effectively to mould the opinion of influential persons.[20]

This conclusion may be a bit too sweeping. We have already indicated that in the pornography field the orchestration of public opinion has been very important. At the same time, SPUC and LIFE had considerable success in the 1970s in using constituency pressure to persuade MPs to support at least the principle of a bill to amend the Abortion Act. Nevertheless, Richards is clearly right to imply that the moulding of parliamentary opinion, and parliamentary organisation to that end, is more important. Obviously those opposing the John Corrie Abortion (Amendment) Bill in the 1979/80 Session were helped by the private members' bill procedure. However, the bill was debated for four days at Report stage and, if the pro-abortion lobby had been poorly organised, it *might* at least have reached the House of Lords. In fact the lobby had learnt well from prior experience. They had a well-organised whipping system to ensure enough Members were present to keep debate going and compete effectively in the division lobbies. They ensured that sufficient amendments were held back from the Committee stage to be tabled on Report. What is more, the formation of the

Coordinating Committee in Defence of the 1967 Abortion Act
(Co-ord) in 1976 ensured effective cooperation between the MPs
and their supporters outside Parliament. In particular Co-ord was
able to ensure that the MPs who most strongly opposed the Corrie
bill were well and consistently briefed by lawyers and doctors. As
we shall see at more length below, such organised opposition was
crucial and was not matched by the interest groups supporting the
bill who concentrated their efforts in the constituencies.

It is much easier then to oppose and defeat legislation. On most
occasions, however, this opposition is less visible than it is on the
abortion issue. Peter Fry's Protection of Animals (Scientific Purposes) Bill in the 1979/80 Session presents an excellent example of
more covert opposition and is worth an extended consideration.[21]
Fry won fourth place in the ballot and was already committed to a
bill in this area as a result of previous discussions with the Royal
Society for the Protection of Animals (RSPCA). Initially Fry wanted
a small bill but the RSPCA put pressure on him to broaden it. They
knew that such a bill would not succeed but they hoped to generate
publicity about the issue and perhaps even persuade the Government to introduce a bill at a later date. Fry had discussions with the
RSPCA, the Home Office, the large pharmaceutical companies, and
the medical profession. His final bill was broad, as the RSPCA had
wanted. It had three main objectives. Firstly, it would substantially
reduce the number of experiments carried out on animals. Over five
million experiments were being carried out annually (i.e. one
hundred thousand a week) and it was clear that in many cases
alternatives to the use of animals were available. Secondly, the bill
sought to ensure that where experiments were necessary – as for
example in cancer research – animals should not suffer avoidable
pain, and should be well treated before experimentation. Thirdly,
the bill aimed to make research by animal experimentation accountable. It wanted to introduce a system of licensing; registration of
premises and their inspection; a Code of Practice; and a require-
ment that the Secretary of State should make an annual report to
Parliament on the operation of the Act.

Some reform of the law was clearly necessary. When the Cruelty
to Animals Act was passed there were only some 50 persons
experimenting on some 500 animals a year. By 1978, these figures
were respectively 19,727 and 5,195,409. Moreover much current
research is beyond the scope of the old Act – for example it does not
cover the transplanting of tumours from one animal to another –

simply because such techniques were not known in 1876 when it was passed. Fry's bill also had widespread support among the public and within the Commons. The bill was debated for four hours at Second Reading and passed without a vote. This was a tactical move by the bill's opponents. If there had been a vote and the bill had received a substantial majority, as its opponents feared it would, then the Standing Committee would have been chosen to reflect that vote. As it was, while Fry suggested some names to the Chairman of the Selection Committee, a number of opponents also put their names forward as being interested in the bill. When the Committee met, a majority of its members were opponents of the bill. This meant that it was only on these occasions on which the Minister and his Parliamentary Private Secretary, who were both members of the Committee, voted with the bill's supporters that they successfully defeated amendments to the bill. Fry and his co-sponsors were so angry about the composition of the Committee that they had a discussion with the Chairman of the Ways and Means Committee but to no avail. The bill was thus emasculated and filibustered in Committee and never emerged for a Report stage.

Who were the bill's opponents? The biggest source of opposition was the Research Defence Society (RDS).[22] This is an organisation which works on behalf of the large pharmaceutical companies. Its role was twofold: to mobilise opinion against the bill; to provide information, and even drafts of speeches. The Society circulated a letter to various scientific and trade associations, advising them that:

... as many individuals and bodies as can be encouraged to do so should write to MPs ... in order to maximise opposition to the Bill in Parliament when it comes up for its second reading ...[23]

So successful was the Society in this, that one MP – John Osborn, Conservative, Sheffield Hallam – even felt obliged to declare to the House that he had come into the issue as an adviser of the RDS and as such had received 'an instructive education'.[24] The influence of RDS on the bill's opponents was generally viewed as so strong that Tam Dalyell, Labour MP for West Lothian, and a principal opponent of the bill, felt the need to protest no less than four times during the debate that he was not part of any commercial lobby, before being told by the Speaker that four denials were enough.[25] That such pressure should be exerted by the drug companies is hardly surprising when one considers that the bulk of experiments on animals are conducted, not to further medical research, but to develop commercial products, particularly cosmetics. In fact there was only minor opposition from the medical profession, on one or two clauses of the bill, and Fry felt that it would have been possible for him to compromise with them. The failure of Fry's bill was clearly due to the fierce and organised opposition it received from the pharmaceutical companies, who have a financial stake in developing commercial products by the cheapest possible means, namely, through experiments on live animals.

So far we have dealt with opposition to bills which was clearly orchestrated by interest groups. However, given the procedure a small number of MPs even without aid from an interest group can successfully oppose a bill. The fate of the Seat Belts Bill in the 1979/80 Session amply illustrates that point. On this occasion, despite the bill receiving an overwhelming majority at Second Reading, it was effectively filibustered both in Committee and at Report stage, largely through the efforts of two Conservative MPs, Ronald Bell and Ivan Lawrence. So individual MPs can play key roles both in the passage of private members' bills and in opposing them.

On alternative strategies

It is hardly surprising that interest groups and individual MPs despair of using private members' bills as a means of achieving legislative change. What alternative strategies are open to them if they want to achieve their aims? Of course, some MPs, sometimes backed by interest groups, are well aware of the difficulties of legislating using the procedure and as such introduce bills with less ambitious ends in view. In such circumstances a bill can serve one or more of three purposes. It can test the level of support for reform in the Commons; force the Government to reveal its view; or more generally help to publicise the issue. However, each of these aims only represents a step towards achieving legislative change. So the interest group or individual MP has to move on from this intermediate strategy. What can they do?

There are a number of strategies open to a frustrated interest group which wishes to promote contentious legislation. They can adapt their bill, or their tactics so that they can achieve at least some degree of success, through the procedure despite its limitations. In contrast they can attempt to get their proposals incorporated into a Government bill. Another approach would involve attempting to effect the *administration* of existing legislation in order to achieve their ends. A final, more long term, strategy would involve an attempt to reform the private members' bill procedure so that it can be used to resolve such issues before introducing legislation. We shall consider each of these broad strategies, and the variants within them, in turn.

1. Adapting the bill or the tactics

There are four variants on this general strategy. A group can adapt its bill, introducing one which is limited in scope and which will either placate most opposition, or allow them, with a good place in the ballot and significant support, to succeed despite opposition. In contrast it can override opposition by changing its tactics: emphasising a sophisticated use of procedure; pushing for Government support and the provision of enough time to defeat attempts at a filibuster; or attempting to influence both Government and public opinion so that opposition to what is potentially a controversial area is swept away in a moral panic. We have dealt with the last three of these variants already and examined their limitations. Here we shall concentrate on the first variant.

It is evident that the larger the bill, the more chance the opposition has of extending debate and defeating it. As we saw, this is what happened in the case of the Corrie Abortion (Amendment) Bill in the 1979/80 Session, despite the fact that it was debated on the floor of the House for 24 hours. Indeed, Marsh and Chambers argue that if the bill had been narrower and less radical it would have had much more chance of success.[26] The abortion issue, however, gives ample evidence as to why the limiting of the scope of a private members' bill is a difficult strategy for groups to adopt.

Certainly, if a group has enough support in the House of Commons, which the anti-abortion lobby clearly has, especially after the 1987 election result, and a sympathetic MP achieves a high place in the ballot, then a single-clause bill will have a very high chance of success. In such a situation there is no chance for the opposition to put down a lot of amendments, the Speaker will prevent too obvious filibustering, and the majority will ensure success in any closure vote. In this way the opponents of liberal abortion law would have little difficulty in obtaining support for a bill to reduce the time limit for abortions from the current one of 28 weeks to 24, or perhaps even 22 weeks. Unfortunately, it is not as simple as that. Most of the anti-abortionists have little interest in a small reduction of the time limit, mainly because so few abortions are carried out after 20 weeks. They are more concerned with changing the grounds for abortion, by removing the so-called 'statistical' argument, or with severing the links between abortion advisory centres and clinics performing abortions.[27] Now, of course, it would probably be possible to draft a one-clause bill dealing with either of these areas, although such a bill would probably provoke, and the Speaker would allow, more amendments to it from the opposition at Report stage than would a time-limit bill. However, this is not the major problem with which this lobby is faced.

Bills on either of these topics would be much more contentious than a time-limit bill, and would by no means be guaranteed a majority in Parliament. At the same time, the anti-abortion lobby inside and outside Parliament cannot agree about the content of such a bill. Different elements within this lobby would like bills dealing with one of these two different areas, and at the same time there are disagreements as to how radical any bill should be. This is an inevitable problem with any large lobby; its members may have broadly similar views, but often differ substantially over questions of strategy and tactics.

2. Relying upon Government

Here, two variants are worth considering. A group can attempt to persuade Government itself to introduce a bill upon its subject of concern. A more limited strategy which has been used recently involves introducing an amendment to a Government bill which incorporates the changes the group wants. Obviously both strategies need the co-operation of Government.

(a) Let the Government do the work

This, of course, would be a preferred strategy of interest groups – it would conserve their resources and guarantee success. Conversely it is not a development likely to be favoured by Government. Indeed, as we have seen, Governments tend to avoid contentious issues because they are most often seen as vote losers, given that any legislation displeases one side and may well not be radical enough to please the other. For example, if the Government decided to legislate to restrict the time limit on abortion, it would displease most of the pro-abortionists and please few of the anti-abortionists, who would prefer changes to restrict the grounds on which abortions are legal. At the same time Governments are always short of Parliamentary time and indeed, as we have seen, often attempt to persuade private members to introduce small uncontroversial Government bills. For these reasons there are few instances of Governments taking up a private members' bill and legislating on the matter themselves.

However, it does happen. One of the best examples concerns the 1956 Clean Air Act. In the 1954/5 Session, Gerald Nabarro, Conservative MP for Worcester, won first place in the ballot. He had made a prior commitment to the interest group involved, the National Smoke Abatement Society (NSAS), to introduce a bill based upon the Report of the Beaver Committee. This was a Government Committee of Inquiry set up to consider the question of air pollution in the aftermath of the London smog of December 1952. In a case study of this legislation, Sanderson emphasises the importance of the NSAS:

A comparison of the Society's memorandum and the Committee's Final Report shows how closely, given minor deviations, the Committee followed the views of the NSAS in reaching its conclusions.[28]

So NSAS had considerable influence on the Beaver Committee's report. However, the bill Nabarro chose to introduce was broader than NSAS wished so their initial attitude to it was ambivalent, although subsequently the Society's Executive Committee passed a motion fully supporting the bill and calling on the Government either to adopt it, or replace Nabarro's bill with its own comprehensive measure.

The Second Reading went much as Nabarro had expected. He immediately established that he was willing to withdraw the bill, after a full discussion, if the Government would promise to introduce its own bill. Mr Sandys, then Minister of Housing and Local Government, responded that the Government could not advise the House to support the bill because it had been hastily prepared, contained drafting errors and lacked the necessary financial provisions. However, he did promise that after full consultation with the interested parties, the Government would introduce legislation based on the Beaver Committee's report.

Sanderson sums up the influence of the Nabarro bill very well:

What was the significance of the Nabarro Bill in the struggle? The Bill openly confronted the Government with a definite proposal. It is true that the Government accepted the Beaver Committee proposals on 25 January and that consultations with the interests concerned were in progress before that date; but it is difficult to say how far these activities were inspired by Mr Nabarro's determination to introduce his Bill. It seems unlikely that the Government contemplated no action, but there is some evidence that the Bill did at least serve to expedite events, although it may not have been quite the 'pistol at the Ministers' backs' envisaged by the *Manchester Guardian*. However, immediately before the second reading, the *Municipal Review* seemed in grave doubt concerning the fate of the Beaver Report, warning that 'in a government office, there is a nice, clean, empty pigeon-hole the same size and shape as the Beaver Report, and there are probably several nice, clean and tidy politicians who ... would like to see this report suitably housed'. Later in the year, the *Review* again suggested that the Report had only escaped shelving because of Mr Nabarro. Sir Hugh Beaver himself thought that Mr Nabarro's action might well have been the decisive factor in persuading the Government to introduce the Clean Air Bill.[29]

There are also more recent examples of this strategy having some effect. In the 1985/6 Parliamentary Session, the Conservative Government introduced legislation to deregulate Sunday trading, although the legislation was subsequently defeated by the defection of a very large number of Government back-benchers. There can be little doubt that the continuing appearance of this subject in private members' bills helped politicise the subject and provide a significant stimulus to the Government. In the last 20 years, six bills dealing with the issue have been introduced into the Commons, although none of these achieved a Second Reading. During the same period, six similar bills were also introduced into the Lords. One of these bills fell at Report stage, while another, introduced by Baroness Trumpington in the 1981/2 Session, successfully completed all its stages in the House of Lords. It fell in the House of Commons as a result of opposition and lack of time. This is a familiar feature of private members' business. Bills are more likely to succeed in the Lords because there is no time limit on debate and as such they cannot be filibustered and 'talked-out' by a handful of members. Of course, when these successful Lords' bills come to the Commons, such tactics can be used to defeat them.

The issue has thus been a recurring one in Parliament in the last 20 years. In the Commons the last bill to deregulate Sunday trading which progressed at all was introduced by Ray Whitney, Conservative MP for Wycombe, in the 1982/3 Session. In February 1983 the bill had a full five hours' debate on Second Reading but was defeated with 205 MPs opposing it while 106 supported it. During the debate David Mellor, Under Secretary of State at the Home Office, speaking on behalf of the Government, supported the bill.[30] He emphasised, however, that the Government believed that the matter was one which should be dealt with by private members' legislation. In the light of this the issue might have been expected to recede in importance. After all the bill was defeated by a considerable majority, and was strongly opposed by a variety of interests. In fact, Leon Brittain, the Home Secretary, set up a Departmental Committee, under Mr Robin Auld, Q.C., to investigate the whole issue of Sunday trading. When the Committee reported at the end of 1984 it recommended that the Government should abolish all restrictions on shop hours in England, Scotland and Wales. Mr Brittain's response to the report was positive if not very definite:

there is widespread agreement that the present law is unsatisfactory and in need of reform. I welcome the report which we will wish to consider carefully, in the light of reactions to it, before reaching any conclusions as regards legislation.[31]

It was something of a surprise, therefore, when the Government introduced its deregulatory legislation. Of course, the supporters of such legislation, both inside and outside Parliament, have been greatly aided by the current Conservative Government's commitment to, and belief in the reduction of Government restrictions on the market. There was no chance of a deregulation bill succeeding under the private members' bill procedure without Government time, even if a majority could have been found for such a bill in the Commons. In this atypical case, however, partly because of interest-groups pressure, and partly because of Government ideology, Government legislation was introduced. The defeat of the bill was an almost unprecedented set-back for the Government. What is more, it must have reconfirmed the predilection to Governments to avoid such conscience issues if at all possible, and made it much less likely that this tactic could be successfully pursued by an interest group in future.

These two examples involve fairly major, and certainly contentious, legislation. In contrast, the fate of the Ground Game Bill, introduced by Tom Hoosen, Conservative MP for Brecon and Radnorshire in the 1979/80 Session, was much less dramatic. Hoosen won 19th place in the ballot. He wanted to introduce a bill to reform the law in the agricultural area given that he represented a rural constituency. He had come across what he regarded as a loophole in the 1880 Ground Game Act. Under this Act tenants were not allowed to shoot rabbits on the land they rented. He introduced a bill to remove this anomaly. The bill was nodded through on Second Reading, briefly discussed in Committee – where the right to shoot hares was added to the bill – and given an unopposed Third Reading. Opposition to the bill only surfaced in the Lords where supporters of the RSPCA used the debate to raise wider issues of animal welfare. The bill was thus effectively filibustered in the House of Lords. However, the issue had been publicised and the Government decided to include the main provisions of the bill as a sub-clause of the 1984 Wildlife and Countryside Act.

On the Sunday opening issue, the efforts of the interest groups and the MPs involved helped persuade the Government to establish a Committee. This might appear a promising avenue for interest groups. They could use the private members' procedure as a springboard to the establishment of a Select Committee, Royal Commission, or Departmental Committee to consider the issue with which they are concerned. Then, if the Committee reported favourably, the Government might decide to introduce legislation. In practice this has not proved a profitable strategy largely because such committees are often used not as a means of reaching a decision, but rather as a means of delaying, or avoiding, a decision. We saw above how such a tactic was used by the Government in relation to Robert Taylor's Affiliation Orders and Ailments Bill in the 1979/80 Session. However, once again, the best example of a referral to a Committee being used by Government to attempt to defuse a contentious private members' bill involves the abortion issue. In the 1975/6 Session James White, Labour MP for Glasgow (Pollok), introduced an Abortion (Amendment) Bill which represented the first major attempt by the anti-abortion lobby to repeal the 1967 Abortion Act. The bill successfully obtained a Second Reading with 203 MPs supporting it and only 88 opposed (a majority of 115). After this, however, it was agreed without a vote and with active encouragement from the anti-abortionist lobby to refer the bill to a specially created Select Committee. This meant that the legislative stages of the White bill were suspended and it lapsed at the end of the parliamentary session.

Almost as soon as the Select Committee was established, it became clear that its 15 members were deeply divided, with nine members strongly in favour of the main provisions of the White Bill, and six against. Initially, however, the Committee concentrated upon the widespread abuse of the Act which both sides felt could be effectively controlled by administrative action. This enabled them to reach agreement on nine recommendations before the end of the Parliamentary Session. These recommendations were all accepted and acted upon by the then Secretary of State for Social Services, Mrs Barbara Castle.

The Government had given an undertaking that, if the Select Committee had not completed its work by the end of the Session, it would be re-established, but the Government prevaricated and the Select Committee was only re-established, with the same membership, after a debate and vote in the Commons in February 1976. At this stage there was an unusual development. The minority of six who were against any significant changes in the 1967 Act resigned because they felt that the Committee, by its very composition, was sure to recommend the emasculation of the original Act. Only one of the six vacancies thus caused in the Committee's membership was filled, but the rest of the Committee continued to take evidence and produced two further reports before finally completing their deliberations in November 1976.

The major report of the reconvened Select Committee contained 15 recommendations.[32] These recommendations were not adopted by the Department of Health and there is no doubt that the anti-abortion lobby believed that the referral of the White bill to the Select Committee had been counter-productive because it defused the issue and produced few, if any, significant changes in the operation of the legislation. It is revealing that when the sponsors of the Powell bill in the 1984/5 Session were offered the chance of having the issue referred to a Select Committee, they refused. Certainly many of the activists involved remembered their experience with the White bill.

(b) Legislating through the back door

In many ways the most interesting development in this area recently concerns the attempt by some lobbies to insert in Government's bills amendments which deal with subjects which have previously formed the basis of private members' bills which have failed. The best example of this so far involves the campaign to make the wearing of seat belts compulsory. There were, in fact, five attempts at legislation in this field before Neil Carmichael introduced the Road Traffic Act (Seat Belts) Bill when he drew second place in the private members' ballot in the 1979/80 Session.[33] The bill received very strong support, with 139 voting for and 48 against, a majority of 91. The bill then had five sittings in Standing Committee and was debated at Report stage for one-and-a-half days. However, as we pointed out earlier, it was very effectively filibustered on Report.

Here then was a classic case of a private members' bill, which had a large measure of support in the House, being defeated by the efforts of a well-organised small group of MPs effectively using private members' procedure. Clearly no bill of this sort introduced under private members' procedure could succeed. However, in this instance the supporters of compulsion found a novel way of escaping from the impasse. Lord Nugent, a long-time supporter of the cause,[34] moved an amendment to the Government 1981 Transport Bill in the Lords. The Government did not oppose the amendment and it was agreed in the House of Lords by 132 votes to 92. When the bill returned to the Commons for its consideration of the Lords' amendment, the Government put a time-limit, a guillotine, on discussion and allowed a free vote on the seat-belts clause. Consequently there could be no filibuster and Ivan Lawrence's motion to reject the Lords' amendment was defeated by 221 votes to 144, a majority for compulsion of 77.

Actually, the 1981 Transport Bill finally contained three clauses which incorporated reforms which had earlier been the subject of private members' bills. In addition to the compulsory-seat-belts clause, Barry Sheerman introduced a clause which required all children under thirteen, who were front-seat passengers, to be restrained by harness, and prohibited children from the age of one from travelling in the front seat.[35] This change was accepted by the Government and was very similar in substance to the private members' bill he had initiated under the ballot procedure in the 1980/1 Session. At the same time a clause dealing with the provision of road humps, a frequent subject of private members' bills,[36] was included in the bill as a result of an amendment moved by two Conservative back-benchers at Report stage.

This, then, appears a promising strategy for MPs or interest groups because Government bills are inevitably guillotined and thus the time problem can be overcome. However, such a strategy can only be successful if the bill/clause has very strong support in Parliament and, more importantly, if the Government, of whatever party, is willing to allow such a clause to be added to one of their bills. Otherwise the Government can merely whip its MPs to oppose the clause and in such circumstances it would have very little chance of success.

(c) *Effecting administration rather than legislation*

Major economic groups have always been more concerned about their contacts with Whitehall than Westminster. In contrast, the smaller and weaker social interest groups with little formal or informal access to the departments have had to concentrate upon MPs and, if they want to change policy, to promote or suggest private members' bills. However, these groups have become increasingly aware of the difficulties, or even the impossibility, of obtaining change through this method. At the same time, the contacts of such groups with Whitehall have not improved, largely because they have little to offer, and few, if any, sanctions which they can exercise in relation to Government policy. For these reasons groups like the anti-abortion lobby have begun to explore other avenues in attempting to influence policy. In the first place, they have inundated the department concerned, the DHSS, with letters and 'evidence' about 'abuses' of the operation of the Abortion Act. More significantly, however, there has been a move towards the use of the courts to test the legislation and attempt to establish, through judicial decisions, a less liberal interpretation of the Act than that adopted by some doctors. These changes in strategy deserve lengthy consideration but two points are important here. Firstly, this strategy has had some, although limited, success. Secondly, it reflects a disillusionment with the inadequacies, as such groups see it, of private-members'-bill procedure.

(d) *Reforming the procedure*

Most interest groups we have talked to, and indeed most MPs we have interviewed, have been critical of private members' procedure. The key problem is that controversial issues cannot be resolved by the procedure as it now stands. Many supporters of groups sponsoring bills are not only baffled by the procedure but also disillusioned. They work hard to promote a bill, and perhaps see it achieve a large majority on Second Reading. Then the bill is lost, not through lack of support, but because of limited time and the concerted opposition of often only a handful of MPs. The anti-abortion lobby provides an excellent example of this growing disillusionment. The Corrie bill was strongly opposed, and by more than a handful of MPs, but it had received overwhelming support at Second Reading, and its supporters in SPUC and LIFE were frustrated when it failed. This leads not merely, or mainly, to a dissatisfaction with the private-members'-bill procedure, which few understand, but to a more general disillusionment with Parliament, and the legislative process. Such feelings will not result in trouble in the streets. However, they do mean that such interest groups turn increasingly to extra-parliamentary means, and in particular to using the courts to achieve the reforms for which they feel they have a mandate, given the votes of MPs at Second Reading.

Of course, it can be argued that non-technical controversial bills should be the prerogative of Government. However, it is clear that governments, largely for party political reasons, are unwilling to introduce bills which deal with contentious social and moral issues like abortion, freedom of information, blood sports, obscenity and euthanasia. These are issues which concern many people but are most likely to be raised, and legislated upon, through private members' bills. Yet, there seems to be little point in Parliament wasting time and money continually debating the same issues because parliamentary private members' procedure and practices do not allow them to be resolved. What is needed is a change in procedure to allow Parliament to reach a definite decision on these issues.

We shall discuss later what changes are appropriate. The point here is that interest groups interested in such issues may be better advised to campaign for a change in private members' procedure first before pushing ahead with their primary aim.

5 Voting on private members' issues: the limits of statistical analysis

We have already seen that votes on private members' bills at Second or Third Reading are rare and becoming rarer (Table 3.1). Nevertheless such votes do present an opportunity to examine what factors affect MPs' voting when they are not subject to party discipline.

Although Britain is a parliamentary democracy the existence of strong party discipline means that policy is made by government and merely legitimated in Parliament. As Norton has documented, there has been a significant increase in dissent on the floor of the House of Commons with many more MPs willing to defy the whip on frequent occasions. Nevertheless any government can be sure of a majority on almost all elements in its legislative programme. This tight, if slightly slackening, party discipline means that on all whipped votes most MPs toe the party line and as such are rarely influenced by other factors. It is thus only on unwhipped issues that we can see more directly the effect of other factors such as ideology, religion, constituency pressures and lobbying on MPs' votes.

It might be argued of course that as there are relatively few free votes in the House of Commons there is little point in examining the factors which affect MPs voting under such circumstances. This view seems short-sighted. MPs retain their consciences and ideological positions, and are subject to constituency and interest-group pressure on whipped issues although such factors are normally submerged under the all-pervasive strictures of party discipline. However, as party discipline decreases, as the signs show it is doing, these factors will become more significant. Given such a development an analysis of the factors which influence MPs in circumstances of free voting may well offer insights into the wider pattern of parliamentary voting in the future.

Our analysis in the chapter is concerned with those three issues which were originally passed using the private-members'-bill procedure in the 1960s and have remained topics of debate and 'free votes' in the House of Commons since. The abortion issue has continued to surface in private members' bills. In contrast capital punishment and homosexuality have not been the subject of private members' bills since they were passed. However capital punishment has been regularly debated and voted upon – with a 'free vote' – because, under the terms of the Murder (Abolition of Death Penalty) Act 1965, the Government has to introduce an affirmative motion every five years so that the legislation can continue to operate. As far as homosexuality is concerned since the Sexual Offences Act (1967) was passed the issue has only been debated and voted upon once. In 1980 an amendment to the Criminal Justice (Scotland) Bill legalised homosexuality in Scotland. Although this was a Government bill there was a 'free vote' on this clause. Homosexuality and capital punishment are thus regarded as private members' issues although many of the votes involved were not votes on private members' bills. These three issues, because they have been the subject of debates and votes in three periods, 1964–70, 1974–9 and after 1979, have the added advantage of allowing us to examine if the factors which affect MPs' voting on such issues have changed over time.

There has been a certain amount of prior research on this problem. Richards, for example, presents a chapter based upon an analysis carried out by Margaret Fuller of voting upon capital punishment, homosexuality, abortion, divorce and Sunday entertainment between 1965 and 1969.[1] However while he offers a good description of the voting patterns his attempts at explanation are hindered by the nature of the statistical analyses which were performed. The analysis is bivariate and offers no measure of the strength of the relationships involved. Rather we are presented with a series of cross-tabulations. While these are interesting they have important limitations. Richards does not control for the effect of third variables in any of his tables. For this reason he consistently offers qualifications to his findings. For example his tables indicate a close relationship between gender and vote with most women taking the liberal position on these issues. However he goes on:

In a sense the table is misleading because there is proportionately a higher number of women members in the Labour Party . . . Thus the women were favourable to reform, not because of their sex, but because nearly three-quarters of them were Labour supporters.[2]

Richards could have dealt with this problem to a limited extent by presenting tables in which he controlled for intervening variables.

This strategy was followed by Marsh and Chambers.[3] However the major limitation of the analysis of Marsh and Chambers, as well as that of Richards, is that it is based upon cross-tabulation. Such a technique does not allow much effective assessment of the *combined* or the *relative* influence of party, gender, religion, age and education on MPs voting in free-vote situations. In order to identify the combined and relative influence of these and other independent variables on the dependent variable(s), the votes, we need to employ multi-variate analysis.

Such an analysis has been undertaken by George Moyser in an unpublished conference paper.[4] He re-analysed the Fuller data, which is the basis of Richards's study, using a multi-variate technique. However Moyser's data and analysis has limitations. Firstly the technique he uses, multiple classification analysis, does not allow any assessment of the statistical significance of his results.[5] Secondly Moyser constructs scales of votes and uses them as his dependent variable. As such he reports no results on individual votes and cannot compare voting on one issue with that on others. Finally, and perhaps most importantly, Moyser only has data on one period, 1965–9, which means, for example, he can say nothing about whether the results he finds are a product of the untypical period he studied.

Our data set contains information on MPs (and their constituencies) between 1965 and 1980 and about the voting behaviour of MPs on abortion, capital punishment and homosexuality during this fifteen-year period. This allows us to examine voting patterns on free votes in three different time periods (1964–70; 1974–9; and 1979–83). As such it is much less likely that the findings we report will be unduly influenced by a single, unusual, session or series of votes. Our results should be correspondingly more generalisable. On occasions we do use straightforward bivariate analysis. However when multi-variate analysis is used the results are generated by the ordinary least-squared regression procedure.[6]

The hypotheses

The aim of this chapter is both to describe and to explain the voting patterns on these bills. What factors influence MPs voting in free-vote situations? We will concentrate upon four sets of factors: the party identification and ideological position of the MP; the personal background of MPs; constituency characteristics and pressure; and the political environment within which MPs are voting. The existing material does allow us to generate a series of hypotheses which we can test using our statistical analysis. These concern three groups of variables: party and ideology; personal-background characteristics of MPs; and constituency characteristics.

Party

All the studies are agreed that despite the fact that these issues are unwhipped, party is the best predictor of vote. So Moyser emphasises:

despite being concerned with supposedly 'non-party' issues, the imprint of party on the general 'liberal-conservative' stance of MPs on moral matters in fact is very strong.[7]

As Richards says, 'Labour and Liberal members were heavily in favour of the reforms while Conservative members were hostile.'[8] Thus our first hypothesis is that: party will be the best predictor of voting on these private members' issues.[9]

Of course there are ideological splits within the political parties, particularly the Labour Party, and they might well be expected to be related to voting on these moral issues. In fact Marsh and Chambers argue that:

the members of the Tribune Group are consistently much more likely to oppose amending legislation [on abortion] than their party colleagues.[10]

For this reason our second hypothesis in this section will be: Left Wing Labour MPs (defined in terms of Tribune Group membership) will be more liberal than their colleagues.

The background characteristics of MPs

As far as Moyser is concerned religion is the next-best predictor of vote, after party:

Next in overall importance, a long way behind party, comes religion.[11]

He found Roman Catholics to be the most 'conservative' group, with Anglicans occupying a central position, while MPs with other religious affiliations were more liberal. Our hypothesis following Moyser will be that: religion is the next-best predictor of vote after party.

Both Richards and Pym regard age as an important influence on vote,[12] with younger members being heavily in favour of reform. Moyser is more definite. He suggests:

age is quite important as an explanatory factor, coming fourth among all those considered. Across the various age groups, the general pattern of association with moral stances, is approximately linear, with the most 'conservative' being the oldest, and the most 'liberal' being the youngest MPs.[13]

Here then our hypothesis must be that age is positively related to holding more conservative attitudes on these moral issues. Moyser's results suggest that no other social-background characteristic has much influence on vote once one controls for other factors, and this is confirmed by Marsh and Chambers. We shall of course test to see if sex, occupation or education have an important impact on voting in our data.

Constituency factors

Both Moyser and Richards suggest that region has an important independent influence on vote. Moyser argues:

The third categorical background factor which exerts a relatively powerful effect upon the general 'moral' stances of MPs is the region of their constituency . . . The two regions where the moral ethos leaves the clearest imprint upon voting in the House of Commons (again excepting Northern Ireland) are Scotland and Wales. In both cases the effect is a distinctly 'conservative' one.

In similar vein Richards argues, without the benefit of multi-variate analysis, that MPs from the South-East were more favourably disposed to most reforms while Scottish MPs in particular were 'remarkably hostile to reform'.[14] The hypothesis here then must be that: region has an important independent effect upon voting.

Marsh and Chambers's material is different in that they pay some attention to the effect of the marginality and the religious composition of MPs' constituencies on their voting. Indeed, at least as far as Labour MPs' voting on abortion is concerned, they suggest that the marginality of a constituency may have considerable effect on voting patterns:

There is in fact a persistent relationship between marginality and voting on abortion. MPs in marginal constituencies are more likely to vote than their colleagues in safe seats. In addition Labour MPs in marginal constituencies are much more likely to support the 1967 Act [than their colleagues in safe seats].[15]

In contrast Marsh and Chambers play down the effect of the religious composition of the constituency, arguing:

There is no obvious . . . relationship between the religious composition of the constituency and voting on this issue.[16]

This material suggests two hypotheses. First: the marginality of the constituency will have considerable independent effect on the voting of Labour MPs on abortion. Second: the religious composition of a constituency will have no effect on MPs voting on these issues.

None of this should suggest that we believe that such a quantitative analysis can offer a full explanation of voting on these social issues. Indeed we shall be crucially concerned throughout this chapter to assess the strength and limitations of this quantitative approach.

Results

This section of the chapter is divided into two main parts. In the first part we shall look at the relative effect of the various background and constituency variables on voting on these issues over three separate periods – 1964–70, 1974–9, and 1979–84. In the second part we shall concentrate on trying to identify and explain the divisions which occur within the two main parties.

Explaining the votes

The 1964–70 period

The results in Table 5.1 tend to confirm most of the hypotheses we have suggested. The standardised regression coefficients are presented with asterisks indicating those relationships which are statistically significant. In this and future tables we are only dealing with those Labour and Conservative MPs who voted, as MPs who do not vote may fail to do so for a variety of reasons. It is therefore dubious to treat abstentions as an intermediary category. We are using seven different dependent variables – the votes upon: the Second Reading of the Steel bill (1966); the Third Reading of the Steel bill (1967); the St John-Stevas Abortion Bill (1969); the Sexual Offences Bill (1967); the Abolition of the Death Penalty Bill (1965); a

Table 5.1 *Explaining voting patterns on free votes in 1964–70 period* Labour and Conservative MPs who voted only

Standardised regression coefficients for:

Variables	Second Reading Steel (1966)	Steel Third Reading (1967)	St John-Stevas bill (1969)	Sexual Offences Bill (1967)	Capital Punishment (1965)	Capital Punishment (1966)	Capital Punishment (1969)
Scotland	0.06	0.10*	0.10*	0.08	0.02	0.05	0.05
Wales	−0.02	0.02	0.03	0.15*	−0.00	−0.03	0.00
Northern England	0.08	0.14*	0.03	0.15*	0.01	0.04	0.01
Oxbridge	0.11	−0.05	−0.05	−0.25*	−0.07	−0.06	0.12*
College	−0.12*	−0.07	−0.09	−0.12	−0.02	0.01	−0.04
No higher education	0.02	−0.06	−0.02	−0.13	−0.05	−0.02	−0.04
Religion	0.63*	0.34*	0.23*	−0.02	−0.02	−0.04	−0.04
Gender	0.01	0.01	0.01	−0.03	0.03	0.04	−0.00
Age	0.02	−0.12*	0.09	0.04	0.05	0.11*	0.07*
Party	0.18*	0.49*	0.54*	0.63*	0.80*	0.74*	0.75*
Lawyer	0.06	0.02	0.01	−0.07	0.00	0.06	0.08
Other profession	0.03	−0.00	0.00	−0.11	−0.00	−0.01	0.03
Business	0.11	0.04	0.06	−0.08	−0.09	0.08	0.08*
Constituency majority	−0.02	0.02	−0.04	0.02	N/A	−0.03	−0.05
R² total explanatory power of model	0.44	0.43	0.35	0.41	0.68	0.59	0.59

* Significant at .05 level.
The coding for Tables 5.1, 5.2 and 5.3 is as follows:
Vote = 0 if Liberal vote 1 if Conservative vote
Scotland = 1 if representing a Scottish constituency; 0 otherwise
Wales = 1 if representing a Welsh constituency; 0 otherwise
Northern England = 1 if representing a constituency in Northern England; 0 otherwise
Age = 1 if born after 1950, 2 if born between 1940 and 1950; 3 if born between 1930 and 1934 etc.
Gender = 0 for female, 1 for male
Roman Catholic = 1 if MP is a Roman Catholic; 0 otherwise
Party ID = 0 if MP belongs to the Labour Party; 1 otherwise
Lawyer = 1 if MP lists occupational background as a lawyer; 0 otherwise
Other professional = 1 if MP lists some profession other than law; 0 otherwise
Business = 1 if MP lists occupation as business; 0 otherwise
No higher education = 1 if MP had no higher education; 0 otherwise
College = 1 if MP lists higher education as college; 0 otherwise
Oxbridge = 1 if MP attended either Oxford or Cambridge; 0 otherwise
Constituency majority = 1 if more than 10%; 0 otherwise

Table 5.2 *Explaining voting patterns on free votes in 1974–9 period*

Labour and Conservative MPs who voted only

Variables	Standardised regression coefficients for:			
	White Abortion Bill (1975	Benyon Abortion Bill (1977)	Braine Abortion Bill (1978)	Motion on capital punishment (1974)
Scotland	0.17*	0.19*	0.17*	−0.00
Wales	0.17*	0.0	0.08	−0.02
Northern England	0.27*	0.13*	0.12	−0.04
Oxbridge	−0.09*	−0.08	−0.07	−0.07
College	−0.02	−0.16*	−0.11*	−0.03
No higher education	0.07	−0.01	−0.03	0.03
Religion	0.20*	0.27*	0.22*	−0.02
Gender	0.17*	0.04	0.05	−0.01
Age	−0.06	0.04	−0.06	0.02
Party	0.51*	0.55*	0.47*	0.72*
Lawyer	−0.06	−0.02	0.01	0.09*
Other profession	−0.06	−0.04	−0.03	0.10*
Business	−0.06	0.06	0.00	0.10*
Constituency majority	0.07	0.03	0.08	−0.02
R² total explanatory power of model	0.36	0.39	0.29	0.54

* Significant at 0.05 level.
For coding see Table 5.1

motion to reintroduce capital punishment (1966); and the affirmative motion on capital punishment (1969).

If we consider the three abortion votes the results are very much as expected. The standardised regression coefficients (or beta weights) offer a measure of the total explanatory power of the independent variables. The higher the beta weight the greater the explanatory power of the variable regardless of sign. As such it is clear from Table 5.1 that party is the best predictor of abortion voting. The only exception, and it is the only one in all the tables we shall present, involves the Second Reading vote on the Steel bill. Here the beta weight for party is 0.18 while that for religion is 0.63. The reason for this is simple. This is the only abortion vote on which the vast majority of both Labour and Conservative MPs supported liberal abortion law (*see* Table 5.8). Subsequently on all votes the majority of Conservative MPs have opposed abortion. On this occasion the Tory MPs voted in favour of the principle of reform probably partly because of the liberal atmosphere prevailing at the time, partly because of the *then* absence of strong opposition to the proposal, but mainly because they thought some reform, but not radical reform, was necessary. When it became clear at Third Reading that the bill was radical, and afterwards when the Abortion Act led to the widespread availability of abortion on 'social' grounds, many reasserted their more usual, less liberal, view and opposed the liberal law.

The second best predictor of voting, and indeed the best in the case of the 1966 vote, is religion. Roman Catholics are considerably more likely to oppose abortion than other MPs. The beta weights vary considerably (from 0.63 down to 0.23) but they are consistently high and significant at the 0.05 level. As far as other variables are concerned none is very important, although Scottish MPs are consistently less liberal than their colleagues, and on two of the three votes this relationship is significant.

The pattern is noticeably different if we consider the two other issues. Here party is overwhelmingly the best predictor and is a better predictor than it was in the case of the abortion votes. In contrast religion has no explanatory power. Indeed Roman Catholics are more liberal than other MPs on these two issues (note the consistent negative relationships) although more of the relationships are significant. No other variable has a great deal of explanatory power on all the votes. However it is noticeable that MPs with an Oxbridge background are more liberal on homosexuality than their colleagues (beta weight −0.25 and the relationship is significant) a result which, as we shall see in Table 5.3, is repeated on the 1980 homosexuality vote. Age also has a limited but significant effect on voting on capital punishment. As we hypothesised younger MPs are slightly more liberal than their older colleagues.

The 1974–9 period

In the second period under consideration we have used four dependent variables. They are the votes upon: the White Abortion

Table 5.3 *Explaining voting patterns on free votes in 1979–83 period*

(Labour and Conservative MP's who voted only)

Variables	Standardised regression coefficients for:			
	Corrie Second Reading (1979)	Corrie Report stage (1980)	Motion on capital punishment (1979)	Homo-sexuality vote (1980)
Scotland	0.09*	0.04	0.01	0.03
Wales	0.17*	−0.03	0.01	0.00
Northern England	0.13*	0.13*	0.04	0.01
Oxbridge	−0.05	0.03	0.15*	−0.14*
College	0.10*	−0.13	0.03	−0.04
No higher education	−0.03	0.01	0.02	0.03
Religion	0.26*	0.23*	0.03	0.07
Gender	0.03	−0.01	0.02	−0.01
Age	−0.05	0.00	−0.06	0.10
Party	0.56*	0.54*	0.67*	0.63*
Lawyer	0.00	0.03	−0.06	0.07
Other profession	−0.03	−0.01	−0.07	0.05
Business	0.04	0.05	−0.08	0.04
Constituency majority	−0.07	−0.08	0.00	0.08
R^2 total explanatory power of model	0.38	0.42	0.46	0.36

* Significant at .05 level.
For coding see Table 5.1.

Bill (1975); the Benyon Abortion Bill (1977); the Braine Abortion Bill (1978); and the motion on capital punishment, 1974.

Once again party is by far the best predictor of vote upon both abortion and capital punishment although it is a better predictor of the capital punishment vote. Religion is an important and significant predictor of abortion voting but has no explanatory power as far as voting on hanging is concerned. On the abortion votes region is the best predictor, with Scottish and Northern MPs consistently more likely to take a more conservative position than their colleagues. However region has no effect on capital punishment voting. There are one or two other significant relationships in the table but they do not appear very important. On the White bill gender has a noticeable effect (beta 0.20) but this is the only occasion in the three tables that it does. On the capital punishment vote occupational background has an effect with MPs who had been lawyers, other professionals or businessmen being less liberal than other MPs. However no similar relationship appears in either of the other periods.

The 1979–83 period

In this period we consider four dependent variables. They are voting upon: the Second Reading of the Corrie Abortion Bill (1979); the Silkin amendment to the Corrie bill at Report stage (1980); the 1979 motion on capital punishment; and the vote on the legalisation of homosexuality in Scotland (1980).

The results confirm the pattern we have previously established. Party is overwhelmingly the most important explanatory variable. Religion is the second most important variable as far as voting on abortion is concerned but has no explanatory value for voting on the other two issues. Region has some explanatory value as far as abortion is concerned with Northern MPs in particular being less liberal than other MPs. On the other two issues only one variable, other than party, has a significant effect. MPs with an Oxbridge background are more likely to be conservative on capital punishment and liberal on homosexuality than their colleagues.

We have to date said nothing about whether the religious composition of a constituency has any effect on voting. Unfortunately we only have data, and far from perfect data at that, upon the religious composition of English constituencies from 1974 onwards.[17] For that reason Table 5.4 presents an analysis of those English MPs who voted. Rather than report the results of all fourteen variables used in the model we merely report the beta weights of those variables where the relationship is significant. As the table indicates the percentage of Roman Catholics living in a constituency does appear to have some influence upon voting on abortion. The larger the proportion of Catholics in a constituency the more likely an MP is to oppose liberal abortion law. However the effect is not consistently significant and it is stronger on the earlier votes.

Table 5.4 *The effect of the religious composition of the constituency on the voting of English MPs 1974–1980*

| Variables | Standardised regression coefficients for: | | | | | | | | |
	White abortion vote (1975)	Benyon abortion vote (1977)	Braine abortion vote (1978)	Capital punishment vote (1974)	Corrie abortion vote (1979)	Corrie abortion vote (1980)	Capital punishment vote (1979)	Homosexuality vote (1980)
Party	0.56	0.63	0.56	0.78	0.69	0.59	0.73	0.64
Religion	0.18	0.25	0.18	NS	0.24	0.22	NS	NS
Oxbridge	NS	NS	NS	NS	NS	NS	0.15	−0.18
North	0.25	0.14	0.12	NS	NS	0.15	NS	NS
Religious composition constituency: percentage of Protestants	NS	NS	NS	NS	NS	NS	NS	NS
Religious composition constituency: percentage of Catholics	0.20	0.25	0.13	NS	NS	NS	0.17	NS
R² Total explanatory power 14 variable model	0.47	0.48	0.37	0.60	0.48	0.46	0.49	0.36

NS = Not Significant
Coding as in Table 5.1 except for:
Percentage Roman Catholics (Protestants) in constituency = 1 if percentage RCs (Prots) in constituency is less than 2 per cent, 2 if it is between 2 per cent and 3 per cent, 3 if it is between 3 per cent and 4 per cent etc.

Table 5.5 *Explaining abortion voting (1966–1980)*

	Total Explanatory Power (R^2) of Model for Vote:							
Model	Second Reading of Steel bill (1966)	Third Reading of Steel bill (1967)	St John-Stevas bill (1969)	White bill (1975)	Benyon bill (1977)	Braine bill (1978)	Second Reading of Corrie bill (1979)	Report stage of Corrie bill (1980)
14-variable model	0.44	0.43	0.39	0.36	0.39	0.29	0.38	0.42
2-variable model (party and religion)	0.44	0.42	0.37	0.22	0.34	0.25	0.34	0.40

Table 5.6 *Explaining voting on the homosexuality issue*

	Total explanatory power (R²) of model for vote	
Model	Vote on homosexuality (1967)	Vote on homosexuality (1980)
14-variable model	0.41	0.36
2-variable model (Party and Oxbridge)	0.40	0.35

Table 5.7 *Explaining voting on capital punishment*

	Total explanatory power (R²) of model for vote				
Model	Capital punish- ment (1965)	Capital punish- ment (1966)	Capital punish- ment (1969)	Capital punish- ment (1974)	Capital punish- ment (1979)
14-variable model	0.68	0.59	0.59	0.54	0.46
1-variable model (party)	0.68	0.57	0.57	0.53	0.44

An overview of the three periods

The overall pattern is clear. There are noticeable differences between the voting patterns on the three issues. Only one variable, party, is a key factor in explaining all the votes we have considered. At the same time it is a noticeably better explanatory variable on capital punishment and homosexuality than it is on abortion. As far as abortion is concerned a two-variable model, using party and religion, has almost as much explanatory power as the fourteen-variable model we initially presented. In fact Table 5.5 indicates both that twelve variables can be removed from the model for all the abortion votes except that upon the White bill (1975) without losing more than 4 per cent of its explanatory power, and that the resultant model is not very powerful. In no case does even our extended model with 14 variables explain more than 45 per cent of the variance in vote. Party is a good predictor of vote but it is a far from perfect predictor. Religion can explain some of the variance not explained by party but not much. If we consider the voting on homosexuality once again, a 2-variable model – in this case party and Oxbridge – has almost as much explanatory power as our larger model (see Table 5.6). When we look at voting on capital punishment just considering party is sufficient to generate an R^2 very similar to that given by the 14-variable model. In both cases there is still a considerable amount of variance to be explained. Obviously then our statistical analysis can only go a limited way towards explaining MPs' voting on these three issues. Party is nevertheless a good but far from perfect predictor of vote.

Intra-party differences in voting

We have seen throughout our presentation of results that party is the best predictor of voting on these free-vote issues. In this section we shall attempt to establish not so much why there are differences between parties but rather why there are splits within parties. Tables 5.8, 5.9 and 5.10 examine the divisions within the parties on all the major free votes between 1965 and 1980 on the three issues we have considered.

These tables highlight an interesting pattern. In general Labour MPs are more cohesive on these issues than Conservative MPs. The index of intra-party cohesion is only above 60 per cent for the Conservatives in relation to four (of eleven) abortion votes and three (of six) votes on capital punishment. In contrast the Labour Party has an index of intra-party cohesion above 60 per cent on all the capital punishment votes, five of the eleven abortion votes and both of the homosexuality votes. In essence the Labour Party is only split on abortion while the Conservatives are split on all three issues. How far does our statistical analysis help us explain these splits?

The results presented in Tables 5.11 and 5.12 are disappointing, particularly as far as the splits in the Conservative party are concerned. The R^2 in Table 5.12 is consistently very low with the eleven variables in the model often explaining less than ten per cent of the variance in voting. As Table 5.11 indicates the model used to explain Labour voting is better, although still not outstanding. It is clear that religion and region are more important explanatory variables when considering the votes of Labour, as distinct from Conservative MPs. Table 5.11 also indicates, as we hypothesised, that ideology is related to voting in the Labour Party with Tribune

Tables 5.8 to 5.10 Intra-party cohesion and inter-party differences on social issues (MPs who voted)

Table 5.8 *Abortion (1966–1980)*

Voted	Inter-party difference %	Conservatives			Labour		
		Pro-** %	Anti-*** %	Intra-party cohesion* %	Pro-** %	Anti-*** %	Intra-party cohesion* %
Steel bill, Second Reading (1966)	15	77	23	54	92	8	84
Steel bill, Third Reading (1967)	51	34	66	32	85	15	70
St John-Stevas bill (1969)	58	20	80	60	78	22	56
White bill, Second Reading (1975)	43	4	96	92	47	54	6
Benyon bill, Second Reading (1977)	55	15	85	70	70	30	40
Braine bill, Ten-Minute-Rule bill (1978)	48	23	77	54	71	29	42
Corrie bill, Second Reading (1979)	52	8	92	84	60	45	20
Report stage, 24-week amendment	34	46	54	8	80	20	60
'Serious' amendment	46	34	66	24	80	14	60
'Substantial' amendment	62	16	84	68	78	22	56
Silkin amendment	61	21	79	58	82	10	64

* Measured by subtracting those supporting a bill from those who oppose it within the party – perfect cohesion is therefore 100% and occurs when all MPs of the party vote in the same way. Intra-party difference is arrived at by subtracting the percentage of Conservative supporters from the percentage of Labour supporters. It can range from 0% to 100%.
** Here, as throughout, a vote for the Steel bill and against the Amendment bills.
*** Here, as throughout, a vote against the Steel bill and for the Amendment bills.

Table 5.9 *Capital punishment, 1965–1979*

Vote	Inter-party differences %	Conservatives			Labour		
		Pro-* %	Anti-** %	Intra-party cohesion %	Pro-* %	Anti-** %	Intra-party cohesion %
Murder (Abolition of Death Penalty) Bill, Third Reading (1965)	81	81 (N 97)	19 (N 23)	62	0 (N 0)	100 (N 163)	100
Sandys' motion concerning re-introduction of capital punishment (November 1966)	78	84 (N 148)	16 (N 29)	68	6 (N 17)	94 (N 252)	88
Murder (Abolition of Death Penalty) Bill (June 1969)	79	82 (N 111)	18 (N 24)	64	3 (N 6)	97 (N 221)	94
Government affirmative motion on capital punishment (December 1969)	74	76 (N 173)	24 (N 55)	52	2 (N 6)	98 (N 272)	96
Anti-capital punishment amendment to Government affirmative motion on capital punishment (December 1974)	75	77 (N 199)	23 (N 59)	44	2 (N 6)	98 (N 293)	96
Government affirmative motion on capital punishment (July 1979)	69	71 (N 228)	29 (N 95)	42	2 (N 4)	98 (N 253)	96

* An 'aye' vote in November 1966, June 1969 and December 1974 and a 'no' vote on the other occasions.
** An 'aye' vote in 1965 and July 1979 and a 'no' vote in June and December 1969 and December 1974.

Table 5.10 *Homosexuality, 1967–1980*

Vote	Conservatives				Labour		
	Inter-party differences %	Pro-* %	Anti-** %	Intra-party cohesion %	Pro-* %	Anti-** %	Intra-party cohesion %
Sexual Offences Bill, Third Reading (1967)	48	50 (N 14)	50 (N 14)	0	98 (N 82)	2 (N 2)	96
Amendment to Criminal Justice (Scotland) Bill (1980)	55	42 (N 52)	58 (N 73)	16	97 (N 141)	3 (N 4)	94

* An 'aye' vote in both cases
** A 'no' vote in both cases

Table 5.11 *Explaining intra-party division among Labour MPs in voting on abortion (significant relationships only)*

Variables	Standard regression coefficients for vote on:							
	Second Reading of Steel bill (1966)	Third Reading of Steel bill (1967)	St John-Stevas bill (1969)	White bill (1975)	Benyon bill (1977)	Braine bill (1978)	Second Reading of Corrie bill (1979)	Report stage of Corrie bill (1980)
Religion	0.79	0.67	0.51	0.24	0.35	0.28	0.42	0.40
Tribune Group membership	NS	NS	NS	-0.19	-0.21	-0.22	-0.27	-0.16
Trade union sponsorship	NS	NS	NS	0.18	0.19	NS	NS	NS
North	NS	NS	NS	0.31	0.19	0.21	0.23	0.19
Wales	NS	NS	NS	0.22	0.15	0.16	0.28	NS
Scotland	NS	NS	NS	0.21	0.25	0.31	0.14	NS
Total explanatory power $-R^2$ of 15-variable model	0.61	0.48	0.31	0.39	0.37	0.29	0.38	0.25

NS – Not Significant
Coding as in Table 5.1 except for:
Tribune Group membership = 1 if MP has ever been a member of the Tribune Group; 0 otherwise
Trade union sponsorship = 1 if MP has ever been sponsored by a trade union; 0 otherwise

Table 5.12 Explaining intra-party differences in voting on social issues among Conservative MPs (significant relationships only)

(a) Abortion vote

Variable	Standardised regression coefficient for vote on:							
	Abortion (1966)	Abortion (1967)	Abortion (1968)	Abortion (1975)	Abortion (1977)	Abortion (1978)	Abortion (1979)	Abortion (1980)
Religion	0.51	0.23	NS	NS	NS	NS	NS	0.22
Age	NS	0.34	0.26	NS	NS	NS	NS	NS
Oxbridge	−0.35	−0.26	NS	NS	NS	NS	NS	NS
Constituency majority	NS	NS	NS	−0.31	NS	NS	NS	NS
Profession	NS	NS	NS	0.20	NS	NS	NS	NS
College	NS	NS	−0.20	NS	−0.22	NS	NS	NS
Total explanatory power – R^2 – of 11–variable model	0.36	0.17	0.12	0.03	0.02	0.03	0.02	0.05

(b) Capital punishment and homosexuality votes

Variable	Standardised regression coefficient for vote on:						
	Capital punishment (1965)	Capital punishment (1966)	Capital punishment (1969)	Capital punishment (1974)	Capital punishment (1979)	Homosexuality (1967)	Homosexuality (1980)
Age	0.27	0.36	0.26	NS	NS	NS	0.21
Gender	0.22	NS	NS	NS	NS	NS	NS
Scotland	NS	0.21	0.20	NS	NS	NS	NS
Oxbridge	NS	NS	−0.26	NS	0.26	NS	−0.21
Profession	NS	NS	NS	0.24	NS	NS	NS
Total explanatory power – R^2 – of 11–variable model	0.08	0.13	0.14	0.03	0.05	0.38	0.09

MPs taking a more liberal attitude on abortion than their colleagues. In contrast none of our analysis suggests that the marginality of a constituency has any effect upon the voting of Labour MPs.

The limits of statistical analysis

Our statistical analysis does throw considerable light on our hypotheses and it provides the starting point for an explanation of voting on these issues. However it is clear that any full explanation of this voting would need to consider the political background to the votes in much more detail.

As far as our hypotheses are concerned the results are mixed. Party is certainly the best predictor of voting and ideology does have some effect on voting in the Labour Party. Of the background variables, religion has the strongest influence on abortion voting but has no effect on voting on other issues. No other background variable has any consistent effect. If we consider the constituency variables, region has the predicted effect but marginality has no noticeable influence. In contrast there is a relationship between the percentage of Catholics in a constituency and voting on abortion which was not hypothesised. Despite all this it seems to us that the major conclusions of our study must be that relatively few quantitative variables affect voting on these issues and that much of the variance in voting cannot be explained using these statistical models.

In order to reinforce the importance of the political context in which votes are taken it is worth considering briefly five of the abortion votes, the votes upon the Second and Third Readings of the original Steel bill; the White bill; and the Second Reading and Report stages of the Corrie bill.[18] As we have already indicated the Second Reading vote on the Steel bill is atypical because of the high proportion of Conservative MPs (77 per cent) who voted and who supported it. In contrast by the Third Reading vote 66 per cent of the Conservative MPs who voted, opposed the bill. It is impossible to explain this change without appreciating that between the two votes the opponents of the bill became better organised and a major anti-abortion interest group, the Society for the Protection of the Unborn Child (SPUC), was formed. This group proselytised particularly among Conservative MPs emphasising that the Steel bill permitted abortion on broad 'social' grounds. This together with the increased publicity given to the medical profession's opposition to abortion on 'social' grounds obviously persuaded many Conservative MPs to change their votes.

The next major change in voting on abortion occurred before the James White bill in 1975. On this occasion 96 per cent of the Conservative MPs who voted supported the bill but more significantly 54 per cent of the Labour MPs did the same. These changes cannot be explained by reference to statistical analysis. Rather they result from the way the 1967 Abortion Act operated, its coverage by the media, and the growth in the size and effectiveness of the anti-abortion lobby. There can be little doubt that the opinion of MPs on the issue in 1975 were considerably influenced by two major aspects of the implementation of the 1967 Act. MPs were surprised by the large number of abortions which were being performed and with allegations that London was becoming the 'abortion capital of the world'. At the same time, and more importantly, MPs were increasingly aware of the 'abuses' in the operation of the Act in the private sector. These abuses were highlighted and exaggerated in the press and very effectively used by SPUC. The pro-abortion lobby had lost its impetus after its success in 1967 and until 1975 the anti-abortion lobby had little opposition. Thus many Labour MPs supported the White bill at Second Reading because they thought it would deal with the 'abuses', and because many were under strong pressure from the anti-abortion lobby in their constituencies. The bill did not progress beyond Second Reading so it is unclear if MPs appreciated how radical the White bill was and whether, if it had progressed, they would have still supported it.

It is also impossible to explain voting on the Corrie bill and particularly the differences between the votes at Second Reading and on Report by reference solely to statistical analysis. At Second Reading 92 per cent of the Conservatives and 45 per cent of the Labour MPs who voted supported the bill. On later votes at Report stage the Conservative support for the bill decreased and Labour opposition increased. The reason for this change is fairly straightforward. Many Labour MPs under pressure from anti-abortion groups in their constituencies, and particularly from Roman Catholic Labour supporters, agreed to support an abortion bill at Second Reading in order to allow the issue to be fully debated but reasserted their opposition to major reform in later votes. Other MPs supported the Second Reading because they believed the major aim of the bill was to reduce the time limit up to which abortions can be carried out. When it became clear that the bill's sponsors were not interested in other clauses of the bill which would have had a much more radical effect upon the law such MPs opposed these clauses at the later stages. In addition as the controversy over the bill progressed the opposition of the medical profession to the bill became clearer and this evidently affected a number of MPs, particularly Conservatives.

Obviously we have only been able to indicate some of the political factors which affected some of the votes upon one of the issues. However this brief analysis should confirm that while statistical analysis can provide an important basis from which to embark upon an explanation of voting a fuller, more adequate, explanation involves a much more detailed consideration of the political background to, and context of, the votes.

2 The case studies

6   A case study of the abortion issue

There can be little doubt that, in the post-war period at least, abortion has been the longest running, and most contentious, private members' issue. Since the passage of the 1967 Abortion Act there have been nine private members' bills which have attempted to amend it, making it less liberal.[1] One bill also attempted to liberalise the position.[2] During this period sophisticated lobbies have developed on both sides so that when Parliament debates abortion the atmosphere in the chamber is highly charged. Such an atmosphere is very untypical of private members' days. The chamber is crowded, Ministers attend and vote, and the public galleries are crowded.

In the main body of the text we have referred frequently to the abortion issue. So some of the material here will have been touched upon in the text. The aim here, as in the other case studies, is to examine how Parliament has dealt with this issue, using the private-members'-bill procedure, over the post-war period. Obviously this will provide a fuller consideration of those points alluded to in the text. However the main purpose of these case studies is to offer a detailed appreciation, a 'feel', of how private-members'-bill procedure operates which will flesh out the bones provided by the aggregate analysis presented in the previous chapters.[3]

Here we shall first identify and describe the bills on abortion which were introduced before 1979. The second section will examine the development of the abortion lobbies in the same period. A third section will then analyse the fate of the Corrie bill, introduced in the 1979/80 Session, which has been the most radical, and most nearly successful, of the bills introduced to amend the 1967 Abortion Act. The final section will then discuss what we can learn about the private-members'-bill procedure from this case study of the abortion issue.

The history of the abortion issue before 1979

There were six attempts at abortion law reform before the passage of the 1967 Abortion Act.[4] Only one bill made any progress and that was a private members' bill introduced in the House of Lords by Lord Silkin in November 1965. It received a Second Reading in the Lords with a majority of 67 votes to 8. The bill was subsequently amended quite substantially in Committee and on Report but in this amended form it received an unopposed Third Reading. Silkin's bill was not introduced into the House of Commons because an election was called and Parliament was dissolved in 1966.

In fact Lord Silkin introduced a very similar bill in the next session but withdrew it when David Steel, Liberal MP for Roxburgh, Selkirk and Peebles, introduced a private members' bill into the Commons. Steel had drawn third place in the ballot and after consultations, particularly with ALRA, he decided to sponsor an abortion bill.

The original bill established four legal grounds for abortion: if there was serious risk to the life of the mother, or grave risk to her physical or mental health or that of the child after birth; if there was substantial risk that a child would be born seriously handicapped; if there was reason to believe that the pregnant woman would be severely overstrained as a mother (the 'social clause'); or if the pregnancy was of a girl under 16, or had occurred as a result of rape. The bill did not require one of the two doctors to be a consultant. It contained no specific provisions about a time limit but relied upon the provisions of the Infant Life (Preservation) Act 1929, which made all abortion an offence after 28 weeks.

The bill, initially called the Medical Termination of Pregnancy Bill, had a full five-hour Second Reading debate on 22 July 1966.[5] It was the first abortion bill to receive a full debate and a Commons vote and was given a Second Reading by a majority of 223 votes to 29. However, as always, this vote was only a first step, and Steel was under considerable pressure to amend his bill before and in Standing Committee.

As we saw earlier, there is no doubt that Steel was influenced by representations from the medical profession, particularly by the RCOG and the BMA. Before the passage of the 1967 Abortion Act both these organisations opposed any major liberalisation of abortion law. The two organisations published reports on abortion in 1966 before the publication of the Steel bill. Both reports recommended that abortion be restricted to circumstances where there was 'serious' risk to the life of the mother, or 'substantial' risk that the child would be born abnormal. When the Steel bill was published the RCOG and the BMA formed a committee to consider it which reported in November 1966. This report condemned outright the 'social grounds' for abortion contained in the bill. It did however recommend that a sub-clause should be added to allow a doctor to take into account a patient's 'total environment'. In addition the report argued that one of the two doctors who approved an abortion should be a consultant, noting that as far as the RCOG was concerned a gynaecologist would be preferable.

David Steel was particularly concerned to reach a compromise with the two professional bodies. He had several meetings with them before tabling his own amendment to the bill based upon their objections. The amendment only allowed a doctor to take into account 'the patient's total environment actual or reasonably foreseeable' when taking a decision on abortion. In addition Steel withdrew the two most directly 'social clauses' in the bill, those which would have allowed abortion if the woman was likely to be totally inadequate as a mother, or if the pregnancy was a result of rape. For this reason a number of the leading abortion law reformers believed that the heart of the bill had been removed.

Despite these concessions the bill was strongly opposed during 12 sittings and 30 hours of debate in Standing Committee. The full range of private-members'-bill parliamentary tactics was used against it by its opponents: a large number of amendments were tabled; speeches were long; and numerous points of order were introduced. Despite this only one other significant amendment was approved which was also supported by Steel. It permitted doctors, nurses and other medical staff to abstain from abortion on the grounds of conscience. However the burden of proof rested with the person claiming this exemption. In contrast the opposition was unsuccessful in introducing an amendment to require that one of the two doctors authorising an abortion be a consultant, despite continued lobbying from the RCOG and the BMA both inside and outside Parliament. Although the opposition had little success in amending the bill in Committee, because of the Committee's inbuilt majority for the bill, they did delay it. This meant that it appeared unlikely to pass through its remaining stages in the single day available. In fact it was only saved because Roy Jenkins, the Home Secretary, and Richard Crossman, Leader of the House, who were supporters of the measure, twice persuaded the Cabinet to give the bill more time.

The Report stage lasted for three sessions and a total of 28 hours. After the Third Reading which lasted 2 hours the bill was finally approved by 167 votes to 83 on 13 July. It then passed through the House of Lords, although not without a number of alarms, and received the Royal Assent on 27 October 1967. For administrative reasons, however, it did not come into operation until 27 April 1968. The final Act allowed for a pregnancy to be terminated by a registered medical practitioner if two registered doctors were of the opinion, formed in good faith, that:

(a) the continuance of the pregnancy would involve risk to the life of the pregnant woman, or of injury to the physical or mental health of the pregnant woman or any existing children of her family, greater than if the pregnancy were terminated, or

(b) that there was a substantial risk that if the child were born, it would suffer from such physical or mental abnormalities as to be seriously handicapped.

Why was the Steel bill successful? This is an important question because without understanding why the Abortion bill passed it is hard to appreciate why subsequent legislation has proved unsuccessful. Its passage was clearly helped by the fact that 1966–7 was an extended parliamentary session and by the liberal atmosphere which prevailed in the 1966–70 Parliament. At the same time while the bill's supporters were well organised its opponents were not. ALRA was an effective pressure group while SPUC was not formed until after the Second Reading of Steel's bill. In addition Steel was a skilled sponsor of the bill which was also supported by public opinion. Nevertheless the real reason why the Abortion Act reached the Statute Book was that the Government gave the bill time. In the Second Reading debate Roy Jenkins declared the Government's view as one of benevolent neutrality – but in the event it was more benevolent than neutral. The majority of the Labour Party supported reform as did the majority of the Cabinet. Roy Jenkins and Richard Crossman were both strong advocates of liberal reform, while the Minister of Health, Kenneth Robinson, had himself previously introduced a bill to reform abortion law. So at every stage the Government lent the bill a hand as it did with other liberal reforms in the same period. When the bill was delayed in going to the Standing Committee which considered private members' bills by the extended consideration of a previous bill, the Government allowed the Abortion bill to go to a Standing Committee normally reserved for Government bills. Subsequently and more crucially it allowed 25 hours of Government time to the later stages of the bill. Without such concessions from the Government the bill would have been successfully talked out by its opponents.

The Steel bill succeeded, but there were signs during its passage that the struggle was not over. The Third Reading vote of 83 against the bill indicated a concern, particularly, although not exclusively, among Conservative MPs, that it was too liberal. In addition it reflected the improved organisation of the anti-abortion campaigners both inside and outside Parliament during the bill's later stages. While SPUC may have been unsuccessful in this instance it grew in both size and experience during its fight against the Steel bill. At the same time the opposition in the Commons to the bill gathered around a few MPs who were to be influential in attempts to amend the Act over the next decade, particularly MPs such as Sir Bernard Braine, Jill Knight and Norman St John-Stevas. The Abortion Act became operative on 27 April 1968. Within 15 months the first attempt to amend it was made, and in all seven amendment bills were introduced before the Corrie bill. Between 1967 and 1975 five amending bills were introduced and Parliamentary voting on those bills which progressed reflected increasing support for amending legislation (see Table 6.1).

As the Norman St John-Stevas bill was a Ten-Minute-Rule bill it had little chance of progressing even if it had obtained a First Reading. No abortion bill is likely to be unopposed, and the Labour Government tacitly supported the Abortion Act, so St John-Stevas's bill was doomed from the start. Indeed St John-Stevas's aim in introducing the bill was restricted to airing the issue in Parliament again and testing the opinion of the House. However, he was denied permission to introduce his bill by a narrow majority.

After the return of a Conservative Government the pressure for reform was kept up by the anti-abortion groups. This pressure was partly responsible for the Government's decision to establish a committee chaired by the Hon. Mrs Justice Lane to consider the operation of the Abortion Act in 1971. The Lane Committee took two-and-a-half years to report after taking evidence from the Ministry of Health and all interested parties.[6] Its report supported the Act arguing that where 'abuses' existed in its operation these

Table 6.1 *Parliamentary voting on abortion, 1966–1978*

Year	Sponsor and type of Bill	Voting (expressed as percentage of those voting)			Number of MPs voting
		for	against	majority	
1966	David Steel, private members' bill (1967 Abortion Act), Second Reading	88 (N 233)	12 (N 29)	+194	252
1967	David Steel, private members' bill (1967 Abortion Act), Third Reading	67 (N 167)	33 (N 38)	+ 84	250
1969	Norman St John-Stevas, Ten-Minute-Rule bill, First Reading	49 (N 199)	51 (N 210)	−11	409
1975	James White, private members bill, Second Reading	70 (N 203)	30 (N 88)	+115	291
1977	William Benyon, Abortion (Amendment) private members' bill, Second Reading	56 (N 170)	44 (N 132)	+38	302
1978	Sir Bernard Braine, Abortion (Amendment), Ten-Minute-Rule bill, First Reading	51 (N 181)	59 (N 175)	+6	356

This table does not include tellers. A vote for the Steel bill and against all the subsequent bills is a pro-abortion vote.

could be best dealt with by administrative, rather than legislative, change. Indeed they recommended only one legislative change: an amendment to the 1929 Infant Life (Preservation) Act which would have reduced the time limit for legal abortion from 28 to 24 weeks.

Despite the Lane Committee's report support for an effort to amend the 1967 Abortion Act was growing and it was against this background that a radical private members' amendment bill was introduced by James White, Labour MP for Glasgow (Pollock). Its sponsors argued that the main aim of the bill was to curtail abuses in the operation of the Abortion Act. Nevertheless, there can be no doubt that, if the bill had become law, it would have resulted in a substantial reduction in the availability of legal abortions in Britain.

The bill had three main elements: (1) it attempted to prevent abuses in the private sector and to prevent referral bureaux being financially associated with abortion clinics; (2) it laid down statutory conditions for the approval of private clinics; and most important (3) it removed the clause in the original Act which provided the basis for the so-called 'statistical argument' for abortions. Under this clause an abortion was legal if on balance the risk of continuing pregnancy was greater than that of termination; anti-abortion supporters believed that this clause allowed some doctors to offer abortion on demand, because one could show statistically that abortion was less risky to all mothers than continued pregnancy. The White bill would have replaced this clause with one specifying that the abortion was only legal if there was a 'grave' risk to life or a 'serious' risk to health.

There is no doubt that the voting on the Second Reading of the White bill in 1975 shocked the supporters of the Abortion Act. The bill was given a Second Reading by a majority of 203 to 88. This was a radical change since the Steel bill and even represented a major revision since the voting on the St John-Stevas bill. Despite this massive favourable vote the bill did not, however, progress further because the sponsors accepted a Government proposal that it should be referred to a parliamentary Select Committee which would consider it in the light of a review of abortion law. With hindsight this appears to have been a successful attempt by the Government in general, and perhaps the Ministry of Health in particular, to defuse the abortion issue and remove any hope that the White bill had of progressing.

In the period between 1967 and 1975 then two patterns are apparent. First by 1969, and the vote on the St John-Stevas bill, many Conservative MPs had reasserted their conservative position and supported amending legislation. Obviously such MPs were reinforced in that conservative belief by the evidence of abuses which grew after 1969. However, few Conservatives changed their view between 1969 and 1975 because in 1969 few Conservatives had taken a liberal stand on abortion. Secondly there was a large swing between 1969 and 1975 in the voting of Labour MPs. The change appears to have occurred mainly because MPs believed that there were numerous 'abuses' of the legislation, but at the same time some Labour MPs voted for the White bill at Second Reading for political or tactical reasons.[7]

The Select Committee which was established to consider the White bill had a majority of members who were in favour of major reform of the Abortion Act. Initially, although the Committee was deeply divided it concentrated upon the area of 'abuses' which both sides agreed could be remedied by administrative action. This meant that the Committee agreed on nine recommendations for administrative action which were accepted and acted upon by the Secretary of State for Social Services, Barbara Castle. The House of Commons voted to re-establish the Select Committee in the next Session. However, almost as soon as the Committee reconvened, its six pro-abortion MPs walked out when it was clear the majority would recommend major reform.[8]

In 1977, William Benyon, Conservative Member for Buckingham, introduced a private members' bill based on the first report of the re-formed, but truncated, Select Committee. The bill would have had less effect on the operation of the 1967 Act than James White's bill. Nevertheless, it would have restricted the availability of abortions in three ways: first, by changing the wording of the provision on eligibility for abortion; secondly, by shortening the period during which abortions could take place; thirdly, by requiring that one of the two certifying doctors should have been registered for not less than five years, and that the two doctors should not be partners. What is more the bill would have affected the operation of the charitable pregnancy advisory services, notably the Pregnancy Advisory Service and the British Pregnancy Advisory Service, by ensuring that no one clinic could advise on, and carry out, abortions. The Benyon bill was given a Second Reading by 170 votes to 132 (see Table 6.1).

The Benyon bill was thus the first amendment bill to reach and complete its Committee stage. It proved an educative experience for the supporters and opponents of reform inside and outside Parliament. The bill reached the Standing Committee fairly late in the Session, and the Committee itself was composed of opponents and supporters of the bill in direct proportion to the Second Reading vote. Thus the bill's supporters had a majority and passed a sitting's motion which ensured that the Committee met frequently, completing its consideration of the bill after ten sittings, including three all-night sittings and 19 Sessions, including one which lasted 11 hours 48 minutes. Given this majority the bill came out of Committee largely unscathed but there was not time available for its Report stage, and the Government refused to give it time, so that it fell at the end of Parliament. Nevertheless the Benyon bill was important particularly for the pro-abortion side because of what they learnt from the experience. Indeed MPs from both sides who were on the Committee told us that the Benyon supporters had outmanoeuvred their opponents at the Committee stage. In particular the liaison between the parliamentary and extra-parliamentary wings of the pro-abortion lobby, and the briefings provided by the interest groups to the MPs, were nothing like as good as they subsequently became.

In the next Session Sir Bernard Braine introduced a Ten-Minute-Rule bill, the provisions of which followed closely those of the Benyon bill. Sir Bernard was given leave to introduce the bill, with 181 voting in favour and 175 against. Once again then we can see that a significant change in parliamentary opinion had occurred between 1975 and 1978 with support for amending legislation decreasing.

It is not difficult to explain the changing views of those, mostly Labour MPs, who moved away from support for amending legislation. By 1977 there was ample evidence that many of the 'abuses' in the operation of the 1967 Act were being removed. In the debate on the White bill, the DHSS had made clear for the first time the steps it was taking to prevent abuses. The Department had also accepted, and acted upon, the initial, unanimous, recommendations of the Select Committee on the White bill. All this meant that the private clinics were much more tightly controlled, that taxi-touting was dramatically reduced and that standards in the private sector were radically improved. This action was made very clear to MPs in the debate on the Benyon bill by Roland Moyle, Minister of State at the DHSS. The Department's action on 'abuses' obviously influenced some MPs. Indeed 11 MPs who supported White and opposed Benyon and/or Braine, and replied to our request for information, gave the curtailment of the 'abuses' as the reason for their changed vote.

The Corrie bill

After the 1978 vote, opinion in the House appeared evenly divided. The two sides had learnt a great deal from their experience on the Benyon bill although it is probable that the pro-abortionists had learnt more, particularly about the problems of organisation in Standing Committee. However both sides at this time awaited the outcome of the forthcoming election knowing that, given past voting patterns, if the Conservative Party won a comfortable majority at such an election, the chances of a successful amendment to the Abortion Act would increase substantially.

When the Conservatives won the next election and John Corrie won first place in the 1979 private members' ballot and decided to introduce a bill to restrict abortion the stage was set for a major parliamentary event. Certainly the contention generated in relation to this bill is unrivalled in the post-war history of private members' business.

When John Corrie won first place in the ballot it was not immediately clear that he would introduce an abortion bill and neither of the abortion factions were certain of his intentions. He was not one of the MPs whom SPUC or LIFE would have chosen to win the ballot and when he drew first place neither initially expected him to take an abortion bill. Indeed LIFE's first hope was that Robert Taylor, Conservative MP for Croydon North-West, who drew third place in the ballot, would introduce a bill.

In fact in the Second Reading debate on his bill, Corrie claimed that abortion reform had always been in his mind:

I walked into the House on Wednesday night when the ballot had been drawn, I was told by a press man that I had won it and he asked me what I would do. At that moment I said that I would try to amend the Abortion Act because I had always felt strongly about it. No other person had spoken to me up to that moment. It was my decision made because I wanted to do it.[9]

In addition Corrie gave a more personal reason for his choice:

Let's not pretend I haven't been influenced by the fact that it has taken us fifteen years to try to have three children. A lot of time – while nurses were sweating to see that our child wasn't lost – they have been hurrying off to perform abortions on patients in beds flanking my wife's.[10]

Despite this, John Corrie is a politician and as such he consulted widely with his friends inside and outside Parliament and with interested parties before he decided to take a bill through Parliament which he knew would be strongly opposed.[11] Corrie asserted, as we saw earlier, that he was not influenced by SPUC or LIFE in his choice of bill and certainly neither SPUC nor LIFE have claimed a major role in its drafting. Nevertheless Corrie admitted receiving a large number of letters from supporters of abortion law reform, most of whom were members of SPUC and LIFE, while he was deciding which bill to promote. Such pressure did not force him to take an abortion bill but it must have strengthened his belief that he would receive a great deal of support to offset against the inevitable opposition he would encounter. In the end then his choice probably depended as much on his political judgement as his moral and religious convictions. As such it is not surprising that he took time to make a definite commitment to take an amending bill.

It is clear that even before John Corrie had finally decided on the subject of his bill the two abortion lobbies were mobilised for action. At the end of May Co-ord had written to Corrie urging him not to take an abortion bill while on 8 June they wrote to all MPs asking them not to support amending legislation. In addition they called upon all their members to write to their MPs, to John Corrie, and to the Minister of Health, Dr Gerard Vaughan. SPUC and LIFE's tactics were different. They were more concerned to get their members to write to Corrie and to their MPs urging them to support him, rather than writing directly to MPs themselves. This is a definite strategy as they believe that MPs are most influenced by their constituents' letters. Nevertheless the groups only began to move into top gear after 27 June when Corrie's Abortion (Amendment) Bill received a formal First Reading. At this stage, as we saw earlier, a private member still only has to declare the short title, not the content of his bill, so that over the next two and a half weeks until the full text of the bill was available on 10 June, only three days before the Second Reading, no one was entirely sure of its contents, although rumours abounded. During this period Corrie saw a number of organisations to discuss with them the detailed content of his bill. He talked to SPUC, the BMA and the RCOG.

Corrie does not appear to have been greatly influenced in drafting his bill by the representations of interest groups. Rather he was most influenced by his parliamentary colleagues. All private members' bills are almost inevitably sponsored by a number of MPs from different political parties. An MP agrees to sponsor a bill after discussions with its promoter and in return for his support may request changes in, or additions to, the bill. The sponsors of John Corrie's bill were Sir Bernard Braine, Jill Knight, Elaine Kellett-Bowman, William Benyon, Michael Ancram and Janet Fookes (all Conservative MPs), Leo Abse, James Hamilton, James White and Ian Campbell (all Labour MPs); and Gordon Wilson, the Scottish Nationalist. There is no doubt that Michael Ancram, Jill Knight and Elaine Kellett-Bowman take a more fundamentalist view on abortion than John Corrie. In his discussions with us John Corrie made it clear that the bill was larger in scope than he had originally intended because this was the price he paid for the support of his sponsors. In particular it is evident from our interviews that the sponsors were split on Clause 4 of the bill which dealt with the separation of referral agencies and clinics, a split which was very evident in Committee. William Benyon who played a very active role in Committee and, to a slightly lesser extent, John Corrie had little belief in this clause. However to others like Jill Knight and Bernard Braine it was a key, if not the key, clause in the bill.

John Corrie's bill became readily available in the House of Commons on 10 July only two days before Second Reading. This is unusual. Most private members' bills are published at least seven days before the date of the Second Reading in order to allow time for consultations and discussions between MPs and interested outside parties. It is less uncommon in the case of abortion bills. The James White bill in 1975 was not available until seven days before Second Reading. In fact John Corrie claimed that his secretary delivered the bill to the Bill Office in the House of Commons, which is responsible for printing the bills, seven or eight days before 13 July. This view was in direct contrast to the report in the *Catholic Herald* which suggested that release of the bill was delayed partly because of disagreement among its backers as to what would get passed by the House of Commons and partly to prevent the abortion campaign launching an attack on it.[12] Corrie dismissed this report in the Second Reading debate but it is revealing that a draft of the Corrie bill which was significantly different from the final form was still circulating around the House for comments on 9 July.[13]

When the bill was introduced it was clearly a very radical one. It had four main elements. Firstly it would have reduced the time limit up to which abortions can be legally performed from 28 to 20 weeks. Secondly, it would have tightened up the regulations upon the granting of abortion. The aim was to make abortion legal in fewer circumstances, to remove the 'statistical argument' and to reduce significantly the social grounds for abortion. Thirdly, the bill would have allowed any doctor or nurse to object on 'religious, ethical or other grounds' to taking part in an abortion operation. Fourthly, the bill required the separation of referral agencies from clinics carrying out abortion. This would have severely constrained the work of the charitable agencies, the British Pregnancy Advisory Service and the Pregnancy Advisory Service.

The Second Reading debate which lasted four and a half hours, took place on Friday, 13 June. It was very well attended with the Chamber more than two-thirds full throughout the debate. In the division the bill was given a Second Reading by a majority of 242 votes to 98, the largest majority an amendment bill had enjoyed. No

Table 6.2 *Parliamentary voting on the Corrie abortion bill (1979–1980)*

| Vote | Voting (expressed as percentage of those voting) | | | Number of MPs voting |
	for*	against	majority	
Second Reading vote (1979)	71 (N 242)	29 (N 98)	+144	340
Report stage (1980) – amendment to change 20 weeks to 24 weeks	62 (N 275)	38 (N 172)	+103	447
Report stage (1980) – amendment to delete 'serious' from grounds clause	58 (N 201)	42 (N 145)	+56	346
Report stage (1980) – amendment to delete 'substantial' from grounds clause	50 (N 177)	50 (N 180)	−3	357
Report stage (1980) – Silkin amendment	56 (N 157)	44 (N 122)	+35	279

This table does not include tellers.
*Voting for the Second Reading and against all the amendments on Report is an anti-abortion vote.

one was surprised with the result but most were surprised by the size of the majority. The vote meant that the Standing Committee was composed of 10 supporters and five opponents of the bill. As such the bill's opponents had little chance of amending it in Committee. When the bill returned to the floor for the Report stage it was faced by a sophisticated filibuster. Despite being debated for 4 days and 20 hours it failed to complete its Report stage and was finally withdrawn on 25 March 1980.

Before we examine why the Corrie bill failed it is important to establish that the voting patterns of MPs on the issue changed significantly between Second Reading and Report. As Table 6.2 indicates, the support for the details of the Corrie bill was much less than for the Second Reading.[14]

Of course this change partly reflects the fact that many MPs, particularly although not exclusively, Labour MPs, supported the Second Reading of the bill because they favoured a reduction in the time limit up to which abortion could be carried out, and this clause in the bill was the one which was almost exclusively discussed in the Second Reading debate. These MPs were much less favourably disposed to changes in the grounds for abortion and as such voted for important amendments to this clause. However there is little doubt that opinions in Parliament did change as the bill progressed. MPs who opposed the Second Reading were much more likely subsequently to vote consistently on the issue than were MPs who supported it.

The majority of the MPs we are dealing with who altered their views were MPs who had little prior knowledge of, or interest in, the abortion issue. Many of these MPs were newly elected and voted, or did not vote, at Second Reading when they had little knowledge of the details of the bills, or of the issues and questions involved. The publicity and the lobbying associated with the Corrie bill did much to politicise them.

In particular two aspects of the lobbying were important. First, some MPs only realised after the Second Reading how radical the bill was; they had previously believed that it dealt mainly with the time limit for abortions. This new understanding owed much to the letters and lobbying of the extra-parliamentary pro-abortion lobby. In addition however, the pro-abortion MPs on the Standing Committee lobbied extensively at this stage in order to emphasise the bill's radical elements. Secondly, the role of the professional medical organisations was important. The BMA and the RCOG have opposed all the abortion amendment bills since the White bill. However, before Corrie, many MPs had not been aware of the strength of the medical profession's opposition to any major changes to the 1967 Abortion Act. On the Corrie bill the BMA in particular was much more overt in its opposition and there is little doubt that in the light of the opposition, which was only clearly expressed after Second Reading, some MPs rethought their position on some elements in the bill. As one Conservative MP told us:

There can be little doubt that the medical profession's opposition to the bill influenced the votes of many MPs at the Report Stage. I personally would have voted for a change in the grounds for abortion if it hadn't been clear that the bulk of the medical profession opposed such a change.[15]

Why did the Corrie bill fail? It is not easy for someone without knowledge of procedures in Parliament to understand how a bill which receives overwhelming support in principle at Second Reading can fail to pass. In the case of the Corrie bill the answer at one level is simple: the bill simply ran out of time. However, such an answer begs another question: why did the bill run out of time? Actually the bill had more time than any other private members' bills, which did not receive Government time, in the post-war era. It was considered for four-and-a-half hours at Second Reading, 43 hours in Committee and 20 hours on Report. Indeed this means it had more parliamentary time than most successful *Government* bills. So we cannot simply conclude that it had insufficient time. Rather the point is that when it came back to the floor of the House for Report it had insufficient time to complete its remaining stages. There were three reasons for this: the bill was too large; the opposition to it was too strong and well organised; and the Government refused to give the bill time. We shall look at each of these elements of the explanation in turn.

When the bill came back to the House from the Standing Committee it was still large. It contained eight clauses and represented a very radical attempt to amend the 1967 Abortion Act. This had several consequences. First, the large number of clauses meant that its opponents had ample opportunity to table a wide variety of amendments. Indeed 80 amendments were put forward at Report stage from which the Speaker selected over 50 amendments in 28 separate groupings. If the bill had been reduced in scope at the Committee stage, or even after the first day's debate on the Report stage then such a truncated bill might have succeeded. However it was not until just before the third day's Report-stage debate that John Corrie and his supporters withdrew part of the bill. By that time it was too late.

The bill actually came out of Committee considerably altered, and altered in such a way that it made the opposition's task in fighting it easier rather than more difficult. Almost all of the clauses in the original bill were amended, totally redrafted, or withdrawn. So when the House of Commons saw the bill again it was significantly changed. This allowed the opposition to claim that it was a different, although no less radical, bill. More important, it appeared to influence the Speaker's choice of amendments for Report stage. The Speaker called amendments which had already been debated and decided upon in Committee. One obvious, although unstated, justification for that decision was that the House itself should have a chance to debate the major clauses in a bill which had changed so substantially since they had approved it in principle at Second Reading. The Speaker's choice of a large number of amendments for debate virtually ensured that the bill, in the form it came out of

Committee, could not complete its Report and Third Reading stages in the time available.

The bill's contents influenced its fate in one other way. There is little doubt that many MPs who supported the bill on Second Reading did so because they favoured a reduction in the time limit for abortions. They did so in the belief that many of the other elements in the bill would be removed in Committee; that a compromise would be reached between pro- and anti-abortionists. It is not easy to understand how MPs could have taken this view.

There was ample evidence of the strength of feeling on both sides, and no obvious basis for compromise. However so many of our interviewees reported this as their view, or the view of other MPs they knew, that there can be little doubt this was a popular misconception, particularly among MPs newly elected to Parliament. These MPs were surprised when the bill returned to the floor of the Commons with no evidence of compromise and all of its radical elements intact. In addition John Corrie and his supporters were blamed by these MPs for failing to compromise, or as one MP put it:

There can be little doubt that the supporters of the bill were held responsible for not responding to the obvious desire of the House for compromise and as such for being politically inept.[16]

Of course we are still left with the question: Why was there no compromise? As we have said, there was in fact little basis for compromise. The main supporters of the Abortion Act in Parliament might have been willing to compromise on a bill which merely reduced the time limit for abortion to 24 weeks, but they would accept no change in the grounds for abortion. In contrast the anti-abortion MPs were most anxious to change radically the grounds for abortion and remove the so-called 'statistical argument'. There was therefore no way that there could be a compromise between the two sides. However the bill's supporters could have unilaterally dropped some of the clauses of their bill, in Committee or before Report, in order to improve the chances of getting the rest of it through. Why did they not do so? The second half of the bill was only withdrawn by its sponsors just before the third day on Report by which time it was too late. They did not do so earlier partly because some of them initially believed that they could get all the bill through, and partly because there was no obvious basis for compromise among the bill's supporters. There appears little doubt that there was some complacency among the parliamentary supporters of the bill both because of its overwhelming success at Second Reading, and because there was considerable private members' time available for its consideration on Report. With hindsight it is easy to see this was a mistake, but until the Corrie bill no amending legislation had ever reached Report stage, and so neither side had a clear impression of what would happen. Indeed when the Report stage began many of the pro-abortion MPs themselves thought that the bill would go through in some form.

At the same time however the anti-abortion MPs had no contingency plans nor had they drawn up a coherent strategy on what to concede if necessary. The major reason for this was the divisions which existed on the anti-abortion side. For example John Corrie and William Benyon were most anxious to amend the grounds for abortion, and less concerned with the licensing clause and the restriction of the operation of the charities. In contrast, Jill Knight, Michael Ancram and Sir Bernard Braine were much more concerned with the licensing clause, and were therefore reluctant to drop it. In addition the MPs were constantly under pressure from the extra-parliamentary anti-abortion lobby to hold firm to their principles and not drop sections of the bill. This meant that it was difficult for the anti-abortion MPs to agree a strategy, a problem which was further compounded by John Corrie's illness during the Committee stage. Indeed the absence of cohesion or a coherent strategy was the most important reason for the failure of the bill's sponsors to rescue it at Report stage.

One noticeable feature of the lobbying on the Corrie bill as compared with that on the previous amending bills was the growth of the extra-parliamentary pro-abortion lobby. The activities of the National Abortion Campaign and the Campaign against Corrie meant that there was a much more even balance between the efforts and visibility of the two lobbies in the country. This was reflected by the large growth in the number of pro-abortion groups during the period and by a much more equal distribution between pro- and anti-abortion letters in MPs' postbags than had occurred on previous bills. In addition the pro-abortion lobby was greatly assisted by the efforts of the TUC, the Labour Party and the British Medical Association. The TUC organised a large pro-abortion march while the Labour Party, through its Women's Officer, and the Labour Abortion Reform Committee put considerable pressure on Labour MPs. The continued and outspoken support of the BMA was especially important as MPs obviously take particular note of the medical profession on issues of this sort.

Despite this, however, the battle outside Parliament was fairly finely balanced given the continued widespread support for, and local activities of, SPUC and LIFE. It was inside Parliament that the battle was really won by the strategy, effort and organisation of the pro-abortion lobby. Of course it had the advantage at Report stage in that there was limited time available, a fact which works in favour of the side fighting a defensive action. In such circumstances the lobby defending the status quo merely has to delay and filibuster so that a bill runs out of time. Nevertheless such delaying tactics, while effective, are not easy to organise, nor are they inevitably success-ful. The achievement of the parliamentary pro-abortion lobby was that it drafted enough legitimate amendments to ensure extended debate; that it provided and briefed enough speakers to produce a sophisticated filibuster; and that it organised its supporters so that the voting on Report was always close, and on a number of occasions the Corrie side was defeated. Why was this lobby so effective?

As we have said the parliamentary pro-abortion lobby was an easier task because it was fighting a defensive campaign and as such it could be successful without necessarily having to be victorious in the division lobbies. It merely needed to use tactics to delay a decision and ensure the bill fell through lack of time. In other words the pro-abortion parliamentary lobby did not need to be more effective than the anti-abortion side – although by most definitions they were – they only needed properly to organise their forces and effectively use parliamentary delaying tactics. However, that is easier said than done. In this case the parliamentarians were successful because they were cohesive, tactically skilful and indus-trious, and because they were given great moral and practical support by the extra-parliamentary lobby. The bulk of the parlia-mentary work was done by the five pro-abortion members of the Standing Committee but they were helped by a hard core of other MPs and by the efforts of certain outsiders.

It is difficult to appreciate how much work was involved in organising the parliamentary lobbies on both sides. The Committee sat for 43 hours and the MPs who sat on it were also involved in strategy meetings, in organising the whipping of their parlia-mentary supporters, and the speaking and writing to thousands of outside supporters. However, the situation was much worse for the pro-abortion Members of the Standing Committee for two reasons. First, there were only five of them as compared to the 10 supporters of the Corrie bill. More important, however, it was the pro-abortion side which made most of the running in Committee, speaking much more frequently, and putting down many more amendments, all of which had to be discussed and drafted. This commitment and unity among the parliamentarians was matched by the efforts of the extra-parliamentary lobby. The Co-ord advisers were constantly on hand to help with drafting amendments, and the Co-ord office was continually preparing briefs for MPs, and keeping the extra-parliamentary lobby in touch with what was going on at Committee and Report stage. This unity among the MPs, and between the MPs and the extra-parliamentary supporters, was a notable and crucially important factor in the success of the pro-abortion lobby.

However unity and effort would have had little effect without the skilled use of parliamentary tactics. The five MPs included two, Jo Richardson and Oonagh McDonald, who were extremely knowledgeable on the issue and had had the experience of sitting on the Benyon Standing Committee. They were hardened campaigners on the issue but they were aware that they needed colleagues on the Committee who were not only willing to work hard, but who also had a detailed grasp of parliamentary procedure and the use of parliamentary tactics. It was for this reason that they approached Ian Mikardo, one of the House's acknowledged experts on procedure, to serve on the Committee. They were also helped by the fact that Willie Hamilton, another long-serving parliamentarian, asked to join them. Obviously, right from the outset the pro-abortion lobby was aware that it was going to be largely a battle of parliamentary tactics and there can be little doubt that the lobby proved adept in that battle. In Committee it introduced a series of amendments to ensure extended discussion with the aim of educating MPs as to the radical nature of the bill. At the same time, and more crucially, it kept back for Report stage a series of amendments which could have been brought forward at Committee. The most notable of these was an amendment to introduce a time limit of 24 weeks for abortions rather than the 20 weeks included in the Corrie bill. The aim of this tactic of course was to ensure that the Speaker would call that amendment at Report stage, which he might not have done if the amendment had been moved and defeated in Committee.

Despite this all these efforts in Committee would have been of little use if the pro-abortion lobby could not have ensured extended debate and close votes at Report stage. At this stage it obviously aimed to put down a large number of amendments and filibuster the bill. While it kept back a number of amendments, the Co-ord lawyers drafted a great many more. Even so there was an extended series of debates on Report, and as such a lot of time to fill, particularly as the bill's supporters were committed to speeding up proceedings by speaking briefly and infrequently. What is more the Speaker was obviously alert to the possibility of filibustering. The usual private members' filibuster consists of long speeches by a few opponents of a bill. In this case however the filibuster was less obvious but more effective because it involved a large number of short speeches. In fact 24 MPs spoke against the bill on Report: the average length of the speeches was only 15 minutes. Some of these MPs relied fairly heavily on briefs prepared by Co-ord, but one of the strengths of the pro-abortion parliamentary lobby was that it could rely on so many MPs who were willing to attend and speak.

The other aspect of the pro-abortion parliamentary lobby which was important was its whipping system. Both sides had a very sophisticated and effective whipping system for a private members' issue. However the pro-abortion side was better organised and this fact stood it in particularly good stead on the fourth day of the Report stage. For various reasons it was not until very late that either side knew for certain that there would be a fourth day's debate. However the pro-abortion side had assumed there would be, and had sent out a whip urging its supporters to attend. In contrast the bill's supporters had assumed there would not be a fourth day, had not sent out a whip, and had told their supporters they were free to fulfil other engagements. When finally it became clear that there would be a debate the anti-abortion lobby was left to try to repair the damage. For this reason fewer of Corrie's supporters turned up on the final Friday and the Corrie side lost an important closure vote on the debate on the Silkin amendment. This partly reflected the poor attendance by Corrie supporters which in turn resulted from limitations in the organisation of its whipping.

One other aspect of the pro-abortion lobby's parliamentary whipping deserves particular mention. It whipped only Labour MPs, leaving the canvassing of Conservative MPs to one or two individual Conservative members, notably Bowen Wells, and to an extra-parliamentary group, Tories for Free Choice. In one way this was an important weakness in its parliamentary organisation as there was not a great deal of contact between the pro-abortion wings of the two main parties. However any deficiency in this sense was more than made up for by the fact that the Labour pro-abortion parliamentarians could use the PLP meetings as a major channel of communication with its Labour supporters. During the Committee stage the PLP meetings were used to tell pro-abortion supporters of the progress in the Committee, and at the Report stage PLP members were given an outline of the business and votes likely to occur on the following Friday. The anti-abortion MPs had no equivalent forum. The very fact that such announcements were made at PLP meetings reminded wavering Labour MPs that defence of the 1967 Act was party policy.

The general conclusion here must be that once the anti-abortion parliamentarians had decided not to withdraw sections of their bill before Report its fate lay to a large extent in the hands of the pro-abortion parliamentary lobby. If the lobby organised itself effectively it could defeat the bill given the time constraint. It was notably well organised and this was a major reason for the eventual defeat of the bill.

The issue after Corrie

There has been no *major* debate on the abortion issue since the Corrie bill. However the issue has not disappeared, and will not disappear, from the political agenda. Rather the battle continues on different terrain.

There have in fact been two abortion bills introduced since the Corrie bill fell. Amost before the dust had settled David Alton, the Liberal Roman Catholic MP for Liverpool, Edge Hill, brought forward a Ten-Minute-Rule bill to reduce the time limit for abortion to 24 weeks. As a Ten-Minute-Rule bill it had no hope of success but the pro-abortion lobby feared it might receive overwhelming support, which might encourage a future private members' bill. They need not have worried: Alton's bill was undermined by the anti-abortion lobby. Alton had, of course, consulted prominent anti-abortionists in Parliament and talked to SPUC. However his bill met with little enthusiasm from the politicians and none at all from SPUC, who had little interest in a bill dealing solely with the time limit, particularly if that bill only reduced the time limit to twenty-four weeks.

SPUC's view was that if a one-clause bill was to be introduced it should deal with the grounds for abortion or possibly with the question of conscientious objection to carrying out abortions. For this reason SPUC urged its supporters in Parliament to oppose the Alton bill. A number of MPs who support restrictions to the abortion law approached Alton in an effort to persuade him to withdraw his bill. Alton went ahead nevertheless and introduced his bill on 22 April 1980. His Ten-Minute speech was weak and was replied to by Alex Lyon of the pro-abortion lobby who, in contrast, gave a strong and impressive speech. However as no vocal support was given to the bill at the appropriate time there was no vote and the bill automatically fell.

The Alton bill was a non-event and something of a parliamentary debacle. Nevertheless it did reveal the new direction in which the anti-abortion lobby was moving. Given their experience on the Corrie bill they advocated the introduction of single-clause bills to change the 1967 Abortion Act, though they were not interested in a bill on the time limit alone.

The other bill was entirely different. Jo Richardson, who as we have seen is one of the most prominent supporters of the 1967 Act, introduced a Ten-Minute-Rule bill, the National Health Service Act, 1977 (Amendment) Bill, which would have liberalised that Act by requiring a more equitable provision of National Health Service facilities for abortion. This bill failed to gain a First Reading when 139 MPs supported it while 215 MPs opposed it.

We have already intimated that the tactics of the anti-abortion lobby changed after the defeat of the Corrie bill. In fact their attention switched from the pursuit of direct attempts to amend the 1967 Act. In part they were concerned to use the courts to attempt to establish a body of case law which would ensure that doctors were more circumspect and therefore less liberal in their interpretation of the Abortion Act. At the same time the lobby has pursued other, related, issues in the parliamentary arena. By far the most important example of this strategy involved Enoch Powell's Unborn Children (Protection) Bill in the 1984/5 Session.[17]

Powell introduced his bill in large part as a response to the Report of the Warnock Committee of Inquiry into Human Fertilisation and Embryology. A majority of the Warnock Committee recommended that research might be allowed on any embryo up to the fourteenth day. In contrast the Powell bill would have prevented a human embryo from being created, kept, or used for any purpose other than enabling a child to be born by a particular woman. Powell had not previously been actively involved in the anti-abortion lobby and introduced his bill largely out of his personal reaction to, and rejection of, the Warnock Committee report. However, his anti-pathy to Warnock was shared by both SPUC and LIFE who had campaigned strongly against the recommendations. At the same time both SPUC and LIFE clearly saw the issue as related to abortion. After all, if an embryo has 'rights' in its first 14 days then surely a foetus must have rights in its first 28 weeks. Certainly, if the Powell bill had been passed it would have severely weakened any moral arguments in defence of the 1967 Abortion Act. For this reason SPUC and LIFE organised rallies, petitions and write-in campaigns in support of the Powell bill.

The bill had a majority of 172 in a Second Reading vote on 15 February 1985. However it was strongly opposed. Sixty-five MPs voted against it and a large section of the medical profession[18] and the pro-abortion lobby campaigned strongly against the bill. Powell had only drawn fifth place in the ballot so that his bill would have been delayed in progressing into Standing Committee C. However at this time the Government was not using, and indeed had not used throughout that Session, Standing Committee D for its bills. Powell discussed this with the Government's business managers who did not object to the Committee being used for Powell's bill. Given that there were no Government objections, the Speaker allowed the bill to be referred to Standing Committee D. In Committee, Powell immediately introduced a sittings motion which required it to sit in both morning and afternoon sessions – and as we have already indicated, afternoon sessions have no time limit. This meant that the Committee stage of the bill was completed in two 'days', one afternoon session lasting all night while the other finished at 2 a.m.

Despite this when the bill cleared Committee all the 'remaining-stage' days already had at least one bill down for consideration at Report. For this reason the bill was the second for consideration on 3 May, which was the third 'remaining-stage' day. It was debated for one and a half hours, during which time only the first group of amendments was considered. The bill's opponents' first group of amendments was defeated by a vote of 157 to 82. However given the scope of the bill, the extent and organisation of the opposition and the number of amendments they had tabled, there was no chance of the bill being passed. At the same time no further time was available because other bills took precedence on later 'remaining-stage' days. So it seemed, as often before, that a bill with considerable parliamentary support had been scuppered because of the effective use of the private-members'-bill procedure by its opponents. However, Mr Powell pulled the proverbial rabbit from the hat.

As we saw earlier not all private members' time is allocated for the consideration of bills. Some is set aside for the consideration of motions introduced by MPs who are successful in a motions ballot. These motions are then debated. It was fortunate for Mr Powell that Andrew Bowden (Conservative MP for Brighton, Kempton), a strong supporter of the Powell bill, topped the appropriate ballot. Powell approached Bowden and persuaded him to introduce a motion which if passed would have required Parliament to sit over a weekend in order to complete the Report stage and Third Reading of the bill.

The Powell supporters' belief was that given the overwhelming vote for the bill at Second Reading such a move would succeed. Unfortunately for them they reckoned without the tactical sophistication of the opposition, the antipathy of many MPs to the use of such procedural devices, and the antagonism of the Government to such a move. The Government, which anyway was not happy with the bill, was particularly concerned about the likely future consequences for parliamentary procedure if the Bowden/Powell tactic succeeded. After all, in theory at least, it could have meant a major extension of private members' time and changed the balance between the executive and the legislature. In the end the Government turned a blind eye when Dennis Skinner (Labour MP for Bolsover), used another procedural device to restrict discussion and prevent a vote on the Bowden motion.

In the parliamentary timetable the moving of a writ for a by-election takes precedence on Friday over all other business. By convention the party which is defending the seat moves the writ but on this occasion Skinner ignored precedent and moved the writ for the Brecon and Radnorshire by-election in a Conservative seat. Together with other opponents of the Powell bill Mr Skinner then discussed the joys and problems of the constituency for such a time that Mr Bowden's motion when reached had insufficient time for a debate and vote. Of course, Skinner, a man of vast parliamentary experience, took great pleasure in unearthing a procedural device to beat a supposed master of parliamentary procedure, particularly as their political views are hardly adjacent.[19] At the same time although Skinner did not discuss the tactic with the Government there is a certain irony in a tacit agreement between an MP often referred to as 'the beast of Bolsover' and the Conservative front bench which surely represents one of the unholiest alliances in parliamentary history. Nevertheless, the key point here is that the whole affair indicates how difficult it is for private members to succeed even with procedural innovations given the present parliamentary procedure and the opposition of the executive to increased power for the legislature. What is more, it appears very likely that the Government will attempt to persuade Parliament to prevent this procedural manoeuvre being used in future.

Even here the story is not completed. In the 1985/6 Session, Hargreves, MP for Crewe, won ninth place in the ballot and introduced the Unborn Children (Protection) Bill. As the title suggests this bill was very similar to the Powell bill – in fact the draft bill merely reproduces the Powell bill as amended in Standing Committee. With ninth place Hargreves's bill was inevitably second on the order paper. In this case he chose second place on the second private members' day which meant that his bill was behind Winston Churchill's obscenity bill. As we shall see later, Churchill's bill itself was contentious and the pro-abortion lobby kept a watching brief on the Churchill debate ready to intervene if it was necessary to prolong debate. The Churchill bill took up all five hours available for debate and as such Hargreves was left to put his bill down for consideration on later days. However in each case the bill appeared at the bottom of the order paper and was not discussed.

7 Pornography as a private members' issue

As we have seen throughout this study there is little chance of any contentious issue being resolved through this procedure. However, there is an exception to this pattern. There have been a series of bills concerned with pornography, generally defined, which have succeeded, without opposition, despite the fact that at first, and even second, sight they appear contentious and to some extent ill thought-out.

In this chapter we shall consider this issue paying particular attention to four bills: the 1978 Child Protection Act; the 1981 Indecent Displays Act; the 1984 Video Recordings Act; and the Obscene Publications (Protection of Children, etc.) (Amendment) Bill introduced in the 1985–6 parliamentary Session.[1]

At the same time any consideration of the pornography issue throws some light upon the role of the 'moral majority' in British politics. Martin Durham rightly emphasises that the effect of this 'moral backlash' in Britain has been much less than in the United States. Nevertheless he does conclude by asserting that:

In Britain too, the continued debate over abortion ... and the evident concern over obscenity and censorship, all indicate that issues of family and morality will not go away from British politics either.[2]

We shall return to this broader question in the conclusion.

The 1978 Child Protection Act

As McCarthy and Moodie argue in their detailed analysis of the 1978 Child Protection Act:

Legislative action to tighten up the laws regulating the production and distribution of child pornography cannot be viewed as a uniquely British phenomenon. Indeed, the domestic campaign – Action to Ban Sexual Exploitation of Children (ABUSE) – clearly drew its impetus from initiatives taken in other European countries, in Australia and, in particular, from events in the USA.[3]

Indeed by mid-1977 the American campaign had been widely reported in the British newspapers, and this stirred the interest of Mary Whitehouse, a long-established campaigner in this broad field. In fact McCarthy and Moodie show that most of ABUSE's evidence was drawn from American rather than British studies. However by this time there was a distinct backlash in Britain against the so-called 'permissive society'. At the same time Jim Callaghan's Labour Government was in a difficult position, its Social Contract with the trade unions was becoming less popular and this compounded the usual tendency for support for the Government to fall mid-term. More significantly perhaps, after early 1976 the Government lost its overall majority and came to rely upon the Lib.–Lab. Pact. All this provided fertile ground for the ABUSE campaign.

ABUSE was established as a group to campaign specifically upon this issue. It was however closely integrated with, and sponsored by, Mrs Whitehouse's main political vehicle, the National Viewers and Listeners Association, an interest group which we will deal with at some length later in this chapter. In November 1977 Mrs Whitehouse wrote on the subject of pornography to 270 editors of provincial and religious newspapers. As McCarthy and Moodie emphasise:

[This] tactic is useful because provincial newspapers tend to be less liberal in their editorial line than the major dailies or London-based periodicals, so that the likelihood of a sympathetic response is greater. Secondly, provincial newspapers are more likely to print matter of this sort because it is sent by a controversial national figure and because it may have local implications. Thirdly, by writing to religious newspapers, Mrs Whitehouse was virtually ensuring that her 'moral crusade' would be announced from pulpits throughout the country within the week and that churchgoers, among the most vocally supportive of this issue, would quickly make their views known.[4]

The Labour Government's position at this time was clear. They opposed any legislative initiatives in the field until the Home Office Departmental Committee, established to re-examine the pornography law, and chaired by Professor Bernard Williams, reported. At the same time most of the evidence produced by ABUSE was based upon American experience and the police view throughout the period, and during the passage of the Child Protection Act continued to be, that no legislative change was required.

Despite all this the ABUSE campaign did help create an emotionally charged atmosphere which provided the background against which they searched for an MP with a high place in the ballot who was willing to introduce a private members' bill. The top placed Conservative in the 1977/8 Session ballot was Cyril Townsend, MP for Bexleyheath. ABUSE approached him, as did a large number of other groups. After considerable discussion Townsend decided to introduce a bill and ABUSE provided him with legal advise and a well-developed publicity machine. However, Townsend decided to remain financially independent from ABUSE and was fortunate when a sympathetic law firm agreed to draft the bill for the £200 provided from public funds to assist the first ten MPs in the ballot with the cost of drafting their bills.

There was one major disagreement between Townsend and Mrs Whitehouse. The latter, together with ABUSE, wanted the draft bill to deal with written as well as photographic material. Townsend resisted this because he felt this would make the bill larger, more complicated, and thus more vulnerable to defeat. Despite this, as McCarthy and Moodie show, the bill's sponsor acknowledged the importance of Mrs Whitehouse's role:

I was conscious that without massive public opinion on my side the Home Office would win the day . . . if there had not been massive public opinion and, in particular, some one and a half million signatures on a petition collected by the ABUSE campaign, I do not believe we would have the bill on the Statute Book.[5]

Mr Townsend had won fourth place in the ballot so his bill was debated first on 10 February 1978, the fourth private-members'-bill day. Over 400 MPs were present at the debate, which lasted 4 hours 8 minutes, another reflection of the interest in the issue generated by ABUSE and their write-in campaign to MPs. However, by far the most important feature of the debate was that despite the fact that the Government saw no need for the bill and indeed that the need for it was never clearly established, and despite it involving censorship and thus challenging key 'liberal' values, no MP spoke against the bill.

At the end of the debate there was no vote so the bill does conform to the general pattern we have identified. Here the question is: why did a bill which was non-technical and potentially contentious pass without opposition? The answer to this question is reflected in an interjection made in the Second Reading debate by Sir Andrew Bennett, Conservative MP for Torbay:

One Hon. Member commented that he was looking in the tea room for a hero who would oppose the bill, not because he wanted it opposed but so he could get it fairly on the record that he was voting against it.[6]

The atmosphere generated, which may best be described as a 'moral panic', meant that an MP would have needed to be a 'hero' to oppose the bill. Indeed in this case the 'moral panic' affected not only MPs but also the Government. Certainly the Government contained no heroes. Despite their belief that any legislative change should wait until after the publication of the Report of the Williams Committee and their view that the legislation was unnecessary and badly drafted, the Government did not oppose it. Indeed when Ian Mikardo objected to the bill's remaining stages being taken on the nod, merely by shouting 'object', because he felt the bill had been significantly amended in Committee and the House should have had a chance to consider those amendments, the Government stepped in and provided extra time for the consideration of the bill.[7] The bill passed its Report stage and Third Reading unopposed. It was amended in the Lords and those amendments were debated for 2 hours 6 minutes on the last 'remaining-stages' day.

Once again McCarthy and Moodie sum up the bill's passage well:

The Government was in an embattled minority position in the House of Commons, there was the prospect of an early election and the Conservatives had made a drive on the law and order issue. Added to this, the emotiveness of the issue conspired to give the opposition in Parliament and outside, a strong advantage. It is clear that, despite the Government's very real misgivings, a decision was taken in the Cabinet that it was not an issue on which to face the combined opposition of the Conservative Party, the House of Lords, the press, ABUSE and Mrs Whitehouse. Ministers found themselves in the untenable position of explaining the inadequacies of the Bill and then indicating that they would not be opposing it.[8]

The Indecent Displays (Control) Act 1980

The Indecent Displays Control Bill was in most ways the least interesting and certainly the least radical of the bills under consideration in this chapter. 'Indecent displays' was a continuing subject of Parliamentary debate throughout the 1970s. In the 1972/3 Session, Sir Gilbert Longden, Conservative MP for Hertfordshire (SW) won eighteenth place in the ballot and introduced the Public Indecency Bill. Despite its low position it was debated for over one and a half hours on the second 'remaining-stages' day that Session because the one bill which was ahead of it on the order paper only took up two hours of the time available. Nevertheless the sponsor withdrew the bill when the Government indicated it intended to legislate in the field. The Conservative Government did introduce a bill, the

Cinematograph and Indecent Displays Bill in the next Session. This bill, however, fell when the General Election was called in June 1974. Since then there have been five bills introduced which have in effect reproduced sections of Part II of the bill.[9] Peter Cormack, Conservative MP for Staffordshire South West, introduced a Ten-Minute-Rule bill in the truncated Session of 1974 and a Standing Order Number 39 bill in the next Session. Neither made any real progress,[10] nor did W. Rees-Davies's Ten-Minute-Rule bill or Rory Bradford's Indecent Displays (Northern Ireland) Bill in the 1975/6 Session.

The next two bills dealing with this subject fared rather better. In the 1978/9 Session, Hugh Rossi, Conservative MP for Hornsey, obtained second place in the ballot and introduced his Indecent Displays (Control) Bill. This was debated for over four hours on the Second Reading but fell in Committee when the 1979 general election was called. Nevertheless, despite the fact that a number of MPs believed that any bill should be delayed until the Williams Committee reported, and despite some debate over the problems of defining indecent, there was clearly support for a bill on the issue in the House. It was not surprising therefore when Brian MaWhinney, Conservative MP for Peterborough, who drew seventh place in the next year's ballot, introduced a similar bill. As 1979–80 was an extended session there were seven days available for Second Reading debates. The MaWhinney bill was debated for 3 hours and 53 minutes on the seventh day and given a Second Reading. This meant of course that the bill would have been late going into Standing Committee. However a week before the Second Reading debate the Government published the Williams Committee's report. As a result the bill's sponsor was under considerable pressure from some MPs, and particularly from the Government, to withdraw his bill so that the matter could be fully considered in the light of that report. MaWhinney, after some deliberation, withdrew the bill before it went into Committee.

It was against this background that Tim Sainsbury won first place in the ballot for the 1980/1 Session. Sainsbury gave some consideration to sponsoring an abortion bill but finally settled for a bill to control indecent displays, partly as a result of a prior interest in the issue.[11]

The bill he introduced was less broad than most of the others previously introduced. Sainsbury discussed his bill with a number of interested MPs, the Festival of Light, the National Federation of

Newsagents and representatives of the publishers of 'girly' magazines and sex-shop operators. In addition he had extensive talks with the Home Office about the subject. Nevertheless the bill followed very much the pattern laid down by previous bills and approved by Parliament. It was debated for 3 hours 27 minutes and given an unopposed Second Reading. The bill subsequently progressed through the legislative machine with few problems and with the fairly active support of the Government. Once the bill achieved a Second Reading, Sainsbury had discussions with Home Office civil servants about how to improve its drafting. In addition these civil servants gave him access to departmental briefings on the bill and provided him with information throughout the Committee stage. Indeed while this bill did not originate in the Home Office, and so was not a 'Government' private members' bill, it was strongly supported by the Government. In fact Sainsbury suggested that he had been promised that if there was a closure vote at Report stage the Government might informally deliver the pay-roll vote – that is strongly encourage Ministers and Parliamentary Private Secretaries to support the bill. Once again the key feature of the debates on this bill was that there was no opposition on the grounds that the bill involved censorship. It is true that the bill was less contentious than the others we discuss in that chapter and that the groundwork for it had been laid down in previous bills and debates. Nevertheless it did involve some infringement, however justified, of individual liberties. Certainly it is difficult to imagine such a bill succeeding with no opposition in the 1960s when a much more liberal atmosphere prevailed both inside and outside Parliament.

The Video Recordings Act 1984

The first thing to emphasise about the Video Recordings Act is that it easily passed. There was no vote on the bill at Second or Third Reading – so no one appeared to oppose the principle of the bill. In this way it appears to confirm the general pattern discussed throughout this book. Yet it was not a narrow uncontroversial bill and the real question to pose once again is: why was there so little opposition?

Graham Bright won first place in the ballot in the 1983/4 Session and decided to introduce a bill on the subject of 'video nasties'. The aim of his bill was to prevent and restrict the sale and rent of 'video

nasties'. As such it involved, like the other bills we have considered, a restriction – many, of course, would say a quite justifiable
restriction – on individual freedom, involving the censorship by the
State of what people could view in their own home. There is no
doubt that the restriction of individual freedom by the State has
often inspired considerable opposition among libertarian MPs.
Certainly the majority of back-bench opposition to legislation
enforcing the compulsory wearing of seat belts was based upon
such an argument. In addition Parliament has usually contained a
number of MPs willing to oppose censorship in most, if not any,
forms. Indeed such an argument was reflected, if palely reflected,
in the Second Reading debate by Reg Freeson, Labour MP for Brent
East, who argued:

Some honourable Members accept completely and enthusiastically the
general objectives of the Bill but are worried about state intervention and censorship and control. We wish to see the objectives pursued
in legislation, but with the good British approach which supports
self-regulation and does not involve the state unnecessarily in censorship.[12]

In fact it is worthy of note that it has been argued that this was the
first pro-censorship bill to be even *considered* by Parliament in
peacetime since the 1843 Theatre Act.

The bill then was potentially contentious but the five-hour
Second Reading debate was bland, the bill was given a Second
Reading unopposed and there was absolutely no concerted opposition to its principles through its later stages. There were two
strongly contested votes at Report stage, which suggests that some
MPs were far from happy at least with details of the bill, but the
Third Reading was again unopposed. The fact that it had been
given a relatively smooth passage might indicate prolonged and
detailed consideration of the matter establishing a clear need for the
bill. In fact, however, the issue had been scarcely considered and
one could question its necessity. Certainly any comparison
between the evolution of the Video Recordings Act and that of the
major liberal reforms achieved by private members' bills in the
1960s indicates clear differences. As Richards says after reviewing
the passage of that legislation:

As it is, the law is slow to change. Basic legal principles are decided by
Parliament. For various reasons, some political, some procedural, law
reform is not easily achieved on controversial aspects of human behaviour.
There is heavy in-built bias in favour of the status quo.[13]

In addition Richards stresses that the interest groups involved with the issues needed independent inquiries to lend credibility to their particular cause:

But the plain fact is that Parliament does not rush ahead on conscience issues. All the measures discussed in this book were preceded by a report of some kind. Capital punishment had a Royal Commission. Departmental Committees had considered homosexuality and Sunday Observance. A joint Select Committee had reviewed theatre censorship. The Law Commission had reported on the divorce laws. Documents had been issued by the established church on homosexuality, abortion and divorce. It seems probable that no (controversial moral) private members' bill could succeed without some preliminary inquiry of some kind.[14]

There are then quite considerable differences between the Video Recordings Act and the social and moral legislation passed during the 1964–70 period. For example, the campaign for homosexual law reform spanned a ten-year period. The need for reform was established by a Government inquiry, yet the Sexual Offences Bill only passed in 1967 because of extensive Government help and against the background of continuing determined opposition. In contrast the Video Recordings Act, while it received tacit Government support, had no backing from any official inquiry, required no Government time and succeeded with no opposition.

Of course the Video Recordings Act was not as far-reaching a piece of legislation as the liberal reforms of the 1960s. However as we have seen it did involve controversial 'values'. What is more the need for the legislation was hardly clearly demonstrated. Indeed the only 'evidence' to show the widespread harm caused by such videos was exaggerated and histrionic press reports, individual cases quoted by doctors and child psychiatrists and, later, the much-criticised Parliamentary Group Video Inquiry Report, *Video Violence and Children*.[15] What is more, given the popularity of videos one might have expected that any bill imposing restrictions on the sale of video tapes would meet with considerable resistance. None of this is meant to suggest that the Video Recordings Act was an unnecessary restraint on individual liberty. Rather it is important to establish the way in which the bill was passed. It was quickly conceived and rushed through Parliament. In Parliament, as we shall see later, highly emotive speeches created an atmosphere in which anyone who opposed the bill on libertarian grounds was likely to be strongly attacked.

Here we have the outline of what we view as the main reason for the bill's facile success, and it returns us to a theme which we discussed in examining the Child Protection Act. Both bills succeeded in an atmosphere of 'moral panic'. However, in order to look in more detail at this process we need to establish the role of three groups of actors: the Government, the interest groups, and the media.

(a) The role of the Government

As we saw in Chapter 3 the Government play a variety of roles in relation to private members' bills. The Video Recording Bill was not a 'Government' bill, but the Government did play a key role. They gave Bright assistance in drafting the bill and played an active role in its Committee stage. In an interview Bright, while naturally emphasising his own role, paid tribute to the Government and acknowledged the help of the Home Office in drafting the bill.[16] This access to the Home Office parliamentary draftsmen was crucial, particularly given the fact that the bill was large by private members' standards containing twenty-one clauses. Indeed, Bright estimated that to have the bill drafted by a private parliamentary draftsman would have cost him between £9,000 and £10,000 – this seems to us a considerable over-estimate – while Bright was only entitled to £200 from public funds towards the costs.

The Government's support for the bill was clear in the Second Reading debate. The attendance was unusually good and indeed the Prime Minister was present for Mr Bright's speech while the Home Secretary stayed for the entire debate. The Government spokesman, David Mellor, the Under-Secretary of State for the Home Office, fully endorsed the bill. However when the bill reached Committee the Government began to play a more active role as Martin Barker has shown.[17] Indeed at Committee the Government's representative, Mr Mellor, spoke for considerably longer than Mr Bright (see Table 7.1).

In fact in Committee the Government pushed Bright to make his bill more radical – a move which he successfully resisted. Why did the Government give such strong support? The first obvious answer is that the Government supported the values which underpinned the legislation. Indeed their Campaign Guide issued before the 1983 General Election asserted: 'The Conservative Government has been active in its efforts to see that pornography and indecent displays are properly controlled.'[18] In fact later in the same docu-

Table 7.1 *Length of speeches of major committee members on Bright bill (1984)*

(Hansard column inches)

Before Christmas			After Christmas		
Date	Bright	Mellor	Date	Bright	Mellor
23 Nov.	54	57	18 Jan.	5	114
30 Nov.	34	64	25 Jan.	21	84
7 Dec.	54	46	1 Feb.	39	39
14 Dec.	17	52	8 Feb.	11	90

ment they even claimed some credit for two private members' bills in the same broad area: 'Two Conservative private members' bills received strong support from the Government. Mr Timothy Sainsbury's bill, now the Indecent Display Act 1981, controls public displays and Mr Peter Lloyd's Cinematograph (Amendment) Act 1982 closes a legal loophole by extending licensing to commercial cinema clubs.'[19] There was no mention in this campaign document published in April 1983 of a 'video nasties' bill. This is significant. It is clear that this 'problem' only became an 'issue' after a press campaign and intensive lobbying in the early months of 1983. The Government's response to this new 'issue' was reflected in the 1983 Conservative manifesto:

We will also respond to the increasing public concern over obscenity and offences against public decency, which often have links with serious crime. We propose to introduce legislation to deal with the most serious of these problems, such as the dangerous spread of violent and obscene video cassettes.[20]

Martin Barker argues that the Government's response to this issue is best understood as an attempt to re-establish its tarnished image as the party of law and order. Barker suggests that, in the aftermath of the Brixton and Toxteth riots in 1981, the Government was keen to show that it could prevent crime. The issue of 'video nasties' represented a perfect opportunity for the Government to improve its image without increased expenditure. This argument is certainly worth considering but we do not find it totally convincing, partly because this is not the only example of this process at work. In contrast we shall argue that a key pressure group, the National Viewers and Listeners Association (NVALA), and the media played the key role in focusing attention on to the problem and magnifying it out of proportion to its actual scale. They created a 'moral panic' which swept along with it a Government which was anyway susceptible to the values on which it was based and swept away almost all opposition inside and outside Parliament.

(b) The interest groups

The Video Recordings Act generated intense activity among interest groups. In fact, Graham Bright claimed that he received over twenty thousand letters and attended three hundred meetings. Here we shall concentrate upon three groups: NVALA, the National Society for the Prevention of Cruelty to Children (NSPCC), and the National Campaign for the Reform of the Obscene Publications Act (NCROPA).

The National Viewers and Listeners Association was set up in 1965, by Norah and Basil Buckland and Mary and Ernest Whitehouse, the original aim being to launch a 'Clean-up Television' campaign. The 'video nasties' campaign was a logical extension of this, although since its inception NVALA has broadened its interests to include other forms of entertainment.

Certainly NVALA has had an effect on the field of public entertainment but it would be wrong to deduce from this that the organisation has nationwide support from all the cultural and ethnic groups within society. Indeed Geoffrey Alderman in a review of British interest groups claims:

Although a highly articulate group, it cannot claim to be representative of the community. Research suggests that its support is mainly middle-class, female and elderly, that it is over-represented by those in rural areas, the clergy, the older-established professions, small businessmen, traders and shopkeepers.[21]

Despite this the impact NVALA had on the fate of Bright's bill should not be underestimated. Their influence was largely due to the effectiveness of their campaign. They were aware of the 'problem' of 'video nasties' from the outset, and the campaign began in earnest in the run-up to the General Election of 1983. During this period, Mary Whitehouse visited some sixty key marginal constituencies, speaking with all of the candidates running for election, and trying to convince them of the necessity of introducing private members' legislation dealing with the subject. Significantly, the slogan NVALA campaigned under was: 'Children at risk, vote for the candidate who will fight for decency.' Fortunately for NVALA, one of the candidates Mrs Whitehouse met was the MP for Luton South, Graham Bright.

Rather ironically NVALA also made effective use of the video recorder. They produced a video which used clips from certain 'video nasties'. This was shown twice daily at the Conservative Party Conference in 1983. The same video was later shown in the House of Commons prior to the Second Reading debate (by the Metropolitan Police) in the House of Lords and even in the European Parliament at Strasbourg. During the campaign, *The Listener*, NVALA's newsletter, urged its members to write to their MPs and Euro MPs, stressing the need for their support for the bill.

Overall NVALA fought a highly successful campaign, due to a highly effective lobbying of MPs by a vociferous leader, who is herself something of a media superstar. This status helped to gain wide coverage in the media, who were all too willing to latch on to a 'moral panic' of this nature. The effectiveness of NVALA's campaign was reflected in the Second Reading debate in the House of Commons. Of the 26 members who spoke during the debate, six made explicit references to the showing of the 'nasties' video and David Mellor called its preparation and showing a 'masterstroke'. Perhaps more importantly 16 of the speakers made references to the 'threat to the nation's children' theme which was the focus of the NVALA's campaign.

The role of the NSPCC was important because its involvement lent an air of respectability to the campaign to ban 'video nasties'. Certainly the statements issued by the NSPCC tended to be less panic-stricken and doom-laden in tone, and they were also less histrionic in their attacks on the defenders of 'video nasties' than the NVALA. The NSPCC's influence, then, stemmed from its status. In contrast the NVALA's influence owed most to its organisation, its effective parliamentary lobbying and its use of the media. The atmosphere of the Second Reading debate, its tenuous and mistaken assumptions and highly emotive language, certainly owed more to the campaign style of the NVALA and the media rather than to the more measured style of the NSPCC. Phrases such as 'corruptors of youth' and 'purveyors of filth' and words such as 'degrading', 'disembowelling', and 'gratuitous violence' crop up time and time again. The net effect was to narrow down the argument so that anyone opposing the bill risked being associated with the 'purveyors of filth' and the 'corruptors of youth'.

NCROPA were the only interest group to mount any opposition to the bill. Indeed, Graham Bright went so far as to say that they were the only interest group totally to oppose the bill, and that they were 'living in a world of their own'. NCROPA was set up by David Webb in 1976, with the aim of achieving: 'the complete repeal of the Obscene Publications Acts, as well as considerable amending legislation to a number of other relevant Acts'.[22]

Not surprisingly perhaps given the prevailing atmosphere NCROPA had no influence at all. Most MPs were content to label this interest group as misguided, although some saw it as potentially evil. In this vein Mr Geoffrey Finsberg, who was the most vocal critic of NCROPA, claimed during the Second Reading:

I shall read one or two extracts from one of the most monstrous letters that I have ever received in thirteen years' membership of the House. The letter was sent to me by a body called NCROPA.[23]

He continued his attack on the organisation during the Committee stage where he called it a 'weird' organisation and said:

The basis of that organization is clear. I doubt whether any normal people would wish to give credence to any comments from NCROPA on the Video Recordings Bill here.[24]

The opposition to the bill was thus very weak. Apart from NCROPA what other opposition there was came mainly from what might loosely be termed 'intellectuals and academics'. Indeed this may be reflected in the strong anti-intellectual stance taken by supporters of the bill throughout its parliamentary passage. The best example of this trend came from Jerry Hayes, who, speaking in the Second Reading, saw 'the enemies of the bill' as, 'middle-class people who sit on bean-bags wearing Gucci accessories in their Hampstead flats'.[25]

This view was echoed by Donald Anderson at the Committee stage in the Commons:

If I had to choose between the views of the ivory-towered Oxbridge philosopher and those of police officers in the field, magistrates and those who dealt daily with the effects of the torrent of filth that daily poured across our country, I know whose judgement I should respect.[26]

This highly emotive, anti-intellectual, anti-academic argument is important, for this, combined with the 'moral panic' generated in the media and the emphasis upon the 'threat to the nation's children', closed the circle. It became almost impossible to oppose the bill, and those who did so were strongly attacked. As *The Guardian* rightly put it: 'anyone getting in the way too quickly risks being lumped together with the child-molestors and sadists'.[27]

(c) The media and the Parliamentary Group Video Inquiry

Even a brief examination of the popular newspapers in the early part of 1983 quickly establishes the role they played in creating an atmosphere which we have called a 'moral panic'. Cohen in an interesting discussion of such mass manipulation argues:

The media have long operated as agents of moral indignation in their own right: even if they are not self-consciously engaged in crusading or muck-raking, their very reporting of certain 'facts' can be sufficient to generate concern, anxiety, indignation or panic. When such feelings coincide with a perception that particular values need to be protected, the preconditions for new rule creation or social problem definition are present.[28]

That is what happened in this case. The media highlighted some 'facts' many, if not most, of them supplied by the NVALA, and some later taken from the Parliamentary Group Video Inquiry Report. Such a picture fitted well with the Government's commitment to law and order and the 'preservation of family values'. It struck a chord with the electorate and as such became a minor, yet important, election issue.

The press campaign on the 'video nasties' issue began in 1982, reaching a peak at around the time of the General Election in June 1983. The *Daily Mail* took an especially strong stand but most other papers expressed similar attitudes, if in a less vehement manner. The stories used the type of phrases we have already come across in the Parliamentary debates. Purveyors of filth were undermining family life as we know it. Perhaps the main theme dealt with in the stories emphasised that the continual exposure of adults to such videos, and any exposure of children, led the viewer to wish to try to emulate what he had seen. This was another important component of the Second Reading debate in Parliament. Indeed, David Mellor, the Government spokesman, argued:

A society that regards sadistic degradation on film as entertainment cannot complain if reality comes to mirror those shocking scenes. If it is pleasurable to watch a video of somebody being slowly hacked to pieces or even eaten, there must always be the fear that some might be tempted to do it for real.[29]

This was merely a sophisticated rendering of an argument consistently reproduced in more lurid language in the popular press. It was unsupported by any respectable quantitative evidence. In contrast only *The Guardian* and *The Financial Times* among the newspapers had the temerity to express reservations about the bill.

A second wave of popular-press hysteria followed the publication of the Parliamentary Group Video Inquiry Report, *Video Violence and Children*. The report was not the work of an official Parliamentary Committee, rather it came from what might loosely be called a coalition of 'moral entrepreneurs'. The only academic initially involved in the study was Brian Brown, head of the Television Research Unit of Oxford Polytechnic, where the research was carried out. He, however, resigned before the report was completed because of the way the research was manipulated. In fact Brown claimed after the bill was passed:

the PR campaign, the distortion of truth, the manipulation of the public mood – for whatever reason it was done – certainly worked. A major piece of legislation has been discussed amidst an atmosphere of moral panic.[30]

Graham Bright disassociates himself completely from this report and indeed argues that it may have damaged his case because it was so extreme. Certainly it can have had no effect on the views of MPs at Second Reading. However, we would argue that while the report may have had some direct influence in the later stages of the bill's progress its major significance was that it provided more ammunition which the interest groups and media could use to feed a 'moral panic' which already existed.

In fact the conclusion McCarthy and Moodie drew from their case study of the Child Protection Act could just as easily be applied to the Video Recordings Act. In the following lengthy quote only the title of the bill need be replaced.

All the other issues, such as abortion law reform, homosexual law reform ... found their way into investigative committees; countless parliamentary questions, the lobbying of MPs, media campaigns and all other conventional tactics open to pressure groups. In no case was a bill bulldozed through Parliament in the sort of atmosphere in which the Child Protection Bill was. In nearly all of these cases there were strong, active, and identifiable counter-interests involved. That, in itself, ensured that meaningful debate would take place in the media and Parliament. It also ensured that the onus was placed quite firmly on reformers to present unassailable facts.

This was demonstrably not the case with the Child Protection Bill. Fact was largely eschewed in favour of emotive supposition, the actual was ignored in favour of the potential and the remotely possible was selectively interpreted as imminently probable.[31]

The Obscene Publications (Protection of Children, etc.) (Amendment) Bill 1985/6

We have seen to date that two private members' bills in particular which we might have expected to be opposed were passed with no opposition largely due to the generation and influence of 'moral panic'. In contrast, Winston Churchill's bill introduced in the 1985/6 Session reflects the limits of the constraint imposed by such 'moral panic'. Churchill won second place in the ballot and introduced a bill which sought to amend the 1959 Obscene Publications Act in a fairly significant way. So this bill was considerably more radical than any of the others we have considered. The bill would have tightened up the law on the sale of 'obscene' publications to people under 18. At the same time, however, in its original form approved at Second Reading, the bill aimed to remove the immunities given to radio and television in the 1959 Act. More specifically it stipulated that any article or broadcast would be illegal, being deemed obscene, if it was available to children under 18 and depicted visually, in an actual or simulated form: 'acts of masturbation, sodomy, oral/genital connection, lewd exhibition of genital organs, or excretory functions, cannibalism, bestiality, mutilation or vicious cruelty towards persons or animals'.

There is little doubt then that this bill was radical. However, as Churchill indicated in introducing his bill, he saw it as a further step along the road taken by those three bills already discussed. At the same time Mary Whitehouse and the NVALA were again involved in proselytising about the bill and provided Churchill with information and advice throughout.[32] Nevertheless because the bill was more radical it provoked much more opposition. This opposition was reflected in the very different atmosphere which prevailed in the Second Reading debate on the Churchill bill compared to that when the other bills were discussed. Churchill immediately acknowledged he would face opposition and made reference to the power of the media and the position of various pimps and pornographers, stating: 'I am taking on not one but two enormously powerful vested interests'. Such an approach may have been a tactical mistake, however Churchill's words immediately point to a key difference between his and the previous bills. The interests of the 'pimps and pornographers' had been affected by the previous legislation but while they may have considerable economic resources they have little, if any, political influence. In the less liberal 1980s no MP is willing to stand up and defend the interests of pornographers and as we saw, none did when the three previous bills were considered. However, the artistic and media interests are a very different matter. Many of the groups who, as we shall see later, opposed the Churchill bill, had excellent contacts with Government and the Establishment. As such MPs felt much less reluctant to come out and be counted on this issue as they could argue, many would say quite legitimately, that they were defending artistic freedom not licence.

In the debate most of the bill's supporters pointed to a perceived growth in the presentation of sex and violence upon television. Many reported that they had large post-bags in support of the bill, a campaign which of course was in large part orchestrated by the NVALA. The main thrust of the bill's advocates is well summarised in a quote from Mr Churchill:

There is a mounting body of evidence to suggest that the growing tide of violence and obscenity to which society is being subjected is, to a significant although unquantifiable degree, responsible for many of the cases of violence and sexual assault regularly perpetrated into the constituencies of every MP.[33]

Once again, as was the case with earlier bills, most of the 'evidence' cited in support of this argument was partial, anecdotal, or American.

The bill's opponents argued that the bill was unnecessary either because the link between television and violence was unproven or because existing legislation required the broadcasting authorities to deal with the matter. In addition a number of MPs emphasised the difficulties which would be involved in administering the legislation. Indeed much of the opposition was directed against the list of proscribed acts and the consequences this would have for artistic freedom.

However, the major difference between the Second Reading debate on the Churchill bill and those on the other bills was that it ended in a vote. The bill was given a Second Reading by 161 votes to 31, a majority of 130. If the bill had subsequently passed it would have been the first private members' bill which had been voted upon at Second Reading to do so, without the Government providing time, since 1959. At the same time while there was significant opposition in Parliament there was also substantial, growing and organised opposition outside. Given all our previous evidence, the bill was doomed, and so it proved.

Because the bill directly impinged upon questions of artistic freedom and the activities of broadcasters, it was met with consistent and integrated opposition from the theatrical, film, and television professions. As Michael Winner, spokesman for the Directors' Guild of Great Britain, and a strong opponent of the bill, so colourfully put it:

What is it [that joins] together such unlikely aliens as the Guild of Newspaper Editors, the British Academy of Film and Television Arts, the Association of Cinematography and Television Technicians, the Arts Council, the Directors' Guild and every other guild, institution and union connected with the arts? What is it that has the choreographer, Sir Kenneth MacMillan, joining in protest with representatives of the Tate Gallery, the National and Royal Shakespeare Theatres and the Royal Opera House?[34]

The answer of course was the Churchill bill, and even if we allow something for Mr Winner's rhetoric, it was clear that this bill, unlike the others we have discussed, provoked strong criticism from the outset.

This opposition to the bill reached its height during the Committee stage. It was perhaps best reflected in the annual conference of the British Academy of Film and Television Arts (BAFTA) in February. BAFTA had established a subcommittee to consider the bill and Michael Grade, Controller of BBC 1, and chairman of the subcommittee, attacked the bill for being ill-considered and rushed through without sufficient consultation or public debate. He was followed by 'the great and the good' in the industry who without exception spoke against the bill. The tone was perhaps best summed up by the naturalist David Attenborough who said of Mr Churchill's list of proscribed actions: 'The praying mantis does at least three of these simultaneously'.

Of course, the fact that there was élite opposition to the bill was not sufficient by itself to prevent its passage. It was also crucial that, clearly at least in part because they were affected, the media's attitude to the Churchill bill was very different to its view of the other bills. The popular press, which had been so virulent in support of the Video Recordings Act, was much more circumspect about the Churchill bill. Perhaps more significantly, at least as far as MPs were concerned, the bill was strongly opposed by the 'quality press'. *The Guardian* and *The Times* both carried editorials which condemned the bill as an unnecessary, and 'bad', bill. In addition the élite opposition probably also had some effect on the Government's attitude to the bill. David Mellor, the Home Office Minister responsible for the bill, had given it a guarded welcome at Second Reading, and indeed Margaret Thatcher herself voted for the bill to progress. However, even at this stage Mellor cast doubt on the need for the provisions on broadcasting and the Government remained non-benevolently neutral throughout.

As a result of this pressure, particularly from the artistic community, Churchill amended his bill substantially in Committee. Standing Committee C met four times to consider the bill and sat for a total of 9 hours 32 minutes. Those who voted for the bill at Second Reading outnumbered its opponents by 12 to 1 which ensured that the bill would pass through the Committee unamended by its critics. However, the bill was changed in substantial ways by its sponsor. When the bill came out of Committee it was well over twice as long as the bill approved at Second Reading. This was mainly because Churchill introduced an amendment to clause 1 of 53 lines and seven sub-sections. This amendment dealt with technical matters and was suggested to Churchill by the Government which was concerned that the drafting of his legislation was consistent with the provisions of the 1984 Cable and Broadcasting Act. This is worth noting for it is fairly typical of Government's involvement with private members' bills. Departments keep a close watching brief on any bill which affects them and often play a key role in redrafting the bill before, in, and after, Committee. They are particularly concerned to ensure the compatibility between bills.

Despite this the major change introduced by Churchill involved Clause 2 of his bill. On 21 February, before the second meeting of the Committee, he tabled an amendment which deleted the existing Clause 2 and replaced it with a new one. The aim of this amendment was to abandon the list of proscribed acts in favour of a wholly new clause which required that in obscenity cases the courts should 'have regard in particular to the probability of it being viewed or heard by children or young persons under 18 years'. When faced with this amendment Ian Mikardo (Labour, Bow and Poplar) was vociferous in his objection:

the amendments before us today [would] wipe out the key clause of the Bill. The one thing that makes a difference between what the Bill proposes and what has been previous practice [i.e. the list] would be wiped out by the amendments. The clause around which three quarters of the debate on Second Reading revolved will disappear, and we will have an entirely new clause. It will certainly be a very different bill.[35]

In a similar vein *The Guardian* argued:

At a stroke this amendment changes the whole approach of the bill from concentration on particular acts which are deemed to be obscene to a new definition of obscenity itself.[36]

The bill was thus changed in Committee but it remained a large and radical bill. Churchill had clearly changed the bill, after discussions with the NVALA, which he acknowledged in his speech, as a result of criticisms from the artistic establishment. However, the changes did little to satisfy opposition. They were too little and too late.

The bill came back to the floor of the House for its Report stage on 25 April. It took up all the time available for debate that day but had no hope of success. The Speaker arranged the amendments into four groupings and by the end of the debate only one group had been debated and voted upon. Perhaps the major surprise was that on two occasions the bill's supporters failed to succeed with closure motions. The first closure motion was moved by Churchill after two hours' debate and while it was supported by 76 votes to 18 it failed to receive the 100 votes necessary under Standing Orders. This meant that debate continued on the first group of amendments which would have amended the bill so that it did not affect the responsibilities of the Governors of the BBC, or the duties of the members of the IBA, under the Broadcasting Act 1981. This amendment was defeated after three hours' debate by 76 votes to 23, a majority of 53. After this vote Mr Churchill offered to accept all the other amendments on the order paper so that the bill could progress. However, the bill's opponents, not surprisingly, declined this offer and the debate continued on the second group of amendments. As time ran out a second closure motion was called but lost when only supported by 79 MPs (with 11 against).

This bill then failed to progress when it was talked out. It failed partly because it was more radical than its predecessors. It failed mainly because it was opposed both inside and outside Parliament. It represents an interesting case because it illustrates the limits of 'moral panic'. The NVALA campaigned just as strongly on this bill as on others. The write-in campaign they organised was as effective as previously with most MPs reporting a large number of letters supporting the bill. Mrs Whitehouse was as active as a media performer and letter writer as she had been previously. However, the manipulation of 'moral panic' requires a 'captive' proselytising media which fans, feeds and sometimes generates it. On this occasion the media's role was much more circumspect with the popular newspapers ambivalent and the quality press strongly opposed. Nevertheless the key point is that such legislation can only be successful using the private-members'-bill procedure if it is unopposed. The previous bills we have examined, while they may have restricted individual freedom, mainly affected the organised interests of pornographers. This bill hit at the artistic establishment, a lobby which is well organised with privileged access to Parliament and Government. MPs felt few qualms about attracting censorship in this case.

8 The seat-belts issue

The seat-belts issue is one which is significantly different from the others we have discussed. The issue has not been dealt with solely through the private-members'-bill procedure. Rather the Government has been directly involved, so that the first five bills introduced on the subject were Government bills and the compulsory wearing of seat belts was finally approved by Parliament as a clause in a Government bill. However at the same time, as we shall see, the matter was the subject for a private members' bill, the Carmichael bill introduced in the 1979/80 Session, which played a major role in the campaign in favour of compulsion.

Attempts by Governments to legislate in this field proved notably unsuccessful. In 1961 the Government introduced legislation to require cars built after 1 April 1965 to be fitted with seat belts.[1] However despite this legislation and periodic advertising campaigns, the usage rate never topped 40 per cent, and for this reason pressure built up to make the wearing of seat belts compulsory. Of course transport has never been a priority political issue in the House of Commons. There were five Government bills which attempted to introduce compulsion in the period between 1973 and 1979. However each attempt petered out in failure, failure which, given the dominance of the executive over the legislature in British politics, itself indicates the ambivalence with which successive Governments viewed the issue. Two of the bills were introduced in the Lords and three in the Commons. Four of the bills came to the Commons late in the Session which reflects their low priority, all votes on the issue were free votes, and the Government never used a guillotine motion to restrict debate. So despite the fact that these were Government bills they were talked out, or voted out, in much the same way as are private members' bills.

The Lords regard it as something of a tradition that they initiate 'legislation on the vital subject of road traffic'.[2] It came as no surprise, therefore, that the first proposal for compulsion should begin life in the Lords. It was an unsuccessful debut. The proposal did not appear in the original Road Traffic (1973) bill although Lord Montague did indicate his intention of introducing the measure at Committee stage.[3] Apparently to the Government the proposal was an afterthought rather than a policy priority. It was in all respects a half-hearted attempt. The main discussion in the Lords centred around other clauses in the bill but at Committee stage those opposing compulsion aired arguments which reappeared throughout subsequent debates: compulsion involved a restraint on individual liberty, and there would be problems of implementation and enforcement. Indeed the seat-belt clause was not introduced in Committee.[4] Despite this when the clause was discussed at Report stage 14 peers spoke in support and five against and the clause was approved with Government support without a division. At Second Reading in the House of Commons the clause was only discussed for 27 minutes and the bill was given an unopposed Second Reading. However, the bill fell when a General Election was called.

The next four attempts at compulsion were even more inglorious. In the next Session the Road Traffic (1974) Bill was introduced by the Government into the Lords with a clause requiring the compulsory wearing of seat belts. The Second Reading debate only contained a brief mention of the clause and it was subsequently approved in a Committee of the Whole House by 66 to 55.[5] However it was negatived by 79 votes to 72 at Report stage[6] and the bill thus went to the Commons without the seat-belts clause. When the bill came to the House of Commons it was initially considered by a Second Reading Committee.[7] Here Fred Mulley, Minister of Transport, gave ample evidence of the Government's ambivalence and indecision when he argued:

(In normal circumstances) I would wish to ask the House to reinsert that clause, but I think we must be realistic, and in the short time now available to us . . . and having regard to the fact that the Committee stage of the Bill is due to be taken on a Friday, it would be absolutely wrong to ask the House of Commons to come to a view about seat belts on a Friday when we all know that it is the only day that any of us have to make engagements in our constituencies and, therefore, all Hon. Members who might wish to take part in such a debate could not be expected to be present. I think, too, that the public generally would take a very poor view of an important matter of this sort being determined at the end of a parliamentary session with probably less than a full attendance of Hon. Members.

In order to facilitate the passage of the measure, therefore; I do not propose to put down an amendment on seat belts on this occasion, although I must say that I found it extremely odd that another place, having inserted the clause in the previous Bill, on this occasion, after it had accepted their view and put it in my Bill, took it out. But this is something that we have to live with, and I think that the House generally would wish that that matter should perhaps be dealt with separately in the next parliamentary session. That certainly will be my intention if I have any influence in these matters.[8]

As we have said the quotation amply illustrates the Government's attitude towards compulsion. The Minister was willing to sacrifice the seat-belts clause partly to ensure the passage of the rest of the bill. He claimed that time was limited but if the Government had chosen it could have introduced the bill into the Commons much earlier. It did not, which itself reflects the low priority afforded to transport bills. Such bills often originate in the House of Lords and more importantly they frequently arrive in the Commons late in the Session and thus threatened by lack of time. The quotation also makes it clear that Fridays, the day on which private members' bills are considered, are regarded as days on which important issues are best not dealt with owing to the low level of attendance. The Committee accepted the Minister's advice and the bill was given a Second Reading before proceeding to a CWH. In the CWH Jerry Wiggin (Conservative: Weston-Super-Mare) sought to reintroduce the seat-belts proposal as a new clause arguing that he wished to 'restore what the Government should be restoring'.[9] However the issue had clearly become politicised and there was a feeling among most MPs that the matter was one which should be considered separately rather than as one clause in a larger bill. As such many who favoured compulsion voted against the new clause which was defeated by 65 to 3. The bill then passed quickly. All the subsequent bills dealt solely with the seat-belts issue.

The next bill reveals even more clearly the Government's ambivalence. When the Labour Government was returned it introduced a seat-belts bill. This time however it was introduced in October just after the election and thus at the beginning of the 1974/5 Parliamentary Session. However, Fred Mulley, who was reappointed as Transport Minister, made it clear that his main aim was to air the issue. So when the Second Reading debate was adjourned after less than an hour's debate the bill was not reintroduced and was thus allowed to fall. It was 18 months before the Labour Government reintroduced a bill. When it did so the bill was debated for six hours at Second Reading, 14½ hours in Standing Committee, and over six hours at Report. It still failed to progress because the Government was unwilling to guillotine debate or to grant the bill more time. The Labour Government made one last attempt to introduce a bill in 1979.[10] However again they did not pursue the bill, but allowed it to fall.

Overall these five Government bills show a very unusual picture of Parliamentary proceedings. Despite the existence of strong party discipline four of the five bills fell because the Government was unwilling to press on against strong opposition. It indicates that a Government which is not fully committed to legislation can be caught between a rock, shortage of time which is of its own making as such bills are usually introduced late in a session, and a hard place, opposition which is encouraged by the Government's decision to allow a free vote and not impose a guillotine.

Given the failure of five Government bills it was perhaps surprising that when Neil Carmichael (Labour: Glasgow, Woodside) won second place in the private members' ballot for the Session 1979/80, he chose to introduce a similar measure. Certainly the bill had no real hope of success. It was a contentious issue as the previous debates had shown and those previous debates had also ensured that the opposition to compulsion was better organised than it had been initially. In addition the Conservative Party victory in the 1979 Election meant that there were now more libertarian MPs. The situation was also exacerbated by the fact that the Corrie Abortion (Amendment) Bill was the first balloted bill in the Session which meant that two controversial bills were competing for the limited time available. Despite this Carmichael sponsored the bill because transport was his major interest and he felt that this was one area where lives could be saved without much extra cost.[11] At the least he hoped that the debates on the bill would publicise the issue and perhaps put pressure on the Conservative Government to introduce a bill.

The bill Carmichael introduced was exactly the measure introduced by the Labour Government in the previous Session. The Second Reading debate involved a repetition of many of the arguments made before. The bill's opponents criticised it for restricting individual liberty, 'big brotherism', extending the powers of the executive, and being virtually unenforceable. Its supporters argued that it would save lives with little or no cost to the taxpayer. The speech of Norman Fowler, Minister of Transport, was again revealing.[12] Fowler himself had been a long-standing opponent of compulsion and a major protagonist in earlier debates. However he declared that the Government was neutral upon the issue although worried about the question of exemptions. This in itself is strange. Fowler argued that wide consultations would be necessary on the subject of exemptions, yet the Ministry of Transport had been involved with five attempts to legislate in the field in six years. If such consultations had not previously occurred it would either suggest incompetence or, more likely, that the Department was never totally committed to the legislation. Despite his reservations the Minister said the Government would not stand in the way of the legislation if it was passed, while knowing full well that it had little or no chance.

The opposition for the back-benches was led by Ivan Lawrence and Ronald Bell who were intent on delaying and defeating the bill. In fact the former announced his intention to delay 'this dreary, preposterous piece of legislation' because it was 'yet another precedent for freedom being interfered with by the legislation of this House'.[13] Of course a bill cannot be filibustered at Second Reading if it has a full day's debate, as Carmichael's bill did having second place in the ballot, for the Speaker will always accept a closure motion. Carmichael's motion was successful with 139 voting for and 48 against. The bill's Second Reading was then approved by 143 to 59.[14]

The bill then went to Standing Committee C whose 18 members comprised ten Conservatives and eight Labour MPs. The bill was supported by eight at Second Reading, opposed by four, and six had not voted. The Committee had five meetings and there was some attempt to filibuster it, particularly by Ivan Lawrence. A number of attempts were made to amend the bill but it remained largely intact. The bill came back to the House for its Report stage on 22 February 1980, to face determined and well-organised opposition.

The Report stage occupied one and a half days and six and a half hours. Only two clauses were discussed, both new clauses introduced by opponents of the bill. In all over 80 per cent of the time for debate was taken up by the bill's opponents. The first clause (new Clause 2), moved by Sir Ronald Bell, would have delayed any implementation of the bill for six months. It was debated for two and three-quarter hours before the Speaker accepted a closure motion which was approved by 100 votes to 34.[15] The clause was then negatived by 98 votes to 41. Subsequently Gary Waller

(Conservative: Brighouse and Spenthorpe), another major opponent of the bill, introduced another clause (new Clause 4) which
would have required a report on the operation of the legislation to
be produced within two years of its passage and annually there-
after.[16] This debate lasted for two hours until business was
adjourned for the day. The Speaker on several occasions had to
threaten the bill's opponents that they were straying off the subject
of the amendment but nevertheless the filibuster was very
effective.[17]

Few private members' bills have a second day on Report.
However, only one bill was out of Committee ready for consideration on the fifth 'remaining-stages' day available. This day, the
Concessionary Travel for Handicapped Persons (Scotland) Bill,
only took up two and a half hours of the time available, so that some
time was available for a further consideration of the seat-belts bill,
which was second on the order paper for that day. Nothing had
changed. The discussion of the new Clause 4 resumed as did the
filibuster. The debate was monopolised by the bill's opponents and
the clause was discussed for another one and three-quarter hours.
At this stage Ivan Lawrence himself moved a closure well aware
that there were not a hundred supporters of the bill there to ensure
its success. In fact only 45 MPs voted for closure while 12 opposed it
so debate on Clause 4 continued for a short time until the sitting was
adjourned. No more time was available in the Session as the Corrie
bill occupied the next 'remaining-stages' day and subsequently new
proposals emerged from Committee. So the bill fell.

The fate of the Carmichael bill again demonstrates how easy it is
for a few MPs to block a controversial private members' bill. Success
is usually based upon the determination and organisation of a
minority rather than the numerical superiority of the majority. In
addition it becomes more easy to block a bill the more often it
appears, for as we also saw when considering the abortion issue,
such repetition allows a bill's opponents to improve their organisation and sophisticate their tactics. In such circumstances the
debate has little or no effect on the outcome. After the Carmichael
debate it was clear that legislation to introduce compulsion would
not be successful using the private-members'-bill procedure. So the
supporters of compulsion turned to other avenues.

In fact the campaign re-emerged in a familiar setting, the House
of Lords. Lord Nugent of Guildford introduced the Road Traffic
(Seat Belts) Bill (1980).[18] He attempted to convince the House of the

value of the measure. In opposition Lord Balfour of Inchrye asked the House to reaffirm its three previous decisions and reject the bill. In all 32 Lords spoke, 20 in favour and 12 against. The long list of speakers reflected the contentious nature of, and the emotion generated by, the subject. Despite this only 108 Peers voted when an amendment to delete the bill was defeated by 72 votes to 36.[19] The bill was thus given a Second Reading but Lord Nugent decided not to proceed with it given 'the well-known vulnerability of (this type of bill) to any opposition in the House of Commons'.

Two months later in January 1981, Normal Fowler, Secretary of State for Transport, introduced his Transport bill (1981). Although its main aim was to remove the state from business, there were provisions for road safety measures. In the Second-Reading debate, David Ennals (Labour: Norwich, North), argued that this was a golden opportunity to include the compulsory use of seat belts and give it the essential Government support, without which it would never succeed.[20] The bill was given a Second Reading and sent to Standing Committee E.

During the Committee debate Barry Sheerman (Labour: Huddersfield East) introduced a clause which was similar to his balloted private members' bill which had not progresssed in the 1980–1 Session. This required all children under the age of 13, who were front-seat passengers, to be restrained by harness. In addition, children under the age of one year would be prohibited from travelling in the front seat. The finalised amendment required all children under the age of fourteen, travelling in the front seat, to be restrained by harness. This was accepted by the Government since it embodied the recommendations of a report published in the autumn of 1980 by the Child Accident Prevention Committee. It was included in the Transport bill as new Clause 27.

When the bill returned to the floor for its Report stage, David Ennals was anxious to introduce an amendment to require the compulsory wearing of seat belts. However the amendment was not put down soon enough[21] and the Speaker, aware that the Government would guillotine the bill, and thus that the time for debate was severely limited, decided not to choose the clause for debate.

The restricted timetable only allowed one hour and eight minutes for the discussion of new clauses. Nevertheless a new clause was introduced which allowed local authorities to build road-humps (or sleeping policemen) on certain highways in order to slow traffic.

This had been the subject of a number of previous private members' bills. The last had been introduced by Anthony Grant (Conservative: Harrow Central) in the 1979/80 Session. It had been passed through its Second Reading, Report and Third Reading stages with no debate but fell when delayed in the House of Lords. Although it was an unopposed bill its supporters felt that its passage would be quicker and easier if it were to be incorporated in the Transport bill. So Grant moved an amendment at Report stage which became new Clause 16 and was accepted by Government.[22]

When the Transport bill went to the Lords it thus contained two clauses introduced by back-benchers which had been the subject of private members' bills. Lord Nugent welcomed the bill, especially Clause 27, but indicated his intention to introduce a new clause at Committee stage relating to compulsion. In reply, Lord Bellwin, Parliamentary Secretary of State, Department of the Environment, stated that the Government support for Clause 27 should not be construed as support for compulsion in general. The Government's view was that the:

duty to care for children who are not old enough to look after their own safety override factors which must be considered in relation to the compulsory wearing of seat belts by adults.[23]

The Committee stage was taken over three days.[24] On the third day Lord Nugent introduced Amendment 79, which sought to introduce the mandatory use of seat belts. It was similar to his private Peers' bill. Lord Bellwin replying for the Government said that although the Government recognised the need for seat belts this was a cross-party issue and a free vote would be allowed.

The opponents of compulsion had found a new source of argument. Professor John Adams had recently published a paper which argued that the use of seat belts encouraged drivers to take greater risks. His comparison of countries with mandatory usage and those without showed that the latter were much better off in terms of accidents. However Lord Underhill stated that there was now:

much support for the new clause from a variety of quarters, the overwhelming majority of respected organizations favoured compulsion as the most effective means of getting drivers to comply with recommendations.[25]

On this issue 18 Lords spoke, 11 for and 7 against; 132 voted in favour of compulsion while 92 opposed, a majority of 40.

On the second of the two days given to the Report stage, Lord Monson moved most of 26 amendments in an abortive attempt to weaken the effects of the proposal. The majority were designed to restrict the scope of the clause by making it applicable to specific categories of driver, for example learners, rather than to motorists as a whole. In general such amendments were trivial and ultimately withdrawn. During the Third Reading Lord Monson again raised these amendments but Lord Bellwin retaliated by assuring the House that these perceived difficulties were of minor importance only and were catered for within the framework of the bill.

Two important issues did arise. An amendment was introduced to ensure that each person alone was responsible for wearing or not wearing a seat belt. Secondly it was decided to allow a three-month period for consultation with interested parties and then to extend from two to three years the period after which an initial report on the operation of the legislation should be prepared. The question of compulsion had been the predominant one discussed at Third Reading. Despite numerous attempts to introduce amendments the bill remained almost intact after 3 hours and 24 minutes of debate. The bill then returned to the House of Commons for consideration of the Lords' amendments.

The bill was guillotined again when it returned to the Commons. The debate on seat belts lasted two and a half hours. Much of the debate centred around the merits of Professor Adams's work. Altogether 15 MPs spoke, with eight in favour of compulsion and seven against. The Government remained neutral and allowed a free vote. Ivan Lawrence's amendment to delete the clause was finally defeated by 221 votes to 144, a majority in favour of compulsion of 77.[26] Thus the Minister of Transport was now given powers to introduce regulations for the compulsory use of seat belts. The laws had been successful because the Government had guillotined the whole bill so that filibustering was ruled out.

The Minister of Transport laid provisional regulations before the Commons on 8 December 1981. These regulations were widely circulated to the public and to interested organisations for comments. Some of these suggestions were then incorporated in the first draft which was approved by Parliament on 22 July 1982.[27] Mrs Lynda Chalker, Under-Secretary of State for Transport, was adamant in the debate that it was the regulations, rather than the principle involved, which should be discussed. Although several speeches tried to introduce arguments against seat belts, there was little controversy and the regulations were approved by 181 votes to 59. The Act came into operation on 31 January 1983.

Almost three years later, on 13 January 1986, David Mitchell, the new Under-Secretary of State for Transport, introduced a motion to reapprove the regulations. He emphasised that this would be the last opportunity to debate the issue which must be decided once and for all. He also pointed out that the seat-belts usage rate had risen to 95 per cent and that the law had been almost entirely self-enforcing. The debate began at 10.49 p.m., late at night as has been common when this issue is discussed. It took place under Standing Order Number 3 (Exempted Business) which allows only one and a half hours for debate. The House finally accepted that the regulations be made permanent by a massive 217 votes to 25, a majority of 192.[28]

This case study illustrates a number of key points. Firstly, on issues of this sort, conscience issues as the Government chooses to call them, the arguments put in successive debates are repetitive, and overall the debate has little influence upon the vote. Secondly, we can see again how a limited number of well-organised MPs can defeat legislation, even Government legislation, if the Government has little commitment to it. Thirdly, if a Government is committed to, or neutral about, a proposal, then the introduction of a new clause into a Government bill is a potentially useful strategy for an MP or an interest group who have failed to achieve their ends through private members' business. In the end the 1981 Transport bill contained three such clauses.

9   The smoking issue and private members' bills

We have seen throughout this book that controversial issues are unlikely to be resolved through the private-members'-bill procedure. In this chapter we shall examine the smoking issue which has been a regular subject of private members' bills. As might be expected, given the aggregate patterns we have identified, none have passed. However the issue is of particular interest not only because it shows how a powerful lobby can effectively stifle legislative change but also because it demonstrates that private members' bills, far from forwarding the cause of their supporters, can be used to advantage by the Government and/or the bill's opponents. Indeed it is probably the case that the anti-smoking lobby would be better served by ignoring the procedure and concentrating their efforts elsewhere; more specifically upon the education and orchestration of public opinion.

Before 1950 there was little awareness in this country of the dangers of smoking. Indeed even in 1949 the Cancer Standing Advisory Committee (CSAC), in an effort to play down the fear of this disease, recommended that no cancer publicity be undertaken by the Minister.[1] Their reasoning was twofold: they wished firstly to protect the public from an unfounded phobia; and secondly to prevent a demand for services which an already overburdened NHS was unable to meet.

However as the diagnostic ability of doctors improved, and with it the recognition of the dangers associated with smoking, the medical profession was forced to take notice. So Horace Joules, a leading clinician, requested the CSAC report and placed the matter before the Medical Research Council. The MRC report stated that the Council was 'satisfied that the case against smoking as such is proven, and that no further statistical inquiry on the general aspect of that problem is necessary'.[2] On 28 June 1951, the issue entered the 'political' arena when the Minister was pressed for his views on the connection between smoking and lung cancer.[3] But it was soon apparent that Governments in general, and Ministers in particular, lack the necessary political will to attack the problem directly and to instigate a campaign which would, ultimately, result in legislation designed to restrict cigarette consumption.

While the medical profession became increasingly committed to the restriction of smoking then, the political will necessary to legislate was still lacking. At first the Government could claim that the evidence that smoking damaged health was limited. However this argument was soon undermined and there is little doubt that the major reason for the Government's subsequent reluctance to legislate has been its dependence upon the revenue derived from tobacco sales. This is clear from the statement of Ian MacLeod, the Minister of Health between 1952 and 1954, who declared that:

Smokers, mainly cigarette smokers, contribute some £1,000 million pounds yearly to the Exchequer and no one knows better than the government that they simply cannot afford to lose that much.[4]

This response is also, as we shall see, indicative of the response of subsequent governments.

In more recent years, and particularly since the election of the first Thatcher Government in 1979, the growth of 'libertarian' views in the Conservative Party has also strengthened opposition to the anti-smoking lobby. Such a view which emphasises individual rights and rejects the 'nanny state' is certainly reflected in the debates on anti-smoking bills in the post-war period.

Since 1945 only one piece of legislation has been passed which restricts the advertising of cigarettes – the 1964 Television Act. This legislation limited, and subsequently banned, televised cigarette commercials. Apart from this successive Governments have refused to take legislative action and instead have consistently supported voluntary agreements, reached in private between departmental officials and the tobacco industry. The Government attitude was succinctly expressed by David Ennals when in 1977, as Secretary of State for the Social Services, he called for a campaign of 'constant persuasion, repeated warnings, advice, help and education' in what he regarded to be the war against smoking rather than the cigarette smoker. He recognised the dangers of smoking but argued that people should be free to choose for themselves. He thus resisted all pressures to deal with the issue by legislation.[5]

This then is the context within which private members' bills have been introduced in this field. Governments have consistently refused to sponsor legislation. Rather, together with the tobacco companies – a very strong economic interest – they have developed a closed policy community in which secret negotiations take place and from which the anti-smoking lobby, even the British Medical Association which in other fields is very powerful indeed, are effectively excluded. The anti-smoking lobby have abundant evidence to support their case, they have strong professional backing, and a significantly proselytising pressure group, ASH.

ASH (Action on Smoking and Health) was formed in 1971 under the auspices of the Royal College of Physicians (RCP) and is partially funded by the Department of Health and Social Security (DHSS).[6] Despite this it is an 'outsider' group excluded from the negotiations between the DHSS and the tobacco companies and generally kept at arm's length by the Department. It thus has little chance of persuading Government to introduce legislation, or indeed of affecting the Department's administration of existing legislation, let alone its negotiations with the companies. So ASH is left with two major strategies. It can attempt to pass legislation through the private-member's-bill procedure or it can aim to influence and change public opinion and smoking habits, so that in the medium, or long, term public pressure on Government builds up to place legal constraints on the production and advertising of tobacco.

All our aggregate data suggests that the use of the private-member's-bill procedure by ASH and individual MPs who support the anti-smoking lobby is likely to prove of very limited utility. Any such move is strongly opposed by the tobacco companies and their supporters in the House. In addition however the Government can, and does, suggest that smoking is a matter of conscience and as such is a matter which should be left to the private-members' procedure although there is no chance of the issue being resolved in this manner.

In this way the use of procedure by the anti-smoking lobby almost serves to legitimise the existing arrangements. At the same time the Government can point to its negotiations with the tobacco companies as an example of pluralism at work (which it clearly is not because major interested parties are excluded), with the companies being forced to make major concessions. This again serves to provide an ideological underpinning to the existing arrangements.

One other point is important here before we examine the bills which have been introduced. The debates on the bills have proved a very important propaganda platform for the pro-smoking lobby rather more than for the bill's supporters. They have been more effectively organised and better briefed in Parliament and their speeches have generally been longer, better, and more frequently reported. So the anti-smoking lobby have not really been able to use the debates as a way of influencing parliamentary or public opinion, a function which such debates can sometimes perform even if a bill has no hopes of success.

The parliamentary campaign to make the House and the public more aware of the dangers of smoking and to achieve legislative change began on 12 February 1964 when Laurie Pavitt (Labour: Willesden West) sought leave to introduce a Ten-Minute-Rule bill, the Cigarettes (Health Hazards) Bill to make it illegal to sell packets of cigarettes which did not bear a printed warning about the dangers of smoking. It was the first of four bills, all of which failed to make any substantial headway even though it was described by its sponsors as a 'very small contribution towards the solution of a very large problem'.[7]

Pavitt assured the House that the bill did not attack personal freedom but rather sought to make the public more aware of the gravity of their actions. In an effort to pre-empt possible opposition he stressed that his bill would not reduce advertising nor would it limit the number of public places where smoking was allowed. This strategy was an attempt to defuse the issue by stressing to his colleagues just how uncontroversial the proposal in question was in order to make it more acceptable to the majority of MPs who were present.

Pavitt was given leave to introduce his bill. He was clever and fortunate enough to put it down for Second Reading on a day on which it followed two uncontentious bills. Despite being third on the order paper it was debated for eighty minutes. The bill, however, was clearly contentious and a large number of Conservative MPs were present. The opposition was indirect. A number of MPs, most from constituencies with tobacco interests, stressed that the manufacturers were willing to enter into voluntary agreements. Others criticised the bill as a restriction of individual freedom with John Biggs-Davison (Conservative: Chigwell) going furthest, claiming that the bill's spirit: 'is socialistic in the worst sense of the word'.[8] The bill fell when the Speaker would not accept a closure motion.

Subsequent bills were interesting because of the responses drawn from those MPs indirectly involved with the industry, through their constituency connections. Using the facility provided by the Ten-Minute-Rule procedure opponents replied to the sponsor's speeches. Michael English (Conservative: Nottingham West, John Player and Sons) replying to Laurie Pavitt's speech introducing his second bill, rejected Pavitt's methods, suggesting that whilst sales would not be severely affected small companies would ultimately suffer at the hands of the larger companies.[9] In a rather more personal attack Robert Cooke (Bristol West, W. H. and H. O. Wills) accused John Dunwoody, the author of the third bill, of using the time as a publicity opportunity for the views he held.[10] In neither case was a vote urged since it was quite clear that further progress was unlikely. The fourth bill received an unopposed First Reading but subsequently did not progress.

Thus in an era of 'liberal reform' when the great moral issues of capital punishment, of abortion, and of homosexuality were decided by initiatives from the backbenches it proved impossible to resolve the smoking issue. This was despite the fact that the pathway to reform had been laid by both political parties. The Conservatives had reached agreement with the industry over the nature and content of advertising. Labour struck even bigger blows. Firstly they declared their intention to mount a publicity campaign warning of the dangers of smoking. Subsequently in August 1965 they announced cigarette advertising would be banned from the television screen. No other legislation to restrict advertising was forthcoming, not because of the efficacy of voluntary agreements but because of the entrenched position of a powerful economic interest.

On 2 March 1965 the Postmaster General, Anthony (Wedgwood-) Benn, in reply to a question from Philip Noel-Baker, informed the House of Commons that this ban would come into force on 1 August 1965, under the aegis of the Television Act 1964.[11] He added that cigarettes were not alone in being banned from the television screen; there were precedents: money lending, betting and patent medicines were all on the list of prohibited subjects. The response from the industry was immediate. The promotion of cigarettes was carried out with renewed vigour. The initial decline in sales, following the television ban, was reversed within three months, due mainly to the reintroduction of coupons as a promotional gimmick. It was soon evident that the attempt by Government to constrain the industry had failed since sales began to soar. So it was in

October 1967 that Kenneth Robinson once again announced his intention to curb advertising, but this time through the use of legislation.[12] However by the end of 1967 political resolve began to weaken. Although Kenneth Robinson declared his intention to legislate against cigarette coupons, the proposals which followed twelve months of fruitless negotiation and sought to bring pressure upon the tobacco industry, were never introduced into the House. Significantly Michael Hatfield argued at the time, that it was expedient to drop the matter as it was 'politically inopportune at a time when the (Labour) Government had run into a fair degree of unfavourable publicity over the breath test'.[13]

The General Election of 1970 returned a Conservative Government which in effect removed the direct threat to the industry, returning to a system of voluntary agreements. The new Secretary of State for Social Services, Sir Keith Joseph, emphasised that legislation would be 'a significant and dangerous diminution of corporate and personal freedom'[14] although he described the Government as being 'absolutely determined to secure a sharp fall in the suffering associated with cigarette smoking'.[15] He claimed that the satisfactory conclusion of negotiations regarding the printing of a warning – 'WARNING SMOKING CAN DAMAGE YOUR HEALTH' – on each cigarette packet and all promotional material vindicated the Government's approach. The strength and legitimation of the policy community in which such secret negotiation occurred was reinforced when Joseph paid tribute to the responsible and helpful way in which the industry had approached the discussions.

During this Government, Sir Gerald Nabarro introduced his Tobacco (and Snuff) (Health Hazards) Bill which to date has been the most interesting of all the anti-smoking proposals. A brief consideration of its fate illustrates clearly how effectively the Government can and does manipulate the private-member procedure. Sir Gerald's bill introduced on 15 December 1970 was a Ten-Minute-Rule bill.[16] It was much broader than previous proposals. Additional pressure was applied to Parliament three weeks later with the publication of RCP's second report. It was an opportune moment because the Government was at the time involved in the previously mentioned negotiations with the tobacco manufacturers regarding the printing of the health warning on each packet of cigarettes. It offered the Government a perfect form of pressure against the companies, a threat of legislation over which the Government could claim neither responsibility nor control.

With unusual haste Nabarro's bill received a Second Reading 'on the nod'. This in itself was peculiar given the controversial nature of the bill and the fact that, as we have seen, only one member need shout 'Object' when the bill is called in order to prevent its further progress.

This is the only occasion on which no representative of the tobacco lobby *overtly* opposed the bill. However it did not mean that Parliament was prepared to accept the proposal. On 16 March, Sir Keith Joseph announced the negotiations with the industry were complete, agreement had been reached and the bill's demands were met.[17] He recommended that the sponsor withdraw his proposals to allow the immediate implementation of the voluntary measures otherwise manufacturers would procrastinate while Parliament sought a legislative solution.

Sir Gerald criticised Sir Keith. He argued that while Government measures had no contractural validity whatever, his bill, supported by both parties, had statutory implications and covered tobacco and tobacco products, including cigarettes. In reply, the Secretary of State for the Social Services emphasised:

that in the light of the voluntary agreement the industry has reached with the Government and which will be put into effect quickly, the Government do not think there is a need for legislation. We hope . . . that Sir Gerald will see fit to withdraw his bill.[18]

This advice was rejected. The bill passed through its Standing Committee stage successfully only to meet opposition on Report. Government support at this stage, and in particular the provision of extra time, could have ensured success, but none was forthcoming. This was anyway unlikely given the rigid policy adopted by the Conservative Party not to give time to back-bench bills. In fact the Government opposed the bill. The Secretary of State declared:

The Government do not regard the bill as necessary because voluntary agreement is only an ingredient in the campaign which lies before us[19]

Undeterred Nabarro pressed ahead and, with peculiar good fortune, received an almost unprecedented amount of private-member time; time was available to continue the Report stage during three private-member days. Even so this was insufficient for success and eventually time ran out. Sir Gerald's reaction was clear.

During the debate he accused those who had participated in delaying tactics as in effect representing tobacco and cigarette constituencies, so that their views merely reflected that there were

Table 9.1 *The interests of speakers on the Nabarro bill*

	Constituency	Ad. Agency	PR Consultants	No apparent connections	Total
Against	6 (55%)	1 (9%)	2 (18%)	2 (18%)	11 (65%)
Minister				1	1 (6%)
For				5	5 (29%)
	6	1	2	8	17

large numbers of workers in those constituencies.[20] As we have seen, given the procedure, organised opposition, especially with, in this case, the tacit support of Government, has the advantage over organised support because it is so easy to filibuster a bill. Here despite a successful Second Reading and Standing Committee, a success encouraged by Government because it enabled them to bring pressure to bear on the tobacco industry, it proved impossible to progress further in the face of delaying tactics used by opponents aware of the shift in Government attitude.

It is worth examining Sir Gerald's claim that opposition stemmed from representatives of constituencies with tobacco interests and was in effect orchestrated by representatives of the tobacco industry. As Table 9.2 indicates, during the three Report-stage days 21 speeches were made by 17 MPs; four individuals, including the sponsor, made two speeches each.

Table 9.1 shows that 12 (71 per cent) speakers, including the Minister, opposed the bill at Report stage while only 5 (29 per cent) spoke in favour. More importantly 6 (55 per cent) of the 11 MPs opposing came from constituencies in which a cigarette factory, or a subsidiary of a tobacco company, was located. Only two speakers had no apparent constituency or personal interest.

Quite clearly the largest number of speakers were opposed to the motion but there is little clear evidence that individual MPs filibustered. It is likely, however, as was the case with the Corrie Abortion bill,[21] that sufficient opponents were present to allow several short speeches to be made thereby serving the same purposes as a few long ones, but attracting far less criticism. An examination of Table 9.2 shows that speeches against the proposal were on average 20 minutes in duration, some five minutes shorter than those in favour. In fact, Laurie Pavitt's speech on the third day of Report proved to be the longest of all, although the two speeches of Sir Derek Walker-Smith's totalled 64 minutes (37 minutes and 27 minutes respectively). Opponents spoke for 54 per cent of the time available, of which the major share was taken by the Minister who availed himself of 14.8 per cent of the available time to express the Government's dissatisfaction with the bill.

Of course we cannot with certainty conclude that those MPs who opposed the bill were promoting the interests of the companies. Some, while recognising the dangers of smoking, may have felt a duty to protect their constituents' employment. Others with libertarian views would advocate voluntary agreements rather than state intervention. Nevertheless the strength of the opposition to bills like Nabarro's is clearly very strong. What is more a consideration of this bill amply illustrates the tobacco companies' preferred strategy. The companies made some concessions to Government in their negotiations. This served to legitimise the voluntary agreements and allowed the companies to pose as being aware of their social responsibilities. Yet the concessions they made were much less than would have been imposed on them by the Nabarro bill. It is also important to emphasise that the voluntary agreement acted as at least as much, and probably more, of a constraint upon Government as upon the companies.

This in part explains why the anti-smoking campaigners were very disappointed with the outcome of the Nabarro bill, despite the fact that they achieved some of their ends through the voluntary agreement. However they were undeterred and switched their attention to the advertising and promotion of cigarettes. The next seven bills, five Standing Order Number 39 and two Ten-Minute-Rule bills, sought to prohibit advertising. Only two went beyond First Reading, although none progressed substantially. There was a division on John Parker's Cigarettes (Prohibition of Advertising) Bill (1971–72),[22] a Ten-Minute-Rule bill. Parker was given leave to introduce his bill with 132 voting in favour and 72 against, but it failed to progress further.

The return of the Labour Party to office in 1974 gave the anti-smoking groups a misplaced cause for optimism. Barbara Castle, the new Secretary of State for the Social Services, favoured strong action entrusting this task to her Health Minister, Dr David Owen. His approach to the industry was more direct. He argued that legislative backing for voluntary agreements was essential.

Table 9.2 *Time spent debating the Nabarro Bill in hours and minutes*

Number of speakers in brackets

	1st day	2nd day	3rd day	Total	Average minutes per speech	Average minutes per person	Longest speech	Shortest speech
Against	0.42 (2)	2.57 (8)	0.40 (3)	4.19 (13) (54.2%)	20 mins	23.5 mins	1.04	0.05
Minister	0.53	0.18	0	1.11 (2) (14.8%)	35 mins	71 mins	0.53	0.18
For	0.23 (1)	1.00 (3)	1.05 (2)	2.28 (6) (31.0%)	25 mins	29.5 mins	0.45	0.08
Total	1.58 (4)	4.15 (12)	1.45 (5)	7.58 (21)	23 mins	28.0 mins		

However rather than advocating new legislation he threatened to use Section 105 of the Medicines Act, 1968. This section empowers the Minister to control, by order, any substance which, while not itself a medicine, is nevertheless capable of causing danger to the health of the community.

Owen soon realised that opposition to his proposals came from both inside and outside the House of Commons. Dr Gerard Vaughan and Kenneth Clarke, both future Health Ministers in Mrs Thatcher's Government, opposed this strategy.[23] In addition interests outside, embodied by the industry, indicated that they would be prepared to challenge the validity of his interpretation of the Act through the courts.[24]

The Cabinet reshuffle of 1977 removed the immediate concern of the industry when Roland Moyle replaced David Owen, who was moved to the Foreign Office. The Medicine Act strategy was quietly forgotten, especially when it was leaked that the Prime Minister, Jim Callaghan, was against it. In March of that year the industry agreed to a new health warning which included the word 'SERIOUSLY'. In return the Government agreed to forget about legislation for a further three years.

During this period back-bench activity continued. The Cigarette Sales (Gift Coupons) Bill, again sponsored by Laurie Pavitt, was introduced in the 1975/6 Session under Standing Order Number 37 and debated at Second Reading.[25] The similarities with the Nabarro bill five years earlier were evident. The sponsors were requested by Government to withdraw the motion. They were informed that negotiations with the industry were underway and that the aims of the proposed bill would not fit within the voluntary strategy which the Government was pursuing and to which the industry had agreed. After 1 hour and 52 minutes, one minute before the end of the debating period, Pavitt acceded to the Government request and withdrew the bill which had no hope of progressing. One of the most telling points to be made here is that despite the fact that a large number of bills have been introduced most have been introduced by the same small group of MPs with Laurie Pavitt at the forefront. This fact is also reflected in the reluctance of MPs who win high places in the ballot to introduce bills on the subject, so most bills are Standing Order Number 39 or Ten-Minute-Rule bills which have little hope of progressing at all. In the debate on this Pavitt bill it was again the bill's opponents who made better use of the time available and they used it to put their views to the House.

Indeed, Michael English, veteran of the pro-tobacco lobby, continued to talk even though he acknowledged Laurie Pavitt's willingness to withdraw the bill. However, rather than lose this opportunity he proceeded to pour scorn on the aims of the campaign 'to persuade people that they should not smoke in public but go, presumably, into somewhere such as a public lavatory in order to have a quiet smoke'.[26] The debate ended and it was not for another six Sessions, and under a new government, that the issue was once again debated in the House.

In each subsequent Session some attempt to curb smoking in public places, or to constrain the promotional activities of manufacturers, was made. However no bill was debated until the faithful Laurie Pavitt introduced his Tobacco Products (Control of Advertising, Sponsorship and Sales Promotion) Bill in the 1981/2 Session.[27] One of the undebated bills however is worthy of some comment as the controversy around its fate reveals that MPs themselves are by no means fully aware of the limitations of the private-member's-bill procedure.

In the 1980/1 Session, Laurie Pavitt introduced a Standing Order Number 37 bill, Tobacco Products (Control of Advertising, Sponsorship and Sales Promotion) Bill. This was down for a Second Reading Debate after the Zoos' Licensing (No. 2) Bill. The anti-smoking lobby accused the supporters of the industry of filibustering this bill in order to prevent the Pavitt bill being considered. Certainly 164 amendments to the Zoos' bill were introduced, and Sir Anthony Kershaw (Cons.: Stroud), the parliamentary consultant for British American Tobacco, seemed to give credence to the claim when he stated that neither he, nor 'any of the hierarchy in the House' wanted to see Pavitt's bill progress, 'as there was sufficient private members' time left for it possibly to achieve a Third Reading'.[28]

Given all our preceding evidence such an analysis is highly dubious. We have seen how few Standing Order Number 39 bills succeed, and also that opposed bills do not pass without Government time. It is in fact difficult to imagine any circumstances under which the Pavitt bill could have progressed on that day. The Zoos' Licensing (No. 2) Bill was first on the order paper for consideration of its Report and Third Reading stages. Indeed Pavitt's bill was only third on the list behind a Lords' bill which, however, passed 'on the nod'. Even under normal circumstances the Zoos' bill would have required at least two and a half hours for debate which would have left insufficient time to complete the Second Reading of a contentious issue. It is also extremely unlikely that a closure would have been allowed by the Speaker if the bill had been only briefly discussed. As we saw earlier the Speaker will usually allow a closure motion only when a full day's debate has taken place or if he feels that sufficient time has been allowed to debate the issue. If a topic has been raised and the argument discussed thoroughly on previous occasions in the same Parliament a closure motion might be permitted. However, there had been no such previous extended debate on smoking in the 1974/9 Parliament. Indeed although the smoking issue may, superficially, have a high political profile it has been infrequently debated particularly given the attention that the issue receives in the media. This almost inevitably means that any debate on a smoking bill would last five hours.

The analysis of the anti-smoking lobby, and indeed of Kershaw, appears if anything even more dubious if we briefly examine what might have happened if the bill had received a Second Reading on that day. At this stage there were only two 'remaining-stages' days left; one just seven days later and the final day, 10 July. It is conceivable that following a successful Second Reading the bill could have gone immediately to Standing Committee C, which was not in use at the time, but such a bill would have normally been discussed in Committee for two, if not three, weeks. In fact in 1971 the Nabarro bill required four meetings over four weeks in Committee. Consequently the bill would not have been out of Committee until 28 June which would effectively have left one 'remaining-stages' day available – the day on which Lords' Amendments are normally considered. Thus the chances of a successful Third Reading were minimal given the order of precedence for the consideration of bills on a 'remaining-stages' day; any bill which has at least completed its Third Reading must be taken first. On that day Lords' Amendments were taken first and ended with the completion of the Countryside (Scotland) (HL) Bill at 2.12 p.m.[29] This left just 18 minutes for other bills. On this evidence it is clear that Pavitt's bill had not even an outside chance of being fifteenth-time lucky.

At the same time it is also evident that Kershaw and Colvin, the main supporters of the industry in the House, were not responsible for obstructing the proposal even if this was their desired aim. What is more while Colvin had participated in the Zoos' bill throughout, his involvement was in his capacity as parliamentary representative of the interests of the RSPCA. The key point is that the Zoos' bill was controversial in its own right mainly because it was badly drafted and much amended in Committee. Indeed there were 334 amendments and 11 new clauses introduced in Committee. Overall it is difficult to comprehend how the supporters, or indeed the opponents, of Pavitt's bill thought it had any hope of success. Once again it reveals that many MPs have limited knowledge of the intricacies of private-member's-bill procedure.

By the end of the 1970s the issue of coupons was no longer important as European Community's legislation had made packets of cigarettes containing such material more expensive. Now ASH and its supporters were giving emphasis to the question of spon-sorship by tobacco companies. Once again it was Pavitt who introduced a bill on this subject, the Tobacco Products (Control of Advertising, Sponsorship and Sales Promotion) Bill in 1982 and this was the first bill to be debated for six years. It was a Standing Order Number 39 bill which was debated at Second Reading for just 42 minutes, 32 of which were taken up by the bill's sponsor. Michael Colvin replied and, as would be expected, talked the bill out when the Speaker refused to accept a closure motion.

The defeat of the bill with such ease indicates the limited utility of the strategy which Pavitt, ASH and the anti-smoking lobby have adopted. Certainly the smoking issue has been a consistent subject for private members' bills. However as an issue it does not have a high profile. We have already seen that few MPs are willing to sponsor these bills and indeed the casual observer would be forgiven for concluding that Laurie Pavitt is a one-man campaign. Certainly the issue is seen by a number of MPs to whom we have spoken as a personal campaign, and almost as a 'bit of a joke'.

Since 1982 successive bills have fared badly. There has however been one exception in the general area. On 4 December 1985 John Hare Robertson introduced the Tobacco Products (Sales Restriction) Bill.[30] The bill attempted to restrict the sale of a specific form of tobacco product, Skool Bandits, to children. It was thus a minor bill which merely extended the provisions of the 1933 Children and Young Persons Act to new products. As such it was not opposed by the tobacco industry. Indeed when the Second Reading took place on 31 January 1986, it was obvious that there was no opposition at all to the proposal. It was a bill to which nobody could object given the existing legislation regarding minors and tobacco. It was aimed to protect children because, despite assurances to the contrary, the

United States Tobacco Company had directed much of its promotional activity at the young.

In the House the speeches were short and to the point. Only nine
minutes were required to introduce the measure with just five for a
supporting speech from Roger Sims. In contrast Laurie Pavitt spoke
for 15 minutes as he congratulated the sponsor on his good fortune
in the ballot and explained the need for this measure. Government
approval was expressed by Ray Whitney, the Under Secretary for
Health and Social Security. Within one hour the Second Reading
was agreed. The Committee Stage was completed in one sitting.
The Report and Third Reading stages were also extremely short
lasting under two hours, of which the Third Reading took 1 hour
and 40 minutes.

In less than three hours of debating time, an issue which struck at
the tobacco industry had completed its parliamentary course. This
demonstrates that where there is genuine concern, where
entrenched economic positions cannot be adequately defended,
and where behavioural patterns have not been established, quick
and decisive action can be achieved. Untypically there were no
dissenting voices even from the Government which gave its 'full
support'.[31] In contrast similar attempts to restrict cigarette promotion to adults has met with persistent obstruction. Indeed,
Philip Johnson, writing for the *British Medical Journal*, was moved to
comment that some people must be 'increasingly bemused by the
plethora of proposed smoking legislation' which receives massive
publicity but then 'seems to sink without trace'.[32] Clearly there is no
chance that radical reforms, or indeed any significant reforms, will
be achieved through the private members' procedure given the
nature of that procedure and the organised opposition to such
changes which is orchestrated by the tobacco companies.

In this area we are faced with a major problem which recurs
elsewhere in policy-making: how can you reconcile the economic
activities of companies which are directed towards increasing
profitability with the broader public interest? The answer here, as
elsewhere, is that the compromise which is reached is one which
tends to favour the industry. This results partly from the pressure
group activities of the tobacco companies. They are well organised
with considerable resources, and privileged access to Government.
In contrast the anti-smoking lobby, though increasingly supported
by the medical profession, is poorly resourced and denied access to
discussions between the industry and the Government. Despite

this the main constraint operated by the industry on Government is structural – in two senses. Firstly, the crucial economic position of the companies, both as an employer – particularly in a time of high unemployment – and also as a source of revenue, constrain the policy options open to Government. So even when David Owen was at his most vigorous and threatened to use the Medicine Act to control cigarette promotions the industry resisted legislative change and even defused demands for stronger warnings on packets. The Government backed down for fear of a loss of jobs and revenue.

However the economic position of the industry also has a structural manifestation in the closed policy community composed of the industry representatives and the DHSS ministers and officials which meets annually to discuss a voluntary agreement. This policy-making structure serves to legitimise the status quo both because it implies that the Government is constantly winning concessions from the industry, and because bureaucratic inertia and personal relationships, developed by continuing interaction, make change a step into unknown territory.

Of course it could be argued that the process of negotiation does lead to major concessions being made by the tobacco companies in response to Government pressure, and in the national interest. However it is clear that the voluntary agreements arrived at are not always adhered to, and indeed cigarette 'advertisements' (in the form of hoardings, sponsorships etc.) are still a common feature on our television screens 20 years after they were banned. The example of the introduction of low-tar cigarettes is even more instructive. The companies agreed to print the tar levels on packets of cigarettes in response to Government arguments that low-tar cigarettes would be less damaging to health. However the companies' response was to promote low-tar brands and attempt to ensure that each smoker smoked more of these less damaging brands – thus increasing their profits, reducing cost, but not reducing health risk. In this context the *Lancet* has called for the policy of agreed restraint to be replaced by a statutory ban on all publicity, direct or indirect.

By consistently relegating the matter to the private-members' procedure the Government, any Government, would argue that it leaves the matter open to the people's representatives to decide. In fact by adopting this course the Government absolves itself from responsibility and ensures that no legislation will be passed. This leaves ASH and the anti-smoking lobby in a difficult position. The legislative avenue is in effect closed. So their major chance of achieving progress is by encouraging behavioural change through education. This, however, is clearly a long and expensive process.

Our main concern here is not with how the smoking issue should be, or will be, resolved. Rather, we have shown that it cannot be resolved through the private-members'-bill procedure. Yet, like abortion, it is an important and recurring problem and one which Governments are loath to address. Clearly if it is to be resolved either it will need a change of heart by Government, perhaps brought on by a shift in public opinion, or the private-members'-bill procedure needs to be reformed. We shall turn to a discussion of reforming the procedure in our conclusion.

Conclusion: a proposal for reform?

This study of private members' bills clearly indicates that the procedure is not one through which controversial issues can be resolved. Perhaps the most significant fact of all those we have produced is that no private members' bill which has had a vote on the floor of the House has passed since 1959, unless it has been granted time by the Government. At the same time Governments are less willing to grant time now than in the past. This means that most of the bills passed in recent years have been minor, technical and uncontentious. In fact most have been Government bills in all but name.

Of course one might argue that this does not matter, that private members' bills serve other purposes, and/or that in the British parliamentary system the executive does, and should, control legislation. Certainly, as we have seen, many MPs introduce bills with no hope of success. Their purpose is to publicise an issue in order, they hope, to persuade Government to introduce legislation directly, or influence the public to press for reform which the Government may take up at a later date. This does sometimes happen although it is rare. In fact the most plausible defence of the current system is probably that, even if it results in minor, technical, Government-initiated bills it gives back-bench MPs experience of piloting a bill through Parliament and dealing with civil servants. As such it provides a training ground, offering experience useful to MPs when, and if, they become ministers.

Despite all this it is clear to us that the nature and limitations of the private-members'-bill procedure is merely a reflection of executive dominance in the British system which is itself a reflection of the view of democracy which underpins the institutions and processes of British Government. Any fundamental change in the procedure would only result from a change in the nature of executive–legislative relations which itself would necessitate a move towards a more participatory view of democracy.

The British political tradition

There is no space here to develop a thorough analysis of the British political tradition. However some consideration of the debates about democracy in Britain is important if we are to show how the nature of that tradition underpins executive–legislative relations.[1] As both Beer and Birch show,[2] in the period from 1688 to the end of the nineteenth century, it was the debate about representation which dominated contemporary politics. Until the first half of the nineteenth century, the debate between the Whigs and the Tories concerned the respective roles of monarchs and Parliament, after that the debate between Conservatives and Liberals centred around the franchise. Nevertheless, from the present perspective, the similarity between the Whig and the Tory, and the Conservative and Liberal views appear more revealing than the differences.

In the Tory view the King symbolised and represented the community as a whole. As such they believed that the King should make policy while the Members of Parliament merely expressed the grievances of their constituents. In contrast, the Whigs believed that the *unreformed* Parliament had a crucial role to play both in expressing the various opinions and interests within society, and in reconciling these opinions in order to forward the best interests of the nation. By the beginning of the nineteenth century, however, this debate had lost its relevance. The active role of Parliament in policy-making was accepted, and Old Whigs and Old Tories combined in a defence of the unreformed House of Commons against demands for the extension of the franchise. The point here is that Whigs and Tories, despite their differences, shared an antipathy towards popular sovereignty. They emphasised the need to preserve order and stability with the stress on strong, efficient and centralised, rather than responsive, government.

Of course, early radicals like the seventeenth-century Levellers had advocated popular sovereignty. However, it was not until the nineteenth century that such views came to the fore. As Birch argues:

It is fair to say that Victorian discussions about representative Government were dominated by Liberal ideas and that these ideas, at first held by only a minority of politicians and writers, gradually won widespread acceptance until by the end of the century they had come to constitute the prevailing constitutional doctrine.[3]

So by the end of the nineteenth century Conservatives, Liberals and Socialists alike had accepted the principle and importance of universal male suffrage although of course it was not until 1928 that women received the same voting rights.

Obviously the debate about the franchise was a heated one in nineteenth-century England, and the extension of the franchise was gradual. However, from the present perspective what seems more important is that at no time was the argument about representation broadened. Indeed as Beer argues even to the Liberals:

The member of the legislature was not a delegate sent merely to reflect the will of the people, he was a representative charged with the deliberation on the common good.[4]

Parliament was representative because it was free and fairly elected and MPs and Government could be held accountable at periodic elections. Once elected an MP must be free to take decisions, and a Government free to govern. This obviously raises the notion of responsibility which we shall discuss later. However the immediate point is made succinctly by Birch:

No serious politician has suggested that representatives should be bound by specific instructions from their constituents and subject to recall if they do not follow these instructions.[5]

The British notion of representative democracy is thus a limited one. In fact in the British system the stress has consistently been upon strong, centralised, efficient Government rather than responsive Government. This is clear if we examine the notion of responsibility. Birch argues that the debate about responsibility did not become a prominent feature of constitutional debate until the twentieth century. Yet ideas about responsibility were always implicit, and sometimes explicit, in Tory, Whig and Liberal views of representation. In many respects the same theory of responsibility was implicit in all three theories of representation. The Tories had believed that the supreme authority should be the Monarch, the Whigs believed in a shared authority between the Monarch and Parliament, while the Liberals believed that the House of Commons should be supreme. Yet all saw Government, however constructed, as the arbiter or judge of the 'national interest'. What was needed was a Government capable of strong decisive action to forward that 'national interest'. The public's role, even in the Liberal view, was largely restricted to voting at periodic elections.

Of course by the late nineteenth century and early twentieth century the details of the debate had changed. By then all accepted the dominance of the House of Commons, although there was continuing dispute over the Lords' role, and the key question concerned the relationship between the executive and the legislature. Here of course the Liberal view stressed the doctrines of parliamentary sovereignty, ministerial responsibility and parliamentary control of the executive. In contrast the Conservative view emphasised the necessity for a strong executive in order to ensure responsibility; that is strong and effective Government. Once again while these views were significantly different not even the Liberal view advocated any notion that the Government should be primarily responsible to the population, rather Government should be responsible to Parliament which represented the nation.

The Liberal stress upon the accountability of the executive to Parliament was almost immediately weakened by the development of strong, cohesive parliamentary parties. They developed in order that Governments could ensure majorities in Parliament. Similarly the Conservative and Liberal extra-parliamentary parties were created to ensure the continued election of MPs who supported the parliamentary party. It is this party discipline and cohesion which is the crucial factor which enables the executive to dominate the legislature. Birch sees the development of party discipline and executive dominance as non-ideological:

The present representative system, in which party management play so important a role, does not have ideological origins and cannot easily be justified in terms of a theory about the proper functioning of MPs.[6]

However, this seems to us to be a mistaken view. Indeed, it appears to us that the modern British political system is in fact underpinned by a conservative view of responsibility which can be traced back to old Tory views, together with a limited liberal view of representation. As Birch himself says, the British political tradition emphasised 'first consistency, prudence and leadership, second, accountability to Parliament and the electorate, and third responsiveness to public opinions and demands'. In other words the stress in the British political system is upon élite or leadership democracy rather than participatory democracy; upon the notion that Government knows best.

It is this political tradition, this leadership view of democracy which underpins the institutions and processes of Government. The continued existence of an unfair electoral system, the level of secrecy, and the ineffective nature of select committees, are all defended by recourse to arguments based upon the need to retain leadership, democracy and strong government. Given this view individual MPs would be expected to play a limited role in the legislative process. One would expect limited time to be available to the back-bench MPs and private members' bills to be concerned with trivia, with promoting minor, Government-inspired legislation, or with subjects which Government choose to award. This, of course, is exactly the pattern which we have identified. As we have seen most bills which pass are small, technical and non-contentious. Many, if not most, of these bills are Government bills in all but name. So the Government, which controls the vast majority of parliamentary time anyway, still utilises private members' time to get through minor legislation. Such bills may be useful but they are Government bills and their prevalence indicates once again the very restricted role that the legislature plays in the British system. At the same time this indicates why change is unlikely. Any major reform of the procedure would inevitably involve a shift in the balance of power, albeit a fairly minor one, in the relationship between the executive and the legislature. What is more the executive is well-suited by the present practice as it can achieve minor legislative change without using its own time. For both these reasons the executive is not likely to initiate, or welcome, any radical change. Equally the very advocacy of major change almost inevitably reflects a view that the executive is too dominant in the British system and probably more fundamentally that the British political system is too élitist.

Reforming the system

This means that while observers have pointed to the waste of parliamentary time involved and the arbitrary nature of the ballot few have advocated radical change. Bromhead for example, after a brief consideration of other alternatives, concludes:

It still remains doubtful whether the existing machinery, for all its haphazard character, really is so very inefficient in relation to the achievement of the tasks which it sets out to perform.[7]

This conclusion is based partly upon the difficulty of suggesting any viable alternative which does not involve so fundamental a change in procedure that it might establish a precedent in relation to

Government bills. However it mainly stems from Bromhead's belief that the 'tasks' of private members' bills should be limited. They should deal with minor, technical, but 'useful,' subjects. A shift towards narrower bills was occurring when Bromhead wrote, and this tendency has developed even more in the last decade. It was only in the 1960s that major social legislation dealing with controversial subjects was passed under the procedure. If Bromhead's view that small technical matters are the proper subject for private members' bills is accepted then little change in the procedure, certainly as far as balloted bills are concerned, would be necessary.

The problem is that there are controversial issues which are recurring subjects of private members' bills. Of course it can be argued that large, non-technical, controversial bills should be the prerogative of Government. However, it is clear that Governments, largely for party political reasons, are unwilling to introduce bills which deal with contentious social and moral issues like abortion, animal experimentation, blood sports or obscenity. So these issues, while they concern many people, are most likely to be raised, and legislated upon, through private members' bills. Yet, there seems to be little point in Parliament wasting time and money continually debating the same issues because parliamentary private members' procedure and practices do not allow them to be resolved. In our view what is needed is a change in procedure to allow Parliament to reach a definite decision on these issues.

It appears to us that any effective reform of the system would necessitate the establishment of a Steering Committee to deal with private members' bills. Such a Committee is considered by Bromhead and appears to have been proposed first by Professor Ramsay Muir in his evidence to the House of Commons Procedure Committee in the 1930/31 Session.[8] To be effective this Committee would need to have control over a certain section of the parliamentary timetable. It would also be necessary in our view to recognise the distinction between non-contentious and contentious bills which we have emphasised.

At present, it is the MPs' names which go into the ballot, so that an MP need not have any specific bill in mind, when he or she enters the ballot. Indeed, MPs have a month after the ballot before they even have to declare the short title of their bills, while the full text of the bill is often unavailable until a week before the day of the Second Reading. If, in contrast, MPs had to have their draft bill ready when they entered the ballot, this would ensure that only

MPs with definite ideas and commitments entered the ballot. In addition, it would allow both other MPs, and interested parties outside Parliament, to know immediately the exact contents of all the bills successful in the ballot. If a bill was non-controversial and no MP (or perhaps no small group of MPs) registered opposition to its principles within a short period of time then it could be placed by the new Steering Committee in a different category from those bills which were opposed. Such bills need minutes, rather than hours, of parliamentary time so that if this distinction was established the majority of private members' time could then be given over to opposed bills.

This distinction in itself, however, would not solve the chief problems evident from our analysis. One would also need to prevent the possibility of a controversial bill failing because it was filibustered and ran out of time. This is why the new Steering Committee would need to have control over that section of the parliamentary timetable allocated to private members' bills. We would suggest that the first four or five weeks of time available for controversial private members' bills should be allocated to Second Reading debates. Then the bill which has the most support (or perhaps the largest majority), could go first into Standing Committee. When it came out of Standing Committee the next most popular bill could then go into Committee. However the first bill out of Committee would have to complete its 'remaining stages' before any other bill is considered on the floor of the House. In addition we would suggest that the Steering Committee should have the power to introduce a guillotine motion on the later stages of debate on these bills. Depending upon how much time was available for these bills it is likely that only one, or perhaps two, bills would be fully considered in any Session. However, this procedure would allow the House to reach a decision on some controversial bills if it so wished and was willing to support a guillotine motion. It would probably also be necessary to prevent bills on the same controversial issue being introduced in every Session. A rule which allowed only one bill upon a given issue per Parliament might be appropriate with the Steering Committee taking the decisions as to whether a bill was too similar to one previously discussed.

Notes

Introduction

1 P. Bromhead, *Private Members Bills in the British Parliament* (London: Routledge, 1956).

2 Philip Norton, *The Commons in Perspective* (Oxford: Martin Robertson, 1981), devotes three pages to the subject, most of which is taken up with explaining the procedure, pp. 99–102.

3 On this period see P. Richards, *Parliament and Conscience* (London: Allen and Unwin, 1970) and B. Pym, *Pressure Groups and the Permissive Society* (Newton Abbot: David and Charles, 1974).

4 The Housing (Homeless Persons) Bill was particularly interesting. It was introduced by Stephen Ross, Liberal MP for the Isle of Wight. It laid a duty on local authorities to house homeless people in priority groups – for example those with children, the elderly or infirm, and pregnant women. The Labour Government agreed in the Lib–Lab Pact to provide extra time so the bill – which they strongly supported – could be passed. As the bill was complex it required thirteen hours of debate on the floor of the House and in Committee and would not have been passed without Government support. See A. Michie and S. Hoggart, *The Pact: The Inside Story of the Lib–Lab Government, 1977–78* (London: Quartet, 1978), p. 57.

5 D. M. Hill (ed.), *Parliamentary Select Committees in Action: A Symposium*, Stratchclyde Papers on Government and Politics, no. 24, 1984.

6 See P. Norton, *Dissension in the House of Commons 1945–74* (London: Macmillan, 1975), P. Norton, *Dissension in the House of Commons 1974–9* (Oxford: Oxford University Press, 1980), and equally P. Norton, *Conservative Dissidents* (London: Temple Smith, 1978).

7 P. Richards, 'Private Members Legislation', in S. Walkland (ed.), *The House of Commons in the Twentieth Century* (Oxford: Clarendon Press, 1979), pp. 292–328, and P. Richards, 'Private Members Legislation', in S. Walkland and M. Ryle, *The Commons in the Seventies* (London: Martin Robertson, 1977), pp. 113–28.

8 On the reintroduction of the procedure after World War II see P. Bromhead, *Private Members Bills*, pp. 9–13, esp.

9 I. Burton and G. Drewry, *Legislation and Public Policy: Public Bills in the 1970–74 Parliament* (London: Macmillan, 1981), pp. 214–55.

10 I. Burton and G. Drewry, 'Public Legislation: A Survey of the Session 1968–69', *Parliamentary Affairs*, Vol. 23, 1969/70, pp. 154–83. I. Burton

and G. Drewry, 'Public Legislation: A Survey of the Session 1969–70', *Parliamentary Affairs*, Vol. 23, 1969/70, pp. 308–44. I. Burton and G. Drewry, 'Public Legislation: A Survey of the Session 1970–71', *Parliamentary Affairs*, Vol. 25, 1971/2, pp. 123–62. I. Burton and G. Drewry, 'Public Legislation: A Survey of the Session 1971–72', *Parliamentary Affairs*, Vol. 26, 1972/3, pp. 145–85. I. Burton and G. Drewry, 'Public Legislation: A Survey of the Session 1972–73', *Parliamentary Affairs*, Vol. 27, 1973/4, pp. 120–58. I. Burton and G. Drewry, 'Public Legislation 1973/4' and 'A Parliament in Retrospect', *Parliamentary Affairs*, Vol. 28, 1974/5, pp. 125–53. I. Burton and G. Drewry, 'Public Legislation: A Survey of the Session 1974', *Parliamentary Affairs*, Vol. 29, 1976, pp. 155–89. I. Burton and G. Drewry, 'Public Legislation: A Survey of the Session 1974–75', *Parliamentary Affairs*, Vol. 30, 1977, pp. 161–92. I. Burton and G. Drewry, 'Public Legislation: A Survey of the Sessions 1975–76 and 1976–77', *Parliamentary Affairs*, Vol. 31, 1978, pp. 140–73. I. Burton and G. Drewry, 'Public Legislation: A Survey of the Sessions 1977–78 and 1978–79', *Parliamentary Affairs*, Vol. 33, 1980, pp. 173–209. I. Burton and G. Drewry, 'Public Legislation: A Survey of the Session 1979–80', *Parliamentary Affairs*, Vol. 35, 1982/3, pp. 7–38. I. Burton and G. Drewry, 'Public Legislation: A Survey of the Session 1980–81', *Parliamentary Affairs*, Vol. 36, 1983–4, pp. 436–59.

11 See, for example: J. Christoph, *Capital Punishment and British Politics* (London: Allen & Unwin, 1962); M. McCarthy and R. Moodie, 'Parliament and Pornography: The 1978 Child Protection Act', *Parliamentary Affairs*, vol. 34, 1980–1, pp. 47–62; and J. Gray, 'The Unsolicited Goods and Services Acts 1971 and 1975: A Case Study of the Process Leading to the Enactment of Private Members Bills', *Public Law*, 1978, pp. 242–63.

1 Private members' bills: the procedure

1 Kevin McNamara, H.C. Debs, 23 Nov. 1976, Vol. 794, Col. 741.
2 In fact Mr Biffen, Leader of the House, said: 'The current value of the allowance expressed in prices prevailing at the date of its introduction is £43.35.' H.C. Debs, Vol. 89, 13 Jan. 1986, Col. 441.
3 Mr Biffen, H.C. Debs, Vol. 90, 20 Jan. 1986, Col. 4.
4 At the beginning of the 1969–70 Session, Robin Maxwell Hislop, Conservative MP for Tiverton, regarded as something of a procedural expert, queued all night in order to put down enough motions to book all the time for Ten-Minute-Rule bills for a whole year (from November 1969 to December 1970) for Tory MPs. This was widely regarded as against the spirit of the House and the matter was referred to the Select Committee on Procedure. The Committee recommended a change in the procedure and this was accepted by the House. Now an MP can only hand in one motion asking for leave to introduce a Ten-Minute bill at a time, and only book time up to 15 days ahead.
5 *See* p. 71.
6 P. Bromhead, *Private Members Bills*, p. 25.
7 I. Burton and G. Drewry, 'Public legislation: 1977/8 and 1978/9', claim:

'The increased number of ten-minute rule motions taken to a division continued. More and more, these divisions take place over bills whose titles deliberately flaunt partisan attitudes to contemporary political issues and which are in some sense serious legislative endeavours' (p. 197).

2 The introduction and fate of private members' bills

1 P. Bromhead, *Private Members Bills*, p. 50.
2 *Ibid.*, p. 53.
3 *Ibid.*, p. 54.
4 *Ibid.*, p. 3.
5 I. Burton and G. Drewry, 'Public Legislation: 1977/8 and 1978/9', p. 197.
6 P. Bromhead, *Private Members Bills*, pp. 127–149. Bromhead, however, argues that constitutional reform is an unsuitable subject for a private members' bill.
7 See P. Richards, 'Private Members Legislation, 1977', pp. 119–123, and P. Richards, 'Private Members Legislation, 1979', pp. 307–316.
8 I. Burton and G. Drewry, *Legislation and Public Policy*, pp. 235–8.
9 For example, Burton and Drewry say: '(there are) two distinct categories of private members bills: those securing a place, *preferably a high place*, in the ballot, and those which are unobjectionable'. *See* Burton and Drewry, *Public Legislation 1972–73*, p. 143.

3 The Government and private members' bills

1 So Burton and Drewry are wrong when they say: 'It is common knowledge that some bills are officially drafted under the auspices either of the Law Commission or of a Government department, and handed to sympathetic back benchers (*particularly those who have won a good place in the ballot*) by the whips.' I. Burton and G. Drewry, *Legislation and Public Policy*, p. 214. In contrast Bromhead is right to emphasise: 'It must be remembered ... that it is often the Members with low places in the ballot who bring in bills on behalf of the Government, and that such Members would have not much chance of getting very far with bills brought in on their own account.' P. Bromhead, *Private Members Bills*, p. 24.
2 This section is based upon an interview with Mr McKelvey, 27 Jan. 1981.
3 Interview with Mr Banks, 10 Dec. 1981.
4 For a discussion of the Law Commission see D. Miers and A. C. Page, *Legislation* (London: Skeet and Maxwell, 1982), pp. 42–6.
5 A. Mitchell, 'A House Buyer's Bill: How not to pass a Private Members Bill', *Parliamentary Affairs*, 1986, pp. 1–18, quote p. 1.
6 P. Bromhead, *Private Members Bills*, pp. 86–116.
7 Bromhead merely says: 'If a Minister wants to bring in a minor bill concerning his own Department, and is told that the Government's legislative timetable is so full that no room can be found for his bill, he may try, either himself or through the Whips, to get a private Member

to use a place in the ballot for the bill.' P. Bromhead, *Private Members Bills*, p. 107. He also makes a similar point earlier, *see* p. 24.

8 I. Burton and G. Drewry, *Legislation and Public Policy*, p. 214.

9 It is also worth pointing out, as Burton and Drewry do, that many Law Commission reports become the basis of Government bills.

10 Burton and Drewry, *Legislation and Public Policy*, p. 214.

11 Although the Government may not be very happy with some of the bills which they don't actively oppose but which pass. For example, see M. McCarthy and R. Moodie, 'Parliament and Pornography: The 1978 Child Protection Act', *Parliamentary Affairs*, Winter 1981, pp. 47–62.

12 I. Burton and G. Drewry, 'Public Legislation: A Survey of the Session 1974', p. 174.

13 Interview with Nigel Spearing, 10 Dec. 1981.

14 P. Bromhead, *Private Members Bills*, pp. 102–7.

15 Interview with Robert Taylor, 17 Feb. 1981.

16 Interview with Trevor Skeet, 3 Dec. 1981.

17 See D. Marsh and J. Chambers, *Abortion Politics* (London: Junction Books, 1981). This material is partly based on interviews with John Corrie, 8 July 1979 and William Benyon, 8 July 1979.

18 Interview with Enoch Powell, 6 March 1986.

19 There are two studies of this period: P. Richards, *Parliament and Conscience* and Bridget Pym, *Pressure Groups and the Permissive Society* (Newton Abbot: David and Charles, 1974).

20 On this bill *see*, P. Richards, *Parliament and Conscience*, Chapter 3, pp. 35–62, and B. Pym, 'Pressure Groups and the Permissive Society', pp. 66–69.

21 On this bill see P. Richards, *Parliament and Conscience*, Chapter 4, pp. 63–84; B. Pym, *Pressure Groups and the Permissive Society*, pp. 97–102, and L. Abse, *Private Member* (London: MacDonald, 1973).

22 It is perhaps worth noting that it is possible for an Opposition to allow debate on a bill on one of the supply days on which it decides the topic of debate. In 1973 the Labour Opposition gave up half a supply day for the discussion of Willy Hamilton's Anti-discrimination bill. See Burton and Drewry, *Legislation and Public Policy*, pp. 251–52. In addition, of course, the Commons can vote to suspend Standing Orders and extend debate using the private members' motion procedure.

23 R. Crossman, H.C. Debs, 24 April 1967, vol. 745, col. 1152.

24 W. Whitelaw, H.C. Debs, 18 February 1971, vol. 811, col. 2131.

25 *See* Burton and Drewry, *Legislation and Public Policy*, p. 241.

26 *See* A. Leathard, *The Fight for Family Planning* (London: Macmillan), pp. 190–3.

4 Interest groups, individual MPs and private members' bills

1 Bridget Pym, *Pressure Groups and the Permissive Society*.

2 Bridget Pym, *Pressure Groups*, p. 115.

3 Interview with John Page, 7 Dec. 1981.

4 P. Richards, *Parliament and Conscience*, p. 206.

5 M. Simms and K. Hindell, *Abortion Law Reformed* (London: Peter Owen, 1971).

6 B. Pym, *Pressure Groups*, pp. 117–18.

7 The bill's title was changed to the Abortion Bill because of an amendment tabled by the House of Lords and accepted by the House of Commons, H.C. Debs, 25 October 1967, vol. 751, col. 1780. Two reasons were given by David Steel. First, two bills had been passed in the Lords (1965 and 1966) under the title 'Abortion Bill'. It was natural, he felt, that they should prefer their own title. Secondly, Lord Brooke had pointed out during debate that the term 'termination of pregnancy' could be used up to full term. As the Bill did not provide for abortion in the case of a viable foetus the title 'Abortion Bill' was therefore technically correct.

8 B. Pym, *Pressure Groups*, p. 116.

9 P. Richards, *Parliament and Conscience*, p. 104.

10 A. Barker and M. Rush, *The Member of Parliament and His Information* (London: Allen and Unwin, 1970), p. 55.

11 M. Simms and K. Hindell, *Abortion Law Reformed*, p. 178.

12 B. Pym, *Pressure Groups*, pp. 119–20.

13 L. Abse, *Private Member* (London: MacDonald, 1973).

14 On the Divorce bill *see* P. Richards, *Parliament and Conscience*, Chapter 7, pp. 132–58.

15 P. Richards, *Parliament and Conscience*, p. 157.

16 B. Pym, *Pressure Groups*, p.91.

17 *Ibid.*, p. 91.

18 The *Guardian*, 4 Nov. 1983.

19 *See* pp. 127–31.

20 P. Richards, *Parliament and Conscience*, pp. 205–6.

21 Most of this material is based upon an interview with Peter Fry, 24 Nov. 1981.

22 Peter Fry, H. C. Debs, vol. 973, 16 Nov. 1979, col. 1675.

23 H. C. Debs, vol. 973, 16 November 1979, col. 1722.

24 *Ibid.*, col. 1732.

25 *Ibid.*, cols. 1711 and 1716.

26 D. Marsh and J. Chambers, *Abortion Politics*, pp. 160–2.

27 *Ibid.*, pp. 177–82.

28 J. B. Sanderson, 'The National Smoke Abatement Society and the Clean Air Act, 1956', *Political Studies*, 1961, pp. 236–253, quote, p. 248.

29 *Ibid.*, pp. 250–251.

30 D. Mellor, H. C. Debs, 4 Feb. 1983, vol. 36, col. 557.

31 L. Britain, H. C. Debs, 22 Nov. 1984, vol. 65, col. 392.

32 First Report of the Select Report of the Select Committee on Abortion, 1975–76, HMSO, HC 573–11.

33 Interview with Neil Carmichael, 27 Jan. 1981.

34 Interview with Lord Nugent, 3 December 1981.

35 Interview with Barry Sheerman, 10 December 1981.

36 It had been previously introduced as the Highways (Road Humps) Bill by M. Shaw, Conservative MP for Scarborough in the 1979–80 Session.

5 Voting on private members' issues: the limits of statistical analysis

1 P. Richards, *Parliament and Conscience*, Chapter 9, pp. 179–96.
2 P. Richards, *Parliament and Conscience*, p. 182. Later Richards also argues that Party has an effect on the relationship between age and vote, and education and vote, *see* pp. 184–5.
3 Many of these cross tabulations controlling for third variables were performed by Marsh and Chambers but relatively few are reported. See D. Marsh and J. Chambers, *Abortion Politics*, p. 9 and pp. 194–212.
4 G. Moyser, 'Voting Patterns on "Moral" Issues in the British House of Commons, 1964–9', paper presented to the Political Studies Association Conference, 1980.
5 J. Hibbing and D. Marsh, 'Accounting for the Voting Patterns of British MPs on Free Votes', *Legislative Studies Quarterly*, xii, no. 2. 1987, 275–98.
6 *Ibid.*, p. 9.
7 G. Moyser, 'Voting Patterns on Moral Issues', p. 11.
8 P. Richards, *Parliament and Conscience*, p. 181.
9 For further support for this hypothesis see D. Marsh and J. Chambers, *Abortion Politics*, pp. 195–205, and B. Pym, *Pressure Groups*, p. 103.
10 D. Marsh and J. Chambers, *Abortion Politics*, p. 198.
11 G. Moyser, 'Voting Patterns on Moral Issues', p. 12.
12 B. Pym, *Pressure Groups*, pp. 112–13. P. Richards, *Parliament and Conscience*, pp. 181–2. Actually Pym's analysis relies largely on Richards's evidence.
13 G. Moyser, 'Voting Patterns on Moral Issues', pp. 14–15.
14 P. Richards, *Parliament and Conscience*, p. 187.
15 D. Marsh and J. Chambers, *Abortion Politics*, p. 209.
16 *Ibid.*, p. 211.
17 The data on the religious composition of the constituencies have two major weaknesses. First, they represent the churches' reports of their membership and as such may be inaccurate. Secondly, we do not have data on the religious composition of constituencies but only on the churches' membership in the counties of which the constituencies are part. As such we have had to make the dubious assumption that there is a close relationship between the religious composition of all constituencies in a given county. In addition the data only deal with English counties, and not with Scottish, Welsh or Northern Irish counties. Nevertheless despite their grave weaknesses these are the best data available and they do reveal some interesting patterns. The source of the data is *Prospects for The Eighties* (London: The Bible Society, 1980).
18 For more detail on these changes *see* the next chapter and also D. Marsh and J. Chambers, *Abortion Politics*, pp. 15–35 and pp. 169–77.

6 A case study of the abortion issue

1 The relevant debates were:

Norman St John-Stevas Bill
    H.C. Debs, 15 July 1969, vol. 787, cols 411–24.

Bryant Godman Irvine Bill
  H.C. Debs, 13 February 1970, vol. 795, cols 1653–703
John Hunt Bill
  H.C. Debs, 1 December 1971, vol. 827, col. 460
Michael Gryll Bill
  H.C. Debs, 8 May 1974, vol. 873, cols 403–6 and col. 853
James White Bill
  H.C. Debs, 7 February 1975, vol. 885, cols 1757–868
William Benyon Bill
  H.C. Debs, 25 February 1977, vol. 926, cols 1783–896
  H.C. Debs, Reports of Standing Committee C on the Abortion
(Amendment) Bill, 22 June–12 July 1977
Sir Bernard Braine Bill
  H.C. Debs, 21 February 1978, vol. 944, cols 1213–24
John Corrie Bill
  H.C. Debs, 13 July 1979, vol. 970, cols 891–984
  H.C. Debs, Report on Standing Committee C on the Abortion
(Amendment) Bill, 25 July–18 December 1979
  H.C. Debs, 8 February 1980, vol. 978 (Report State of John Corrie's
bill), cols 929–1015
  H.C. Debs, 15 February 1980, vol. 978, cols 931–2019
  H.C. Debs, 28 February 1980, vol. 979, cols 1715–810
  H.C. Debs, 14 March 1980, vol. 980, cols 1745–828
David Alton Bill
  H.C. Debs, 22 April 1980, vol. 983, cols 221–6

2 Jo Richardson's bill, The National Health Service Act, 1977 (Amendment) Bill, H.C. Debs.
3 For a much fuller consideration of the abortion issue see D. Marsh and
  J. Chambers, *Abortion Politics*.
4 The relevant debates were:

John Reeves Bill
  H.C. Debs, 27 February 1953, vol. 511, col. 2506
Kenneth Robinson Bill
  H.C. Debs, 10 February 1961, vol. 643, cols 853–92
Renee Short Bill
  H.C. Debs, 15 June 1965, vol. 714, cols 254–9
Simon Wingfield Digby Bill
  H.C. Debs, 26 February 1966, vol. 725, cols 837–56
Lord Silkin First Bill
  H.L. Debs, 30 November 1965, vol. 270, cols 1139–242
  H.L. Debs, 1 February 1966, vol. 272, cols 284–356
  H.L. Debs, 3 February 1966, vol. 272, cols 491–557
  H.L. Debs, 7 February 1966, vol. 272, cols 581–601
  H.L. Debs, 22 February 1966, vol. 273, cols 92–152
  H.L. Debs, 28 February 1966, vol. 273, cols 520–76
  H.L. Debs, 7 March 1966, vol. 273, cols 910–20 and 929–46
Lord Silkin Second Bill
  H.L. Debs, 10 May 1966, vol. 274, cols 577–605

H.L. Debs, 23 May 1966, vol. 274, cols 1206–50.

5 The Steel bill was debated as follows:

H.C. Debs, 22 July 1966, vol. 732, cols 1067–1162
H.C. Debs, 2 June 1967, vol. 747, cols 448–436
H.C. Debs, 30 June 1967, vol. 749, cols 895–1102
H.C. Debs, 13 July 1967, vol. 750, cols 1159–386
H.C. Debs, 25 October 1967, vol. 751, cols 1737–82.

6 Report of the Committee on the Working of the Abortion Act (the Lane Committee) 3 vols, HMSO 1974, Cmnd 5579, 5579–1, and 5879–11.
7 On this period see D. Marsh and J. Chambers, *Abortion Politics*, pp. 25–31.
8 See:

Special Reports and Minutes of Evidence of the Select Committee on the Abortion (Amendment) bill together with the proceedings of the Committee, Session 1974–75, HMSO 692–11, 10 November 1975.
First Report from the Select Committee on Abortion together with the proceedings of the Committee and appendices, Session 1975–6, vol. 1: Report, HMSO HC 573–11, 12 July 1976.
First Report from the Select Committee on Abortion, Session 1975–6, vol. 11: Minutes of Evidence and Appendices, HMSO HC 573–11, 12 July 1976.
Second Report from the Select Committee on Abortion together with the proceedings of the Committee, minutes of evidence and appendices, Session 1975–6, HMSO, 737, 22 November 1976.

9 H.C. Debs, 13 July 1979, vol. 970, col. 908. Actually, as always, the Private Members' ballot was drawn on a Thursday (24 May).
10 *Scottish Daily Record*, 10 July, 1979.
11 Some of this material is based upon an interview with John Corrie, 11 November 1980.
12 *Catholic Herald*, 6 July 1979.
13 See D. Marsh and J. Chambers, *Abortion Politics*, p. 95.
14 For more details on the votes see D. Marsh and J. Chambers, *Abortion Politics*, Chapter 5.
15 Personal interview, 19 June 1980.
16 Personal interview, 15 July 1980.
17 E. Powell's Unborn Children (Protection) Bill, H.C. Debs. This material is partly based upon an interview with Mr Powell.
18 On the medical profession's opposition see an anonymous piece entitled, 'A bill that should be stopped', *British Medical Journal*, vol. 290, 23 Feb. 1985, p. 586.
19 This material is based upon an interview with Dennis Skinner.

7 Pornography as a private members' issue

1 The relevant debates were:

The 1978 Protection of Children Act,

H.C. Debs, 10 Feb. 1978, vol. 943, cols 1826–1922
H.C. Debs, 19 April 1978, vol. 948, cols 446–7
The 1981 Indecent Displays (Control) Act,
   H.C. Debs, 30 Jan. 1981, vol. 997, cols 1165–1209
   H.C. Debs, 1 May 1981, vol. 3, cols 1016–72
The 1984 Video Recordings Act,
   H.C. Debs, 11 Nov. 1983, vol. 48, cols 521–80
   H.C. Debs, 16 March 1984, vol. 56, cols 610–23
The 1985/6 Obscene Publications (Protection of Children, etc.) (Amendment) Bill,
   H.C. Debs, 24 Jan. 1986, vol. 90, cols 556–617
   H.C. Debs, 25 April 1986, vol. 96, cols 572–633

2 M. Durham, 'Family Mortality and the New Right', *Parliamentary Affairs*, Spring 1985, pp. 180–191, quote p. 190.
3 M. McCarthy and R. Moodie, 'Parliament and Pornography. The 1978 Child Protection Act', *Parliamentary Affairs*, Winter 1981, pp. 47–62, quote p. 47.
4 *Ibid* pp. 50–51.
5 Cyril Townsend quoted in M. McCarthy and R. Moodie, 'Parliament and Pornography', p. 57.
6 H.C. Debs, 10 Feb. 1978, vol. 943, cols 1914–15.
7 I. Mikardo, 'Child Pornography', *New Statesman*, 26 May 1978, p. 694.
8 M. McCarthy and R. Moodie, 'Parliament and Pornography', p. 54.
9 As the Minister of State at the Home Office, Mr Patrick Mayhew, put it in the debate on the bill:

   'The bill is the descendant – through five generations now, I think, or perhaps at five removes – of Part II of the Cinematography and Indecent Displays Bill introduced by the Conservative Government in 1973'. H.C. Debs, 30 Jan. 1981, vol. 997, cols 1185.

10 The Standing Order No. 39 (then No. 37) bill was actually debated for 12 minutes but ran out of time and the debate was adjourned.
11 Interview with Tim Sainsbury, 3 Dec. 1981. Sainsbury pointed out in this interview and in the debate on his bill that the very first bill he had become involved in when he went into Parliament was the Conservative Government's Cinematography and Indecent Displays Bill. H.C. Debs, 30 Jan. 1981, vol. 997, cols 1168.
12 H.C. Debs, 11 Nov. 1983, vol. 48, col. 527.
13 P. Richards, *Parliament and Conscience*, p. 22.
14 P. Richards, *Parliament and Conscience*, p. 200.
15 The Parliamentary Video Group, *Video Violence and Children* (London: Oasis Projects, Nov. 1983).
16 Interview with G. Bright, 5 March 1985.
17 Martin Barker (ed.), *The Video Nasties* (London: Pronto Press, 1984), p. 12.
18 Conservative Research Department, *The Campaign Guide* (London: Conservative Central Office, 1983), p. 320.
19 Conservative Research Department, *The Campaign Guide*, p. 321.
20 *The Conservative Election Manifesto* (London: Conservative Central Office, 1983).

21 G. Alderman, *Pressure Groups and Government in Great Britain* (London: Longman, 1984), p. 11.
22 N.C.R.O.P.A. membership leaflet.
23 H.C. Debs, 11 Nov. 1983, vol. 48, col. 580.
24 Proceedings of Standing Committee C, 14 Dec. 1983.
25 H.C. Debs, 11 Nov. 1983, vol. 48, col. 570.
26 Proceedings of Standing Committee C, 25 Jan. 1984.
27 *The Guardian*, 4 Nov. 1983.
28 S. Cohen, *Folk Devils and Moral Panics* (London: Martin Robertson, 1984), p. 16.
29 H.C. Debs, 11 Nov. 1983, vol. 48, col. 556.
30 B. Brown, 'Exactly What We Wanted', in M. Barker, *The Video Nasties*, p. 87.
31 M. McCarthy and R. Moodie, 'Parliament and Pornography', p. 61.
32 In fact Mrs Whitehouse claimed:

> '*Our* Bill the result of most careful consultation over many months with an eminent QC and a former judge of very considerable experience, was the first one offered to Mr Churchill immediately after his success in the draw for Private Members' bills'. *The Listener*, 6 March 1986, p. 21.

33 H.C. Debs, 24 Nov. 1986, vol. 90, col. 558.
34 *Sunday Times*, 16 Feb. 1986.
35 Proceedings of Standing Committee C, 26 Feb. 1986.
36 *The Guardian*, 22 Feb. 1986.

8 The seat-belts issue

 1 H.C. Debs, 8 March 1961, vol. 636, col. 456.
 2 H.L. Debs, 15 Nov. 1973, vol. 346, col. 819.
 3 H.L. Debs, 15 Nov. 1973, vol. 346, cols 871–75.
 4 H.L. Debs, 17 Dec. 1973, vol. 348, col. 95.
 5 H.L. Debs, 11 June 1974, vol. 352, col. 379.
 6 H.L. Debs, 25 June 1974, vol. 352, col. 1368.
 7 H.C. Debs, 12 July 1974, vol. 876, col. 1744.
 8 H.C. Debs, 23 July 1974, vol. 877, col. 1533.
 9 H.C. Debs, 26 July 1974, vol. 877, col. 2107.
10 The bill was introduced by the Minister of Transport, William Rodgers. The controversial nature of the issue was demonstrated by the number of MPs who participated in the debate. In all some 27 Members spoke; all 13 Labour supported it while the 14 Conservatives were divided 7 in favour and 7 against. The resulting division in favour of 244–147, on a free vote, gave the Government a majority of 97. See H.C. Debs, 22 March 1979, vol. 964, col. 1830–32.
11 Interview with Neil Carmichael, 27 Jan. 1981.
12 H.C. Debs, 20 July 1979, vol. 970, col. 2238.
13 H.C. Debs, 20 July 1979, vol. 970, col. 2260.
14 H.C. Debs, 20 July 1979, vol. 970, col. 2286–90.
15 H.C. Debs, 22 Feb. 1980, vol. 979, col. 870–72.
16 H.C. Debs, 22 Feb. 1980, vol. 979, col. 871.
17 H.C. Debs, 22 Feb. 1980, vol. 979, cols 856–63.

18 H.L. Debs, 25 Nov. 1980, vol. 415, col. 22.
19 H.L. Debs, 15 Dec. 1980, vol. 415, col. 961.
20 H.C. Debs, 13 Jan. 1981, vol. 996, col. 885.
21 Interview with Lord Nugent, 3 Dec. 1981.
22 H.C. Debs, 14 April 1981, vol. 3, col. 157.
23 H.L. Debs, 7 May 1981, vol. 420, col. 286.
24 The days were 4, 8 and 11 June.
25 H.L. Debs, 11 June 1981, vol. 421, col. 357–59.
26 H.C. Debs, 28 July 1981, vol. 9, col. 1067–69.
27 H.C. Debs, 22 July 1982, vol. 28, col. 627–48.
28 H.C. Debs, 13 Jan. 1986, vol. 89, col. 897.

9 The smoking issue and private members' bills

1 Cancer SAC, 28 October 1949, D.H.S.S., 94200/2/1A cited in Webster, C., 'Tobacco Smoking Addictions: A Challenge to the National Health Service', *British Journal of Addiction*, No. 79, 1984, p. 11.
2 C. Webster, 'Tobacco Smoking Addiction', p. 11.
3 H.C. Debs, 28 June 1951, vol. 489, cols 15–51.
4 Cited in R.C.P. report, *Smoking and Health Now*, 1971, p. 21.
5 *Health Education News*, No. 12, 1977.
6 Payments to Action on Smoking and Health were as follows:

	£
1971–72	19,000
1972–73	6,000
1973–74	3,000
1974–75	6,400
1975–76	18,500
1976–77	31,000
1977–78	41,500
1978–79	59,500
1979–80	70,000
1980–81	80,000
1981–82	112,000

Written response from the Secretary of State for Social Science, Geoffrey Finsberg, to a question from Michael Brown. It was explained that ASH is treated as any other voluntary organisation and under the Health Service and Public Health Act, 1968 submits financial estimates and accounts annually which are scrutinised by the Department. H.C. Debs, 27 Oct. 1981, vol. 10, col. 326.
7 H.C. Debs, 12 Feb. 1964, vol. 689, col. 383.
8 H.C. Debs, 8 May 1964, vol. 694, col. 1688.
9 H.C. Debs, 9 July 1968, vol. 768, col. 222.
10 H.C. Debs, 20 May 1969, vol. 784, col. 1255.
11 H.C. Debs, 23 Feb. 1965, vol. 707, col. 212.
12 H.C. Debs, 23 Oct. 1967, vol. 751, col. 1328.
13 *The Times*, 21 September 1970, p. 8.
14 P. Taylor, *Smoke Rings: The Politics of Tobacco* (London: Bodley Head, 1984), p. 87.

15 H.C. Debs, 23 April 1971, vol. 815, col. 1575.
16 H.C. Debs, 15 Dec. 1970, vol. 508, col. 1121–25.
17 H.C. Debs, 16 March 1971, vol. 813, col. 1189–98.
18 H.C. Debs, 16 March 1971, vol. 813, col. 1194.
19 H.C. Debs, 23 April 1971, vol. 815, col. 1576.
20 H.C. Debs, 7 May 1971, vol. 816, col. 1907.
21 *See* pp. 119–23.
22 H.C. Debs, 19 Jan. 1972, vol. 829, col. 485–8.
23 H.C. Debs, 16 Jan. 1976, vol. 903, col. 814–20, and cols. 855–62.
24 H.C. Debs, 16 Jan. 1976, vol. 903, col. 819.
25 H.C. Debs, 30 April 1976, vol. 910, col. 759–98.
26 H.C. Debs, 30 April 1976, vol. 910, col. 794.
27 H.C. Debs, 9 July 1982, vol. 27, col. 608–15.
28 P. Taylor, *Smoke Rings*, p. 143.
29 H.C. Debs, 10 July 1981, vol. 8, col. 764.
30 Its title was subsequently changed to the Protection of Children (Tobacco) Bill, H.C. Debs, 4 Dec. 1985, vol. 88, col. 311.
31 H.C. Debs, 30 Jan. 1986, vol. 90, col. 1244.
32 P. Johnson, *British Medical Journal*, vol. 292, p. 707.

Conclusion: a proposal for reform

1 For a much fuller exposition of this argument see: T. Tant, 'Freedom of Information: A Challenge to The British Political Tradition', Ph.D. University of Essex, 1986.
2 A. H. Birch, *Representative and Responsible Government* (London: Allen and Unwin, 1979). S. Beer, *Modern British Politics* (London: Faber, 1982).
3 A. H. Birch, *Representative and Responsible Government*, p. 52.
4 S. Beer, *Modern British Politics*, p. 33.
5 A. H. Birch, *Representative and Responsible Government*, p. 227.
6 A. H. Birch, *Representative and Responsible Government*, p. 235.
7 P. Bromhead, *Private Members' Bills*, p. 45.
8 *Ibid.*, p. 43.

Index